DROP ME A LINE

DROP ME A LINE

Being Letters exchanged on Trout and Coarse Fishing

by

RICHARD WALKER

and

MAURICE INGHAM

Illustrated by the authors

H. F. & G. WITHERBY LTD

First published in Great Britain 1953
by MacGibbon and Kee
Second edition 1964

This edition first published 1989 by
H. F. & G. WITHERBY LTD
14 Henrietta Street, London WC2E 8QJ

British Library Cataloguing in Publication Data
Walker, Richard, *1918–1985*
Drop me a line.—New ed.
1. Angling
I. Title II. Ingham, Maurice
799.1'2

ISBN 0-85493-188-0

Printed in Great Britain by
St Edmundsbury Press Ltd, Bury St Edmunds, Suffolk

To the memory of
Hugh Tempest Sheringham

Acknowledgments

THE authors wish to thank Mr. R. L. Marston, Editor of the *Fishing Gazette* for permission to reprint the two articles 'How to Catch Carp', and for his encouragement; Mr. Harry Sheckell, for permission to publish his letters; Mr. D. F. Leney, of the Surrey Trout Farm, for allowing *his* lettres to be published, and for valuable information; 'B.B.' for writing an Introduction, and for being the very best of angling companions; John Ellis, for being there at the right moment, whether with landing-net or camera; and Peter Thomas, Bob Rutland, Trevor Lockhart and a number of other anglers, who have helped in a hundred ways. They would also like to express gratitude to those owners of private estates who have generously allowed them the privilege of fishing in their waters.

M. H. INGHAM
RICHARD WALKER

Contents

		PAGE
PREFACE TO THE 1989 EDITION BY MAURICE INGHAM		3
INTRODUCTION BY FRED TAYLOR		7
PREFACE BY MAURICE INGHAM		11
I	HOW TO CATCH CARP	13
II	NOVEMBER LETTERS	24
III	DECEMBER LETTERS	49
IV	JANUARY LETTERS	67
V	FEBRUARY LETTERS	101
VI	MARCH LETTERS	131
VII	APRIL LETTERS	150
VIII	MAY LETTERS	167
IX	JUNE LETTERS	191
X	JULY LETTERS	208
XI	AUGUST LETTERS	238
XII	SEPTEMBER LETTERS	267
XIII	OCTOBER LETTERS	284
CONCLUSION		293

Preface to the 1989 Edition by Maurice Ingham

THERE WILL be few readers of this book who are not aware that, sadly, Dick Walker died some 3½ years ago, and I regard this re-issue of *Drop Me a Line* as a fitting opportunity to pay my personal tribute to him.

During the 35 years that have elapsed since the publication of the original edition Dick achieved world-wide recognition and acclaim, not only for his outstanding angling achievements but also for his original and invaluable contributions to angling literature. During this time he also earned the respect and affection of countless thousands of anglers, and indeed of non-anglers too, worldwide. I include myself within this number. From the rather formal beginnings of our correspondence, reproduced in this book, our association developed into a very close friendship which continued until his death and I number Dick among my very dearest friends.

Dick was a truly remarkable man in so many respects, but a man nevertheless, not a demi-god, to which status many of his admirers seemed to wish to elevate him. Anyone who has followed his writing in the angling press over the years will be well aware of his intolerance of cant, hypocrisy, blind dogma and outright dishonesty which he condemned with devastating logic and slashing sarcasm, sometimes bordering on rudeness, but Dick was in all things scrupulously fair and honest and he had little patience with those who did not measure up to his own high standards in these respects. At the same time he was extremely generous—sometimes embarrassingly so, both in material things and in the patient guidance and advice which he gave unstintingly to anyone genuinely seeking his assistance. In the Preface which I wrote to the original edition of this book I said that it contains 'the ideas, opinions and experiences of two ordinary anglers'. I would not wish now, after 35 years, to amend that description of myself but in no way could Dick Walker be described as 'ordinary'. He was in a great many respects quite extraordinary and I think I can truthfully say, as was said earlier of another great personality, that 'we shall not see his like again'.

It is fitting and to me, personally, a great joy that Dick's widow, Pat Marston Walker, has agreed to join me in the task of preparing this book for re-publication, and I am most grateful to her for her invaluable contributions.

Some credit for the original publication of this book—if indeed readers regard it as credit-worthy—should be accorded to Peter Thomas, a lifelong friend and fishing companion of Dick's whom many readers will know personally, or vicariously through the frequent references to him in Dick's writings. Being close neighbours Dick showed Pete most of my letters as he received them and on one occasion Pete remarked to Dick that if I had kept all Dick's letters, as he had kept all mine, they could be incorporated into an unusual and interesting book. Fortunately I had kept all Dick's letters—they were much too precious to me to discard—and so the seed was planted which in due course resulted in *Drop Me a Line*.

I would also like to pay tribute to Dick's mother, the charming and redoubtable Mrs E. M. Walker, to whom we are indebted for the title of this book—an inspired choice.

There are one or two passages in the book that call for some comment in the light of changed attitudes and circumstances since the letters were written:

Page 100 The fact that I used a live minnow when trying to catch a large trout is not something of which I am now particularly proud. I can only plead in mitigation that attitudes have changed a great deal in the past 35 years, and that live-baiting was not frowned upon then as it is now.

Page 163 The trapping and shooting of otters is not something that Dick would have advocated or that I would advocate at the present time, quite apart from the fact that they are now an endangered and protected species. I think Dick's outburst, as in his comments about swans, referred to below, was provoked by anger and frustration.

Page 185 The implication that the only good swans are dead ones was in the nature of a private joke between us, and anyone who knew Dick well will appreciate that such a sentiment was quite alien to his attitude to wildlife generally. I think that shortly before that letter was written he must have had an experience of the irritatingly persistent attentions of swans which, as most anglers know, can quickly provoke 'cygnicidal' or suicidal emotions.

MAURICE INGHAM
May 1989

Introduction

D*ROP ME A LINE* is the only angling book that I couldn't put down until I had read it from cover to cover; and whenever I pick it up, I can't put it down until I have read it through all over again.

When I first read it, I knew neither of its authors; now both are personal friends of mine. Not only that; the example set by the book has brought together many other anglers who have been enriched by friendship and by the better fishing they have enjoyed as a result of exchanging knowledge and ideas.

It is undeniable that many men who are now leading angling journalists were encouraged to write about fishing through reading *Drop me a Line*. The spirit of the book is the willingness of both its authors to give freely and without reservation, all the knowledge at their command. Nothing of how they catch their fish is kept secret.

A dozen years have passed since the letters that form this book were written; and in those years, great changes have taken place in angling. Many more big fish are caught nowadays, and no book has done more to inspire enthusiasm for catching big fish than *Drop me a Line*. Many of today's anglers were children when the book was first published; now, in this second edition, those who did not have the chance to read it before, can do so.

FRED J. TAYLOR
[1964]

'And we two will, for that time,
do nothing but angle, and talk
of fish and fishing.'

IZAAK WALTON

Preface

THIS BOOK that you are about to read differs from the vast majority of books in that it was not written with the intention of its being published. You may be interested to learn exactly how it came to be written at all, and I will endeavour to explain.

I have fished since early childhood, but upon my release from the Army after the war, I turned again with renewed interest to angling in general, and to carp-fishing in particular, as it offered the perfect antidote to the mental and spiritual turmoil of the long war years. After the hurly-burly of the barrack square and the boisterous comradeship of the mess I sought the soothing solitude of the quiet waterside, and it was then that I became incurably afflicted with 'carp-fever'. Here indeed I had found the very quintessence of the contemplative man's recreation—the warm scented summer nights and pearly dawns by the quiet pool, pitting my wits against the venerable mail-clad monsters and occasionally succeeding.

Some three summers of carp-fishing in various waters had impressed upon me the inadequacy and unsuitability of my tackle, and many enquiries had failed to solve my problem. Then, at the crucial moment, there appeared in the *Fishing Gazette* two articles on carp-fishing, in which the author explained that he had experienced exactly the same difficulty that I had encountered, and that he had solved his problem by designing and building a rod specially for carp fishing. Here at last was the answer, if only I could prevail upon the anonymous author to pass on to me the necessary information. I need have had no fears!

My letter, kindly forwarded to the author by the Editor of the *Fishing Gazette*, was answered immediately, in what wealth of detail the following pages will show—and my correspondence with Richard Walker has been uninterrupted since that day in 1949.

I should warn you that you will not find this a text-book on angling matters. The letters contained in this volume are simply those which passed between Richard Walker and me during the first years of our correspondence. They are printed exactly as they were written, the only editing being the omission of certain personal and irrelevant details, and they contain the ideas, opinions and experiences of two ordinary anglers. Some of the ideas we have expressed may be new to you, some, no doubt, are very familiar; of parts of the book you may approve, with other parts you may violently disagree; but it is our sincere hope that you will derive as much enjoyment from reading this book as Dick and I did from writing and reading the letters reproduced in it.

And now, let us 'do nothing but . . . talk of fish and fishing'.

MAURICE H. INGHAM

I

Two articles on carp in the Fishing Gazette *prompted Maurice Ingham's first letter*

OF ALL our freshwater fish the carp is probably the least understood by anglers, and before dealing with methods of fishing for it, it would be well to attempt to clear up some of the many misconceptions that exist.

The first is in nomenclature. There are at least four distinct species, and seven or more varieties of fish all of which are known as carp, which can be set out as follows:

Species	*Varieties*
Common carp	{ Mirror carp, Leather carp }
Crucian carp	Prussian carp
Goldfish	
Bitterling carp	

The bitterling is so uncommon as to be negligible. The crucian carp and its varieties differ as much from the common carp in appearance and habits as a roach from a bream. The crucian is a comparatively slow-moving fish, even when hooked; it bites with great delicacy and circumspection; it has no barbules and seldom exceeds a weight of 2 lb. The common carp is probably the fastest of all British fish, bites greedily unless suspicious, is equipped with barbules and often exceeds 20 lb. in weight.

A great many of the misconceptions about carp fishing have

arisen through misunderstandings as to the totally different nature of these two species of fish. Carp fishing proper is the pursuit of the common carp and its varieties, the mirror and the leather carp, and for the purposes of this article the term 'carp' will be used to refer to these three only.

Very many anglers and angling authors seem to regard carp as practically uncatchable and the pursuit of them as dull and unprofitable. In fact, once the correct technique is learned, carp will be found as accommodating as any other fish; as for dullness, this is the last adjective that any carp fisher of experience would apply to his quarry.

Capricious? No more so than other fish. Far less so than barbel, or tench, or trout at the end of June, or even the average run of roach, bream, etc., on a heavily fished water.

Opinions on its fighting qualities are divided. Those who have hooked carp on fine tackle and have been broken aver that carp will only bite when light tackle is used and that they will immediately break. Those whose experience of carp is limited to seeing them cruising about may be forgiven for wrongly assuming that they are sluggish when hooked. In fact, they can travel at nearly 40 feet per second. The few who have successfully landed carp know that no finer fighter swims.

The record carp of 26 lb. caught by Mr. Albert Buckley at Mapperley in 1930, has done the art of angling for carp great harm. It was caught on a No. 10 hook, 4x gut and a 3 lb. breaking-strain line—a magnificent feat on the part of Mr. Buckley. But the part of Mapperley where it was caught is free from snags and weeds, and Mr. Buckley's skill of hand and coolness of head had a chance to prove themselves. Unfortunately, many would-be carp fishers have since assumed that fine roach tackle, having captured a carp of 26 lb., would suffice for lesser fish; weeds, lilies and snags have played their part and the legend of uncatchability has firmly fixed itself in the minds of many.

I often marvel to see men who commonly use size 4 trebles mounted on wire, 18 lb. breaking-strain lines and rods in proportion, to catch 10 lb. pike, attempting to catch carp of corresponding weight and infinitely greater fighting ability on tackle which would be placed in jeopardy by a fish of 3 lb or 4 lb.

Where carp run from 10 lb. to 15 lb. or more, and there ar snags or weeds within 20 yd. of the pitch, it is folly to use tackl which will not stand a pull of 10 lb. I use a plaited undressed line with a 12 lb. breaking-strain and a 2 yd. gut substitute cast of similar strength.[1] The strain placed on tackle when a heavy fish has to be stopped is very great; for example, stopping a fish of 10 lb. travelling at 40 ft. per second in a distance of 10 ft. would result in a pull on the line of approximately 25 lb.—*provided* pressure was applied quite evenly and with no jerks. In practice, 10 lb. tackle in fairly skilful hands gives the angler a reasonable chance of landing his fish. It is as well to remember that, unlike the salmon and trout, carp do not stop when pressure is released. They go off in a mad rush and keep on as long as they can or until they are buried deep in the weeds.

Hooks must be in proportion to the rest of the tackle; strong in the wire, without being coarse, to avoid the danger of straightening, and wide in gape to reduce the possibility of tearing out. The 'Model Perfect' hooks are the best I know, and sizes 2 and 4 are the most suitable where fish run large. They are also about right for the big baits which are necessary in carp fishing, of which more later.

The ordinary bottom fishing rod is not nearly powerful enough for really big carp. As far as I know there is no rod made by the tackle makers which is ideal for the job[2]; as I make all my own rods, this worries me not at all, but it may prove a stumbling-block to others. My favourite carp rod is a double-built split cane in two joints. It is 10 ft. in length, with high Bell's life intermediate rings, a stand-off agate tip and an enormous butt ring, 26 mm. in diameter. The cork handle is 28 in. long, to enable one to tuck the rubber knob into the groin and apply plenty of leverage. For the benefit of those who make rods, the taper is even and goes from 5/32 in. (from 'flat' to 'flat' of the hexagon) at the tip to ⅝ in. at the extreme butt. This is a power-

[1] We now use monofilament lines.
[2] But see B. James & Son of West Ealing.

ful rod which will control a strong fish and at the same time has plenty of action to throw a light bait with no lead. An approximation to it can be obtained by lopping 12 in. off the top of the rod invented by Mr. F. W. K. Wallis for use on the Avon and now made by several manufacturers; or, preferably, by having an extra short top made.

Reels should be chosen with some regard for the great speed and powers of acceleration possessed by carp. This means ability to recover line very quickly; an easily-applied, smooth drag and a left-hand wind (for right-handed anglers); one has not time, in playing big carp, to mess about changing the rod from one hand to the other. The bigger fixed-spool reels are excellent; I use a post-war model, 'Felton Crosswind'. With this type of reel one can cast baits much too light to throw from a rotating drum reel, and with much greater accuracy. When one is waiting for a run, they can be left with the pick-up in the free position, which is much more satisfactory than coiling several yards on the ground. I have another reel, blood-brother to the one Michael Traherne speaks of in his latest book, *Be Quiet and Go a-Angling*, which is used when monsters are expected and snags are numerous. It is really an oversized version of Hardy's 'Eureka' bottom reel —5¾ in. diameter, ¾ in. wide in the drum, with a finger-operated brake lever in addition to the optional check and exposed flange. This carries a plaited line with a breaking-strain of 18 lb. and is used for attempts on Mr. Buckley's record. I may say in passing that several waters are known which contain carp of 30 lb. or more, and that carp-addicts, more than any other specialist anglers, always have in mind the possibility of breaking the record!

Besides the rest of the tackle, a really capacious landing-net is needed. There are those who favour the gaff, but I like to return all the carp I catch alive and uninjured. There can never be too many of these fine, sporting fish. Also, that much neglected item, a rod-rest, is needed. The ordinary forked stick will not do; the line gets nipped between rod and rest, and it is essential that it should run free. Metal rod-rests are preferable, with a top as shown on page 158. The gap at the base of two straight arms is too small for the rod to drop through.

So much for equipment. What of the baits? Carp are not difficult to please in this matter. Their tastes vary on different waters, but I have yet to find carp that would take neither paste nor worms. Where worms are taken, they are probably best for bottom fishing. The bite on worm is usually decisive, the indication being the rapid removal of several yards of line from the reel or coil. Small wrigglers are useless; at least one and preferably two full-sized lobworms on a No. 4 or No. 2 hook is a much likelier bait for big fish. Paste, too, should be fished in large lumps; a piece an inch in diameter is by no means too large. Both paste and worm should be fished on the bottom, and to ensure that all the gut also lies on the bottom, one shot should be pinched on the tackle at the junction of line and cast. Nothing else is used on the tackle. There is no need for a float; there is never any doubt when a carp takes the bait. Where long casts are necessary, Capt. Parker's idea of a wooden ledger is a good one, except that the wood should be weighted to just *sink*. If it is balanced *exactly* it may rise and drift about, and it is important that all the cast should lie right on the bottom, and lie still. It may well be dyed pale olive.

Boiled potato[1] has been much extolled as a carp bait, probably as a result of its success at Cheshunt forty years ago. I could never find any record of its having been very successful elsewhere. I have on occasions caught carp on potato but have always done better with worms, paste or bread. The virtue of potato lies in the fact that it appears to be attractive only to carp and one is thus spared the annoyance of nibblings from lesser fish.

One of the deadliest of carp baits, and the only one to use when carp are feeding at the surface, which is often, is floating crust. The common mistake is to use small crusts, which are hard to cast; and to get over this difficulty anglers fasten contraptions such as pike floats to the tackle, thus removing all hope of success. For crust fishing, nothing should be on the tackle except cast and hook, except when the water is choppy and the line is liable to sink. Then a tiny torpedo-shaped piece of balsa, stained olive-green and varnished, can be fixed at the junction of line and 2 yd.

[1] Interesting, in the light of later experiences.—R.W.

cast by two bits of valve-rubber—but only if absolutely essential. Weight for casting is obtained by using a big crust—a whole french roll is about right for size. It becomes sloppy in the water, and when a carp sucks it in it goes down like water down the plug-hole of the bath. On hot days, when carp are feeding shyly, one can thread the cast through the big piece of bread and put a small piece on the hook. This floats a few inches away from the big bit and is often taken when the larger lump would be refused, or broken up by constant 'coming short' and swirlings, before being consumed piecemeal, a favourite trick of well-fed carp in sultry weather.

The most profitable times to fish for carp depend to a great extent on the type of water in which they live. In deep waters, from evening to mid-morning, and through the night, finds most of the fish feeding. After nightfall the carp will be found close to the bank and a bait fished within a foot or so of grass- or reed-fringed margin will be found most effective. It is well to avoid shining lights. In shallow lakes night fishing is not usually profitable. The fish seem to stop feeding at nightfall and do not recommence until the morning sun is on the water; when they do start they go on until midday or later. The important fact to bear in mind in any kind of water is that carp prefer shallows in normal weather and are usually found only in the deeps when the weather is rough. One often finds anglers choosing the deepest hole they can find in a lake—the most unlikely place, in normal conditions, that they could choose. In waters that are well stocked with carp, observation will tell the angler the feeding grounds of the fish; volumes of bubbles and discoloration of the water are certain signs of activity on the bottom, and heavings and suckings in the weeds tell of activity at the top. Shallows with not too much and not too little weed of the kind that spreads long streamers along the surface, is the ideal place to float bread, and the line is not so noticeable as it would be in open water.

It need never be feared that carp will fail to find a bait if it is obscured by weed or buried in mud. They have a keen sense of 'smell', or, more correctly, ability to detect the flavouring effect of things in the water, and can readily discover, and, aided probably by their barbules, rout out and take, a bait they could not possibly see.

Tactics are of first importance in carp fishing. Before setting up the tackle, it is well to spend time in finding the likeliest spot. Creeping round the lake in soft-soled shoes, one observes all the signs and, having decided on a pitch, stays there. It is important to avoid movement as much as possible, and it is better to spend an hour deciding on a spot than to spend the day shifting about from pitch to pitch in a frenzy of indecision. Carp will not stand being *pursued*. When a big one is spotted, a lump of dough plonked on his head will ensure that he is not caught that day. Far better to watch him for an hour, observe his 'beat', and arrange for a bait to await him when he next passes that way. And it *must* await him. It must not be pulled out and dropped in elsewhere because an even bigger fish has put in an appearance 50 yd. away!

When a carp takes a bait, he usually swims off with it and the line runs out rapidly. With floating bread and greased line, a gentle strike will fix the hook, but with 20 yd. lying on the bottom, a vigorous sideways pull will be necessary properly to embed a hook as large as a No. 4 or a No. 2. Then the fun commences. I would venture to assert that far more carp have been hooked and lost than have ever been landed. There are no rules for playing lightning! One or two tips may help. If a carp cannot be stopped from going into a weed-bed, apply as much pressure as possible and he will not go in far; the weed impedes his progress. Directly he stops, pull as hard as the tackle will bear. He will probably be dragged out before he can get properly 'under way' again. Failing this, handlining works *sometimes*! Always keep pressure on the fish—one reason for a reel which will take in line rapidly—for a carp will rid itself of a hook quicker than any other fish I know if given slack line. He is also an adept both at keeping out of and jumping out of a landing-net. If he is a big one and you eventually get him in the net, drop the rod and take both hands to the job of lifting—or dragging—the fish ashore. I lost an enormous fish once. . . . Drab clothing is an asset at all times and not least when a fish is being coaxed to the net. My debt of gratitude to the Home Guard for their battle-dress is great; I cannot imagine a better garb for an angler and especially for a carp fisher.

I am surprised that more fishermen do not take an interest in carp. Doubtless angling literature is largely responsible; authors of comprehensive works on coarse fishing seem to have successively borrowed from their predecessors and perpetuated misconception and ignorance to the detriment of a fine fish, and one far better suited for stocking still waters than any other, a fact well known to our ancestors. Angling clubs who spend hundreds of pounds annually to ensure that their waters are full of stunted roach and perch would do well to examine the advantages of stocking up with carp instead, always remembering that it must be common, mirror or leather carp and *not* crucians, which they will infallibly be offered by fish breeders, unless they state definitely that these fish are not desired. I look forward to the time when the outstanding sporting merit of carp will again be appreciated, and when informed carp fishers will be numbered in thousands instead of in dozens as at present.

★ ★ ★

My recent article on carp fishing has, I am glad to say, aroused some interest in this fine fish. I have been able to glean some further useful information about the various varieties, for the bulk of which I am indebted to Mr. D. F. Leney, of the Surrey Trout Farm, Haslemere.

The mirror and leather carp are the *same fish*, but there is a wide variation in the size, number and position of the scales, which vary from none to a complete covering; but even when covered with scales, the mirror/leather carp, which is better called by the collective name 'king carp', is distinguishable from the common carp, as the scales are of much greater size. The king carp is really a domesticated variety, bred and cultivated on the Continent for food. It is capable of much quicker growth and greater ultimate size than the common wild carp. In the past injustice has been done to anglers who have captured specimen common carp, as this fish is not distinguished from the king carp for the purposes of records, as it ought to be.

The king carp is more free-biting than the common carp and is more inclined to feed on the surface; it is in fact more suitable in every way for re-stocking purposes and stands travelling and handling much better.

Carp are not easy to breed and in many waters they refuse to breed at all, or the spawn fails to hatch. Perch are great enemies of the newly-hatched fry. For angling purposes, however, non-breeding has its advantages. Where several hundred carp are put in a lake and do not breed, the chances of an angler capturing a specimen fish are far greater than where there is extensive breeding and carp of all ages and sizes are found. While in such cases more fish are caught, the larger and more circumspect fish are seldom taken; the smaller ones nearly always get the bait first. There is no doubt in my mind that the presence in a general coarse fish lake of a number of carp which do not breed but all of which in a few years will, barring accidents, reach weights of from 10 lb. to 20 lb. and possibly even more, is a very distinct asset which would be welcomed by the vast majority of anglers. As I said earlier, king carp will stand a great deal of handling, and a fortunate angler can have his catch weighed and photographed and then returned alive to the lake. I have on numerous occasions taken king carp of from 14 lb. to 17 lb. home in a wet sack, weighed and photographed them and returned them next day, after a night in the bath! A rule, in the case of club-owned waters, to the effect that no carp were to be killed, coupled with prohibition of the use of the gaff, would ensure that even where carp refused to breed, a good head of fish would be maintained for a great many years, each year seeing an increase in their size and the sport which they would provide.

In my article I omitted to describe in detail what is perhaps the most exciting method of all for catching big carp. It is only applicable to waters in which there are reasonable depths; lakes which are largely shallow do not usually respond. The method consists of fishing a floating crust close to the bank during the hours of darkness, during which time carp will, if the water temperature is high enough, patrol the margin of the lake in search of whatever may have fallen in. Lakes which are generally shallow are chilled by the night air, and even in summer the water temperature quickly falls to a point below that at which carp will feed. The chilled surface water sinks, and as there are no reserves, as there are in the case of deep lakes, to take its place, the temperature of shallow waters is speedily lowered. In the deeper waters the temperature is much slower in changing and therefore never reaches so low a level; consequently carp will feed all through the night.

The essential conditions for margin fishing are to choose a spot where the water is at least 2 ft. deep close to the bank, and preferably one where there is some natural screen, rushes, willow-herb, dwarf willows or the like. Failing these a light screen of willow shoots can be fixed up. Among the herbage or artificial screen, a rod-rest is placed. It is preferable to choose a position *towards* which the wind is blowing, provided it is a light breeze; I have never had much success with margin fishing when the wind was at all strong.

No lead or float is used, nor is it necessary to employ any kind of cast. A single eyed hook, size 2, is tied direct to the end of the line which need not even be of high quality; a twisted or plaited flax line is quite suitable, its strength being proportionate to the size of the fish and prevalence of snags or water-lilies. On the hook is placed a piece of crust, 1½ in. to 2 in. across. This is wound to within a foot or so of the top ring of the rod, which is then placed in the rest. The line is then paid out until the crust, but none of the line, is in the water. In lakes where there are no small fish, such as rudd, it may remain there, but where rudd abound it is as well to wind up the crust after five minutes' soaking, so that it hangs clear of the surface, otherwise it will soon be broken up and devoured by the small fish. Small pieces of crust similar to the hook bait in size are then thrown in close to where the hook bait hangs; if they are eaten by rudd they must be renewed. The commotion made by the rudd will attract carp and sooner or later a mighty swirl and a noise like water going down the waste-pipe of the bath will indicate the presence of a feeding carp. This is the signal for the hook bait to be lowered stealthily on to the surface. When it disappears in the same manner as the 'free offering' the angler will require no advice on his subsequent procedure.

While waiting for the carp to arrive, it is essential to show no light, not even a lighted cigarette. The angler should sit tight within easy reach of his rod; no matter how obvious the indications of carp in the vicinity, the actual bite always seems to come with suddenness, and one must be ready to pick up the rod and strike without the slightest hesitation. Playing and landing one of these great fish in the dark is beset with difficulties, but I think, in waters where the method is suitable, that margin fishing is the most productive of all ways of catching carp—most especially on waters which are heavily fished, as not only are the carp more difficult to catch in daylight in such places, but they are more apt to come close in-shore after dark in search of the remains of groundbait, etc., which drift to the margin towards which the wind blows; they speedily learn that this source of food exists and after dark they come along to take advantage of it.

Of carp in rivers little can be said; in fact, there are few, if any, rivers in which carp exist in sufficient numbers to make it worth fishing for them. It may happen that an angler will discover a number of carp frequenting a stretch of river; in such a case the methods applicable to lakes should be equally suitable, except that it will probably be necessary to use sufficient lead to overcome the effect of current in the case of a sunken bait, and to choose a bit of slack water for floating crust.

I am reminded that I have had nothing to say on the subject of groundbaiting for carp. I have never found it necessary or desirable to groundbait extensively for them, except in the very few waters where no fish but carp exist. In such places a course of groundbaiting in a given spot, lasting over a period of many days, will naturally bring the fish together and increase the fisherman's chances. Groundbait should resemble what is intended for the hook; worms and clay when fishing lobs, bread and bran for paste and crust for crust fishing. Cloud groundbaits are quite useless; one must *feed* the carp. No groundbait should be used while actually fishing. Where there are quantities of roach, rudd, bream or tench, it is better to groundbait very lightly or not at all, as although carp may be attracted so will the small fry and they will always take the hook bait first; the splashings caused by their being landed will frighten the carp. Of course, in margin fishing at night this difficulty can be avoided. Where the nuisance of small fish is too great to be overcome by other means, recourse may be had to potato, the method of using which has been described *ad nauseam*. It is an inferior bait and its sole advantage lies in its immunity to the attacks of anything but carp and a very occasional large tench or bream, of a size which may make their capture not entirely unwelcome.

I am convinced that if angling clubs seeking to improve their coarse fish lakes would experiment with carp instead of the more usual varieties, their members would find a tremendous increase in their sport. Most of us hope to catch a big fish; with carp the possibilities are tremendously increased.

'WATER RAIL'

II

November Letters

Louth, Lincolnshire

Dear Sir,

I take the liberty of writing to you, through the Editor of the *Fishing Gazette*, after reading your excellent articles recently published on 'How to catch Carp'.

I am one of the small but happy band of anglers who fish deliberately for carp, and I was most deeply interested and gratified to find in your articles confirmation of my own views on this much neglected branch of the 'noble art'. I am a graduate from the less refined branches of coarse fishing, and although I have met with some measure of success and my tackle in many respects conforms to your suggestions, I have, during the past summer, become increasingly dissatisfied with the rod which I use on these occasions. It is a rod which was designed for less powerful prey, and consequently my whole outfit is unbalanced and I am unable to obtain the full benefit of it.

I am anxious to occupy some of my spare time during the coming winter evenings in making a rod *primarily* for carp fishing and in this respect I would be extremely grateful for any information you are able to give me. In spite of enquiries to a number of sources I have been unable to obtain a detailed specification of a carp rod. The most satisfactory information I have been able to get is for a rod which 'may be found suitable for carp fishing'. I think you will appreciate my difficulty—I wish to make a rod which is designed specifically for the purpose of carp fishing, not just another bottom rod which 'may be found suitable'.

I would, therefore, greatly appreciate any information you are able to give me on the following points: length of rod; length of handle; materials (whether whole cane, built cane or double built cane); the fullest possible details as to taper; the number, spacing and size of rings, type and position of reel mounting, etc.—in fact, the most detailed specification you are able to give me.

Perhaps I should add that from my limited experience I have come to favour a centre pin reel in preference to a fixed spool reel when carp fishing, and my new rod will be used with my old centre pin reel, which I have found very satisfactory. I also use an 11 lb. breaking-strain line of braided nylon.

I trust I am not presuming too much on our mutual interest in carp, but I would again repeat that any information which you are able, at your convenience, to give me will be most deeply appreciated.

Yours faithfully,

M. H. INGHAM

Hitchin, Hertfordshire

Dear Mr. Ingham,

I found exactly the same problem as you have. It is impossible to buy a rod suitable for big carp. I have made two, the design having been worked out in collaboration with 'B.B.', author of *The Fisherman's Bedside Book* and Michael Traherne, who has just had his *Be Quiet and Go a-Angling* published. So you see these rods are really the product of several carp-fishers. (Incidentally, I am sure you would enjoy reading the books I've mentioned, there's plenty of carp-lore in them.)

Both the rods are split cane, ten feet long. One is single-built and the other double-built. I cannot find any practical advantage in the double-built; the action is similar and the only difference is that the double-built rod is a little stiffer in the butt, an effect which could have been obtained by increasing the butt diameter of the single-built job at very much lower cost (or less trouble, if you make your own split cane as I do).

If you intend building up your own split cane, I would recommend you to read *How to Build your own Split Cane Fishing Rod* by G. Lawton Moss, published by Technical Press Ltd. But if you are only going to make one or two rods it isn't worth all the trouble of buying planes, formers, glue, etc., as split cane made to your own specification can be obtained ready built. I recommend J. B. Walker, 4B Prospect Road, Hythe, Kent.

Here are the dimensions of my carp rod:

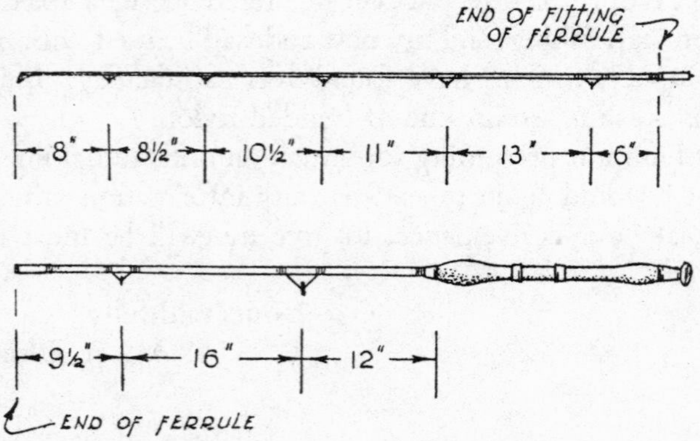

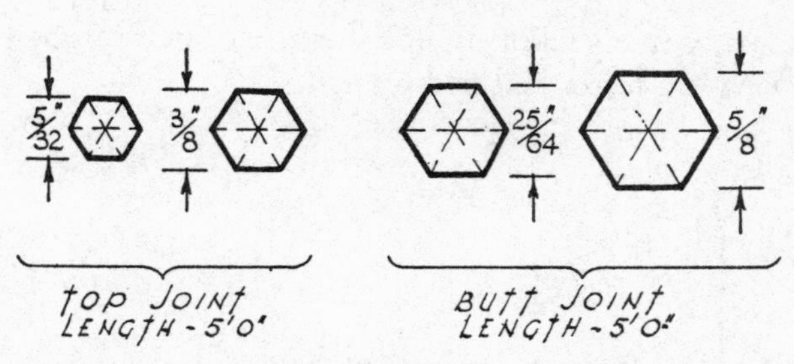

The handle is built up from cork rings and shaped. It is 28″ long. Rings are synthetic agates, with a big one (26 mm.) at the butt, for the fixed-spool reel. The reel fittings, shoulder collar and butt cap are duralumin. You will find all the fittings you need in J. B. Walker's catalogue.

The reel fittings are movable. The taper on both joints is even from one end to the other, i.e. the decrease in diameter per foot run is constant, though not the same on both joints. You must on no account attempt to reduce the diameter of a built-up split cane joint, as this will remove the hard outer skin and ruin the steeliness of the rod. I expect you already know this, but I'll be on the safe side and tell you! Ferrules must be set on very firmly indeed. If possible use a micrometer and ensure a tight drive fit. Dip the ferrules in boiling water to give a little expansion of the brass, then drive on with a hide mallet (or something similar) while still hot.

I don't think the exact number or spacings of rings is very important, nor do I think it necessary to fit lined rings all through. Agate butt and tip are enough, with decent quality metal rings as intermediates.

I think a centre-pin reel is infinitely better than a *small* fixed-spool job. The fixed-spool I use is a biggish one, the Felton Crosswind, which takes 120 yds. of 12½ lb. b.s. braided nylon. Its two advantages over the centre-pin are that one never has to unravel a tangle (in the dark!) caused by casting from the coil in the hand, and that one can set up a simple bite-warning device, thus:

The auto pick-up is left 'off'. A very slight pull on the line causes the stick to fly to the left, and after that has happened the line runs away freely. For night fishing, the stick can be painted white, or have a ferret bell tied on it.

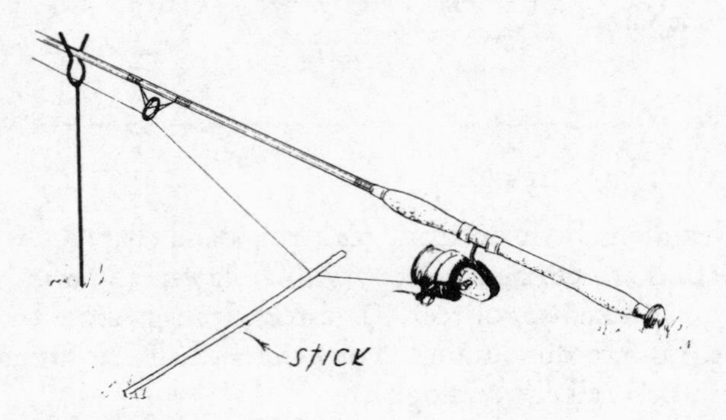

If I were using a centre-pin I would use nylon monofil, but it's rather springy for the fixed-spool. You can dye the monofil with 'Dylon' dye—I use the shade known as 'old gold' which gives a straw colour.

One of these days I intend to have a crack at the carp at Woldale Lake and perhaps Croxby, both in your district. I should be grateful for any information you could give me about these waters, as I hear conflicting reports of them. Croxby was a good water years ago.

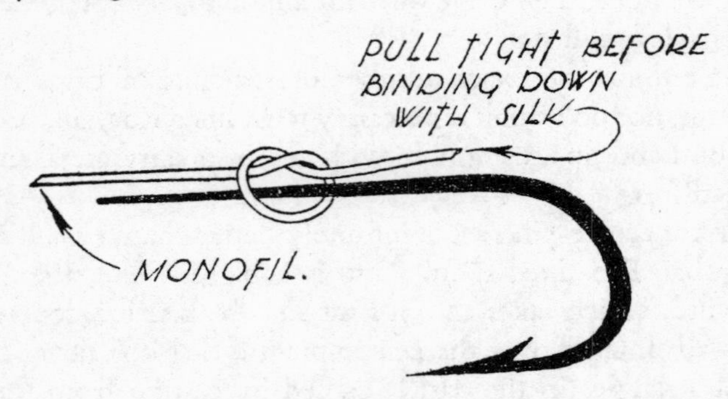

I am enclosing a few Model Perfect hooks, which one cannot get through the normal channels nowadays. If you whip them to monofil nylon, tie a knot in the nylon, or it will slip.

I've long since given up buying hooks-to-gut or nylon: one

can never trust them. I find it far safer to tie one's own. The knot looks a bit clumsy but it holds wonderfully well.

Best of luck,

RICHARD WALKER

('Water Rail')

Dear Mr. Walker,

First of all my most sincere thanks for your long and detailed letter and also for the Model Perfect hooks which you so kindly enclosed. As you anticipated, I had been unable to obtain any and I have had to make do with eyed hooks of very doubtful quality. I am most grateful.

There are two points in connection with the rod on which I would appreciate your further advice. I have already a copy of J. B. Walker's catalogue and I notice that he asks that when ordering built cane customers should give the diameter required by measuring from corner to corner. The sketches in your letter give the dimensions from flat to flat. Should I be correct if I ordered built cane to the dimensions you have given me, or do you suggest that I make the necessary correction to the nearest 32nd" and order accordingly?

The second point is in connection with the ferrule. You suggest that for the dimensions you have given me I should require a ferrule with a diameter (male) of 0.390". The ferrules shown in J. B. Walker's catalogue are graded in ½ sizes which vary by 1/32". According to my arithmetic .390" cannot be reduced to 32nds exactly and I should be pleased to have your views as to the most suitable size, according to J. B. Walker's grading. Do you think I would be safe in ordering the canes to the measurements you suggest and at the same time ask J. B. Walker's to supply a reinforced splint end suction ferrule of the appropriate size to joint the two sections?

Enough of the rod! I will not presume on your patience and generosity any further.

You ask if I can give you any information about Woldale Lake and Croxby. I understand that Croxby Pond enjoys considerable repute as a carp water, but so far I have not had an opportunity of trying my luck there. I made some enquiries during the early part of this year and I was informed that only 40 tickets are issued annually, all of which were taken for this season, and that there is a considerable waiting list for next year.

I am surprised that Woldale is known to you, although any good reports you have heard are well founded. I have known Woldale Lake for a good many years and have fished there quite a lot. One of my earliest recollections of Woldale is of walking around the lake very early one summer morning when I was camping there with the Boy Scouts. The sun had just risen above the trees and was throwing a narrow band of sunlight along one side of the lake. Lined up in this band of sunlight, like pigs at a trough, were some huge carp!—there must have been a score or more. I would not like to hazard a guess as to their weight after all these years, but they were certainly big ones. According to the keeper the lake was stocked with carp some 60–70 years ago and to his knowledge very few have been caught. There are two lakes—the one nearer to the road contains the carp. The farther lake is weedy and badly in need of cleaning, but it also contains some grand fish, particularly tench. I don't know if it has any carp. Referring to the lake nearer to the road—this is fairly clear of weed and even in this exceptionally weedy summer I have only seen two small patches of weed in the middle. It is, at a guess, between 3 and 4 acres in extent, one side very shallow and gently sloping—about 2–3 feet deep at normal fishing distance from the bank. The other (north side) is somewhat deeper but, except at one or two places, fringed by a wide margin of reeds. Whenever I have seen it the water has been a good deep colour.

I have also had some grand sport there with big eels. On one occasion, when ledgering with a small dead roach mounted on a single large hook to wire, I lost five very large eels. In each case the wire, which was new and of considerable strength, was bitten cleanly through an inch or so above the hook! My tackle was amply equipped with swivels and the wire was stranded 'gimp' which I have used successfully for pike fishing, so I think the possibility of kinking can be eliminated. I have also *caught* some good ones there! It is a constant source of surprise to me that more people do not fish deliberately for eels. The fight of a big eel may not give the excitement of a battle with a big carp, but for sheer tenacity and strength I know of no other fish of equal weight which will give the same sport as an eel.

If you do come to have a crack at Woldale or Croxby I should be very pleased to put you up during your stay in this part of the country. Please regard that as a genuine invitation and not merely a gesture, as I would be very pleased to make your acquaintance and to have a chance of yarning with you.

You mention in your letter the possibility of getting a 'birds-nest' when casting from a centre-pin reel in the dark. I have found a satisfactory solution to this difficulty by using an 'Adapta-cast'. I don't know if you have any experience with this little gadget but I have found it a great boon.

In your recent articles in the *Fishing Gazette*, if my memory serves me correctly, you made no mention of how you land your fish when you have played him out. I dislike using a gaff for obvious reasons and I should be pleased to know your views on what you consider to be the most desirable type and size of landing net.

Am I correct in assuming that you are 'R.W.' referred to by Michael Traherne in his book? If so, I envy you your encounter with a potential record-breaker.

I notice in this week's *Fishing Gazette* that you have come in for some criticism for your efforts to popularize carp fishing. I would like to say that in my opinion the selfish attitude of that correspondent is despicable and beneath contempt. Such an attitude is contrary to the traditions of the angling fraternity and compares most unfavourably with your kindness and generosity which are, I assure you, most deeply appreciated by

Yours sincerely,

M. H. Ingham

PS. I have read both the books you mention and enjoyed them immensely.

Dear Mr. Ingham,

I should, of course, have explained that J. B. Walker's ferrule sizes are *not exact* multiples of 1/32″. 0.390″ is one of his actual sizes, but which I am not quite sure, though I fancy it is 6½.

I am sorry about the dimensions of the rod being across flats and not corners. To find dimensions across corners, multiply by 1.155. If you are getting the split cane from J. B. Walker, tell him you want it to the same dimensions as he supplied to me, as I had a set of split cane from him, to make a carp rod for a friend, which came out exactly as I wanted it. It was double-built, by the way, which was unnecessary expense.

A refinement in fitting the ferrule, which is worth the extra trouble, is to glue, on each face of the hexagon where the ferrule is to be fitted, a sliver of bamboo, a fraction narrower than the flat and tapering to nothing away from the end of the joint, thus:

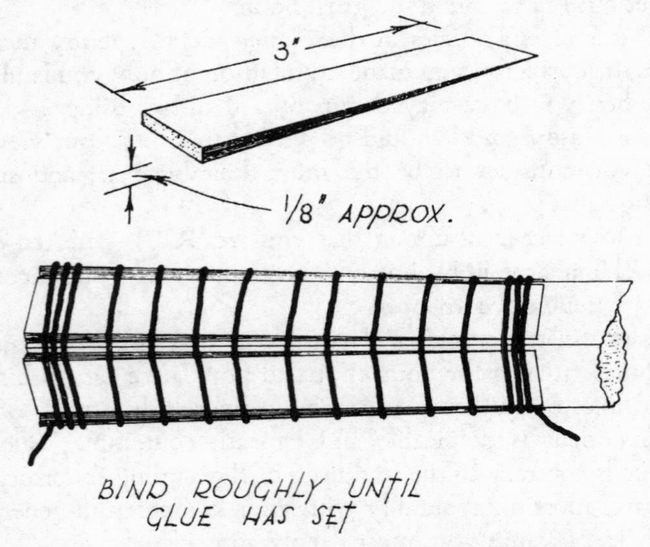

When the glue has set firmly, turn down the whole thing to fit the ferrule, which of course ought to be of such a size that it will just *not* go on the hexagon before the slivers are glued in place. Hardy's adopt this scheme in their best rods; it ensures that the hard outer skin of the bamboo is not taken away to make the ferrule fit. But do not think this is *essential*; it's only a refinement and rather troublesome at that.

You will find Walker's ferrules have four 'prongs' instead of the commoner six. To make them fit nicely on your hexagon, first get a bit of beech dowel, which push in the ferrule; then file down the prongs to a very thin end. The dowel acts as a support to stop the thin edge bending over, and if some of the dowel is filed away in the process, it doesn't matter. The ferrule can then be driven on to the rod and the prongs lightly beaten to the shape of the hexagon with a tack-hammer. Use 'Sylko' for ferrule-prong and ring whippings. It is stronger than silk, although it doesn't look quite so nice. I put an extra whipping of silk in strategic places, over the sylko, which strengthens and improves the appearance at the same time:

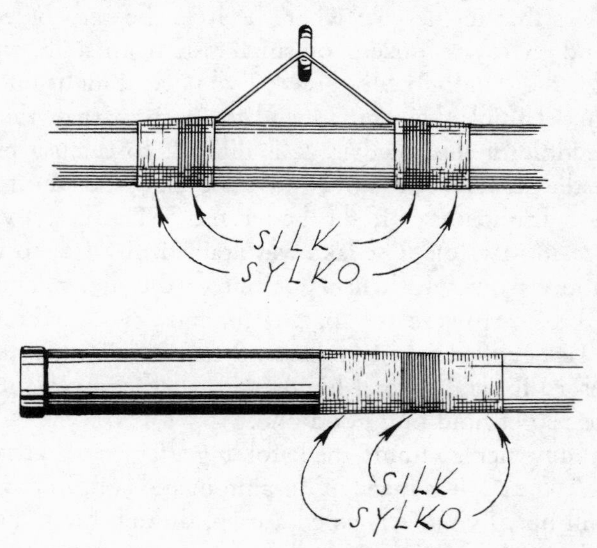

Thank you for the information about Woldale Lake. I will certainly avail myself of your most kind invitation when I get the chance. Next year I have arranged to visit a Warwickshire lake with 'B.B.'.

I fully agree with what you say about eels, and have enjoyed many a tussle with them. Only this year I had three in succession while after the big tench at Compton Verney in Warwickshire, all between four and five pounds, and they all put up a magnificent fight. The fourth bite (and last) turned out to be a tench of 5 lb. 10 oz.; altogether a good evening! Our local club water, which is about 80 ft. deep and 20 ft. ten yards from the bank, contains some monster eels and it is positively uncanny the way they can bite through wire. I have had stout banjo wire bitten. One was found dead this year, its mouth sealed by a big treble. It weighed 9½ lb. There is a tremendous carp in this lake (Arlesey) which I think must weigh nearly 40 lb. I've seen it twice. The lake is so big and deep that the chances of tempting it are slight, especially as the water is gin-clear.

Yes, I am 'R.W.', and still have the hat![1] The big carp I hooked is still going strong. I've seen him several times this year. The difficulty is that in the lake where he lives the carp breed quite freely and there are dozens of small fish from 2 lb. upwards (although they undoubtedly breed, I've never caught one under 1½ lb., and I think they must spend the early part of their lives in the middle of the weeds). It is difficult to catch a big carp there as the smaller ones always get the bait first, the resultant hullabaloo frightening off the better fish. The best I've done there is 12 lb. (twice). The lake was drained in 1942, to recover the rainbow trout which had got out of the upper lake. The biggest three carp were 20½ lb., 21½ lb. and 25½ lb., all returned, and the lake refilled. As I understand there were only about 20 fish over 10 lb. and several hundred smaller, you will see how hard it is to get hold of a good one.

My landing net is a home-made folding affair, with a triangular frame 30″ × 24″. It is made of duralumin and weighs too much! —2 lb. all up. I've never gaffed a carp, though for some queer reason I have no compunction whatever about gaffing pike.

I expect the Adaptacast idea is all right in practice, though in theory there is a likelihood of a lot of twist being put in the line. I am completely converted to the 'Felton Crosswind' and Traherne tells me he has ordered one since he used mine last

[1] A reference to an incident in *Be Quiet and Go a-Angling* by Michael Traherne (Lutterworth Press).

August and fell in love with it. Hardy's 'Altex' No. 3 is probably as good, but I cannot speak from experience. I've had an 'Altex' No. 1 for fourteen years and it's a little gem, though of course quite useless for carp. 'B.B.' has been using a little American Multiplier which he likes, and this year I tried mine (Pflueger Skilkast) on the carp. It is fine for playing a fish, but one cannot cast really light baits, e.g. a single lob from it and it is necessary to cast from coils in the hand, with the ever-present risk of tangles.

I've just remembered that I haven't told you about varnish for your rod. I use cellulose varnish for the whippings, and the best I know is called Banana oil, 'Halfax' brand—made by the Titanine dope people. You can get it from toyshops which sell Model Aeroplane kits and components. Put a turn of transparent sticky tape round the cane on each side of the whipping, varnish the whipping and then, holding the now sticky whipping between thumb and finger, twist the rod once or twice. This sticks down all the 'whiskers' of the silk or Sylko. When the first coat is quite dry (allow 1 hour in a warm room) put on additional coats until the whipping looks as if it is wrapped in cellophane. If you find bubbles or slight roughnesses, rub down with fine glasspaper. If you want the whippings to retain their original colour (cellulose varnish makes the colour go several shades darker) use a mixture of 'Durofix' and amyl acetate for the first and second coats. Then, when all is dry, remove the transparent sticky tape (which will have kept the cellulose off the cane) and give the whole rod four coats best copal varnish, put on as thinly as possible, with a finger-tip. Allow a full fortnight for each coat to dry.

If you are putting on many intermediate whippings you will find it very tedious to do each one with the cellulose, and these can be varnished direct with the copal. Use fine fly-tying silk for these intermediate whippings. If you use white silk, the copal will turn them transparent, a pretty effect. I do not use intermediate whippings at all nowadays, though I must admit they look very nice.

Do let me know if there's any other point you are not sure about. I shall be delighted to help you if I can.

This autumn (1950) 'B.B.'s' *Confessions of a Carp-Fisher* will be published, by Eyre & Spottiswoode.

Sincerely,

RICHARD WALKER

PS. You can save cost on split cane by using a bit of ¾″ beech dowel for the butt of your rod. My single-built rod is thus made. Bore your beech dowel (2 ft. long) six inches deep, to fit the end of your butt joint, which need then only be 3′ 6″ long.

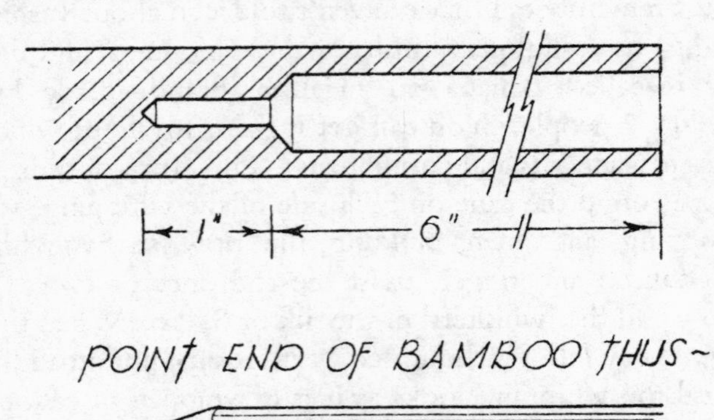

Turn down dowel, taking 1/32″ off all round for full length of bore. Then make 3 cuts like this:

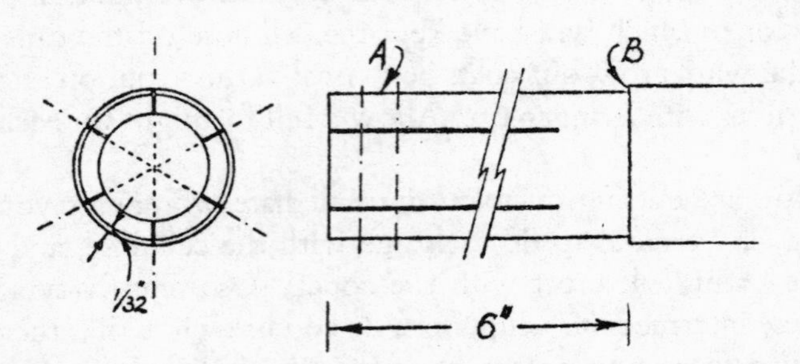

Fill the bore with 'Duroglue' or 'Seccotine', drive the bamboo right home, and wipe off surplus glue. Then bind strong string round at A (above). Finish by whipping with strong thread, starting from B and working towards A. When A is reached remove the string and continue whipping with the thread to within 1/16" of the end of the dowel. Leave a full week to set. The corks will cover the joint; you'll want a few corks of smaller bore to go on the cane.

If you can't get beech dowel or haven't lathe facilities, let me know and I'll send you the butt piece ready bored and turned, though it will be a month or so before I can get at the job.

R. W.

Dear Mr. Walker,

Many thanks for your letter and for the valuable information you have given me. I think I have now got sufficient data to enable me, with the help of one of the standard books on rod making, to proceed with my carp rod and I am ordering the necessary materials from J. B. Walker this week-end.

If you are sure it is not putting you to too much trouble I shall be very pleased to accept your kind offer to supply me with a ready turned butt-piece, and I am ordering a 3' 6" butt joint accordingly. Unfortunately I have not yet been able to equip myself with a properly fitted workshop, as I intend one day to do, and at the present time my bench is the kitchen table and my tools limited to such as can be readily cleared away. I find, as I am sure a good many people do, that clearing away is one of the major trials of my life and I am looking forward to the day when I shall not have to pack up and clear away a partly finished job.

By the way, please don't inconvenience yourself in order to send me the butt-piece in the immediate future. I shall have sufficient work on hand on other parts of the rod to occupy a good many evenings and I am quite content to await your convenience.

You may be interested to hear a little more about Woldale Lake. I had a run over to Woldale this morning for an hour's spinning and incidentally bagged seven pike in the lower lake. Before I came away, however, I managed to corner the keeper and have a chat with him, mainly concerning carp. I misinformed you when

I told you that the top lake was stocked with carp 60–70 years ago. The keeper tells me that the carp were put in about 30–35 years ago. A large number were put in, all about 2 lb. in weight, and since that time few have been caught and the keeper has seen none dead.

I said that by now there must be some fish at least equal to Albert Buckley's 26-pounder and the keeper agreed most emphatically. In fact, he did not agree that that is the record. He said that about twelve years ago he saw a carp landed there which weighed 'an ounce or two under 27 lb.'! I think it may be safe to assume that at least some of the other original fish will have grown at an equal rate, which logically would mean that now there must be fish in that lake approaching 40 lb. That large fish, by the way, was taken on potato.

Re the Adaptacast, I quite agree that in practice as well as in theory, it does impart a twist to the line, which is not taken out when the line is recovered. If many casts were made the amount of twist would become serious, but I only use it when night fishing, when I do not normally have to cast many times and the small amount of twist in the line, whilst not desirable is not serious. It is certainly not an ideal solution, but I prefer it to the danger of a tangle at night when casting from coils in the hand. One day I hope to aspire to a Felton Crosswind, which, with the rod I am about to make, will put me on more equal terms with the big fellows—at the same time removing any possible excuse about the inadequacy of my tackle!

I am looking forward to meeting you when you come to try your skill with our local monsters and if I hear any further information which may be likely to tempt you into Lincolnshire be sure I will let you know. Please regard my invitation as a 'standing' one and let me know whenever you are able to make the trip.

I am looking forward to reading 'B.B.'s' *Confessions of a Carp-Fisher*.

I would very much appreciate your views on the subject of reels for carp fishing. After giving considerable thought to the matter I have decided that if I intend really to concentrate on carp fishing in the future I should equip myself with the best tackle that I can afford. The rod, of which you have given me particulars, should be ideal, and I think that by exercising economy in other directions I can afford to buy a reel which will be worthy of the rod.

Any advice or suggestions based on your wide experience will be greatly appreciated.

Kind regards,

Yours sincerely,
M. H. INGHAM

Dear Mr. Ingham,

There are several fixed-spool reels on the market which I am sure would prove satisfactory for carp, including the Altex III, the Felton Crosswind, and the Mitchell. At present I am using a Felton Crosswind, but I think the other two are both excellent. The main thing is that the reel must hold at least 100 yards of 12 lb. b.s. line. This and the carp-rod make a powerful combination.

Last year I hooked a 12-pounder in very cramped circumstances—between two fallen trees about ten yards apart—and simply clamped down and held it hard, the only possible course. There were one or two close shaves but it was duly landed in just six minutes, a well-conditioned common carp. I am quite confident that given reasonable room, say 50 yards, this outfit would cope with a fish of double that size. These rods are so designed that it is almost impossible to break a 12 lb. line with them—a statement which *sounds* silly, but is actually true.

Of course, in more open water finer lines can be used. In a water like Mapperley I should be inclined to use about 250 yards of monofil line, say .010″ or .011″.

I have often been told that I am heavy-handed on carp and tench, because I make them work as hard as I can for every inch of line they get. This is probably because I commenced my carp-fishing career in the 'deep and weedy clay-pit full of discarded bicycles'! When you are *forced* to stop fish or be broken, you soon develop an acute sense of when a break is imminent and can play a fish just short of that point.

To revert to fixed-spool reels, I find that to grease lines is fatal to casting. Nylon will float quite well without grease. *White* nylon can be dyed a beautiful colour with 'Dylon' dye—'old gold' and 'lime green' mixed 50–50 makes a good colour, or one can get a camouflage effect by dipping half the coil in one colour and the other half in the other, overlapping. This gives:

The same thing can be done with Monofil nylon for casts. I believe it makes a *great difference* to one's chances of success. I am convinced that the secret of success with carp is never to hurry and to take the greatest care over every detail, however unimportant it may seem. I know that careless people often catch carp, but I have caught 73 from 10 lb. to 17 lb., not by cleverness (I'm rather stupid really) but by *taking care* to have everything as right as I know how.

You are entering a field of angling which has very great possibilities which have remained almost unexplored for many, many years. Just consider these points—how many anglers fish for carp—

At the right *time of day*?—Early morning and night.

In the right *part of a lake*?—the *Shallows*, except in rough or cold weather.

With the right *tackle*?—correct rod and line, proper hook, no float or lead.

With the right *bait*, of the right *size*, on the *surface* or *bottom*—*never* hanging?

With soft-soled shoes and from behind cover?

Is it then any wonder that carp have a reputation of uncatchability, and that there are great carp in many waters which can be caught by anyone who goes about the job in the right way?

I haven't the least doubt that you will catch some fine carp and have wonderful sport. Many times I have been given a chance (or challenge!) to take a carp in a lake where 'no one has ever caught a carp' and (given time, because a single day or week-end is not always sufficient) managed to get two or three nice fish. 'B.B.' has had exactly the same experience. If a trout-fisher were set to catch roach in the Lea or even the Thames, I doubt if he would catch many, and might very well call them practically uncatchable. So it is with the coarse-fisherman, who knows his roach and pike, he is beaten by carp, unless he learns the right methods, which he will very seldom trouble to do!

Further thoughts on rod-making—*Never, never* use a transverse pin to secure ferrules! If the ferrule is a good, tight fit, no pin can improve it. If it isn't a good fit, the pin won't save it from rocking on the bamboo, and will only make it more difficult to get off and re-fit properly. The one and only place for a transverse pin is to secure the butt cap.

Varnish. Put copal varnish on with your finger, not a brush. There is no better way of getting a thin, even coat. Never put cellulose on top of copal; copal can go over cellulose but not vice-versa.

Consider the desirability of buying two matched ferrules for your rod. The spare male can be used for an extra top, which may well be stouter than the standard one and can be made at a later date. The female can be kept as a spare to replace the original one, should it suffer damage or become too worn. (Female ferrules are much more susceptible to damage than males!)

Cork handle. When you file this to size, make sure it is round and of even diameter by continually trying it with a gauge as you file. If there is a lot of cork to come off, remove some with a sharp, *wet* knife, which will have to be re-sharpened very frequently. My handles are thus:

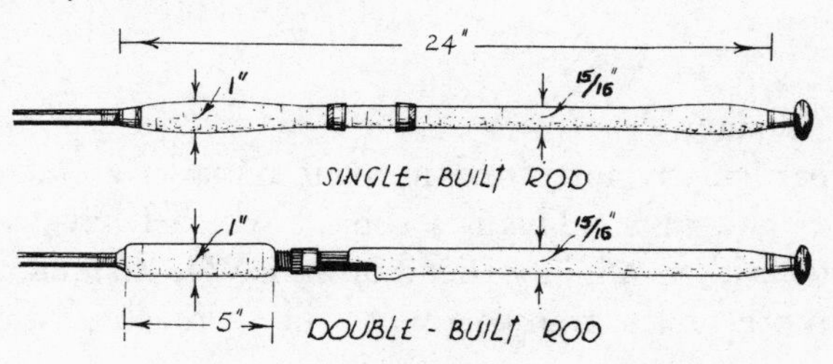

The screw grip on the double-built rod is a dubious advantage —it is more secure, but one is limited to a fixed position for the reel. If I built a third carp rod I should make the handle thus:

with sliding reel fittings. Of course the last two or three corks at the butt end are put on after the rest of the handle has been shaped up and glass papered and the reel fittings slid on. Do not put the shoulder collar or butt cap on until the cork is finished or they will be sure to get scratched. The ferrules go on last of all before rings and whippings. Take care to put the shoulder collar on before the female ferrule!

I use Durofix for the corks—Duroglue or seccotine are liable to go sticky in wet weather. Allow three days at least for the Durofix to dry before shaping the corks, as the air doesn't get to it very easily. I usually leave my corks a fortnight before shaping; there are usually plenty of other rods to be getting on with here!

If you have a shabby old rod in your possession, I would renovate if I were you. The practice will teach you a lot more than I can explain in writing and help you to make a better job of your new carp rod. You might also come across some points which I could tell you about but which I have so far missed.

You are most welcome to write at any time and I shall be very pleased to assist in any way I can. I hope to do the wood handle towards the end of this month.

Sincerely,
RICHARD WALKER

Dear Mr. Walker,

I was particularly interested in your remarks about camouflaged lines and casts. This is a subject which I have discussed many times with an angling friend of mine. He maintains that as nylon is more or less transparent it will be practically invisible when lying on the bed of a lake or river, because it will transmit the colour of the bottom on which it is lying and that provided the nylon cast is long enough it is unnecessary to camouflage either it or the line. This depends, of course, on the degree of transparency or opacity of the nylon Monofil, but as I have yet to see any which is perfectly transparent, I cannot agree with his argument. The slightest opacity will cause the monofil to reflect light and an untreated cast will be revealed as a thread of greyish white lying on the darker colour of the bottom.

A dyed cast will reflect the colour which it is dyed—naturally!—and may also transmit to some small extent the colour of the bottom on which it is lying. This is, in my opinion, preferable to an undyed cast, but it has the disadvantage that unless by some rare chance the dye matches exactly the colour of the bottom, it will be revealed as a *line* of, say, green on a brown bottom.

The camouflaged cast makes no pretence of matching the bottom exactly, but approximates to it. As I see it, the great advantage of a camouflaged cast, and, of course, line, is that it does not show up as a continuous line of non-matching colour. That continuous line is broken and consequently I maintain is less conspicuous.

Could you possibly tell me where I can obtain a white braided nylon line suitable for camouflaging? The only lines I have seen offered for sale have been dyed green or brown. My present line (Milwards' 'Spider Web') is a golden brown, but I suppose that by dipping it as you suggest it could be camouflaged satisfactorily. You recommend 'Dylon' dye. Could you please tell me the makers or where it can be obtained, as I have not seen it in any of our local tackle shops.

I have had a most helpful letter from J. B. Walker, in which he says that he made himself a carp rod to the same specification which you gave me, about the time that you ordered your materials, and that consequently he is familiar with my requirements. Unfortunately there may be some delay before he can let me have the built cane, but I must possess my soul in patience.

I will remember your remarks about attention to detail. With that end in view I have been reading all the available literature on carp lore and I am continually being surprised by the widely divergent, and in some cases contradictory, opinions expressed by experts. Of course one cannot generalize on a subject such as this, and I am prepared to draw my own conclusions, but I would appreciate your views on the question of baits. Again, I would say, one cannot generalize, but everyone I have read seems to have a favourite bait. Albert Buckley swears by honey paste, some by potato and from what I gathered from reading Michael Traherne's book, you and he prefer lob worms for bottom fishing. As far as it is possible to generalize in this matter I would always express a preference for a natural bait and for that reason would choose lob worms, but what may be a good bait in one water would possibly not catch fish in another water. From my limited experience, the disadvantage of the lob worms is that they are attractive to so many kinds of fish, and the disturbances caused by landing, say, an eel can be very annoying when after carp. Do you find that the general efficacy of lob worms as bait for carp outweighs the disadvantage I have mentioned? I should also be interested to know how you hook your worm so as to present it in the most effective manner.

Once again my sincere thanks for your most valuable advice and my apologies for all my questions. Please don't bother to reply by return unless it is convenient to do so.

Yours sincerely,

M. H. INGHAM

Dear Mr. Ingham,

Yes, I fully agree with you about camouflaged casts, especially with nylon Monofil, which in the heavier gauges is most conspicuous—it takes up a certain amount of water and goes whitish as a result. One of these days anglers will realize that because a thing is transparent it is not necessarily invisible. I don't know what the refractive index of nylon is, but rays of light will most certainly be bent by it, even when it is dry, and at the height of its transparency. When it is dyed it becomes no less *visible* but far less *alarming*, in that it more nearly resembles natural things in the water.

My conversion to camouflage is recent and the result of this season's fishing, not only for carp. I belong to a local angling club whose activities are diverse and include dry-fly fishing for trout and match-fishing. Last season I fished in ten matches and came third twice. This season in ten matches I was first six times, second twice, third once. Last season I used 0.006″ nylon undyed; this season I used the same stuff camouflaged.

On the trout stream last year it was hardly possible to fish owing to weed and bushes. We did a vast amount of clearing during the first few months of this year, and from the beginning of the season the water was fished hard and continuously. Although there are several members who are much better fly-fishers than I, my camouflaged casts got the four best fish of the season, 3 lb. 3 oz., 3 lb. 13 oz., 4 lb. and 4 lb. 8 oz.—all marked and known fish which must have seen hundreds of artificial flies before they took mine.

There is a well-known chub-hole at Offord, on the Bedfordshire Ouse. The chub there are very shy indeed and few are caught, though they are seen almost daily. I caught only one last year in about five visits. This year I went three times and caught twelve weighing 28 lb. the lot, best fish 3¾ lb., besides being broken several times. Camouflage again.

I am absolutely convinced that camouflaged casts make a tremendous difference, especially on waters which are much fished.

I don't know who makes 'Dylon' dyes. I got mine from a small general store; I imagine that drapers would stock them. If you cannot obtain the dye locally let me know and I will send you some; it's very cheap, a shillingsworth will last a whole season.

My white braided nylon line was smuggled in from America. I don't know where white lines can be obtained in England, though I have no doubt that they are available. Probably Hardy's would have them. I don't think camouflage of the line is so important as long as the cast is camouflaged.

Plaited flax makes a good material for bottom fishing for carp, if properly dyed. I have done well with eyed hooks tied direct to plaited line, but it is apt to fray during a long fight, as I have found to my cost!

Baits. I refuse to be dogmatic. You will usually find that a man who swears by a particular bait is limited in his experience to one particular water.

Plain bread paste is taken by carp in every water I know. It is not always the *best* bait, but I know nowhere where it is useless. The same applies to floating crust, except that it is useless everywhere in cold conditions or when fish are definitely on the bottom.

Both paste and bread are subject to the attentions of small roach, etc.

Worms—big lobworms—are the best bait of all where they are taken; that is, carp either take them well or not at all. I don't know why this should be, but it is so. On some waters they will not look at lobs—Beechmere, in Devon, for example, is full of carp of all sizes which will take paste or crust well—it is possible to catch five or six in a day, from 2 lb. to 10 lb. or so; but I never heard of anyone catching a fish there on worm. 'B.B.' spent days worm-fishing there without success. The bite on worm, where it *is* taken, is usually decisive and one is not troubled by small roach and rudd. Small perch and eels are a nuisance, but provided you find your feeding carp (bubbles and mud-swirls) you can usually catch one or two in spite of eels and perch.

Potato is a most uncertain bait; I know many waters where potato is quite useless, and none where paste, bread or worms are not better baits. Potato has its uses where small fish or eels are so numerous as to make the other baits impossible to use. I think that extensive ground-baiting would educate carp to take potato more readily, but I cannot say that I am greatly enamoured with it.[1]

I have also taken carp on black slugs, water-lily seeds, bunches of leatherjackets, water snails, land snails complete with shell, and on pieces of water-lily leaf with those queer eggs on, embedded in transparent jelly (I think they are snail eggs, but I'm not sure). Also rush-grubs or flagworms, five or six on a hook.

[1] Note, in view of later experience!—R.W.

You split rushes and find them inside, whitish grubs with burnt sienna heads, and you split of a lot of rushes before you have enough! Carp will take gentles but I've never caught a big one on them. Once or twice I have had a small carp on a bluebottle dapped under trees where the fish were basking on the surface.

Baiting. For short casts I stick the hook in the worm once; for long casts I loop it. For crust, as below:

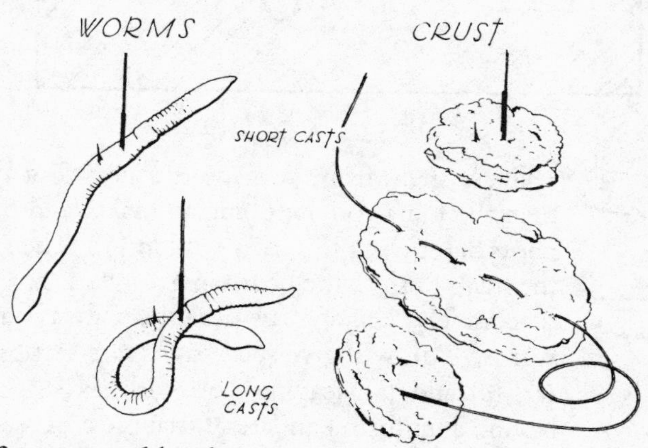

And for potato, like this:

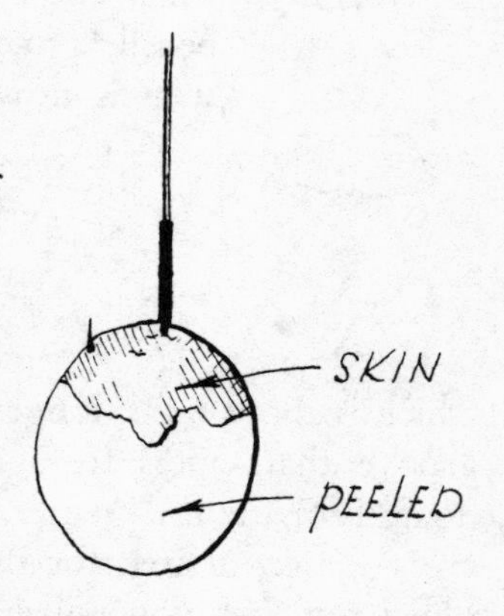

I never use treble hooks, even for potato. 'B.B.' says carp will take boiled beans, haricots, etc. I caught a trout once which vomited a lot of cooked broad beans which had been coming into the river via a pipe from a farmhouse. I think beans have possibilities, but have never tried them. Sticklebacks, perch and trout eat *leeches*; perhaps carp might. I caught a carp of 9½ lb. once which unfortunately died, and we found its stomach full of frog spawn and tadpoles. It was caught, with a view to its spawning in another water, with a landing net. An old keeper once told me that the hardboiled yolk of a bantam's egg was a good carp bait.

In case you would like to try making your own split-cane, here is one method:

Two boards are required. The first is about 3 ft. long and has four grooves, thus:

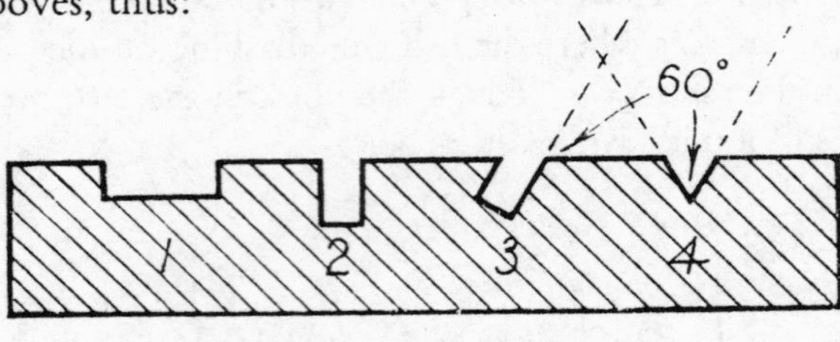

CROSS SECTION

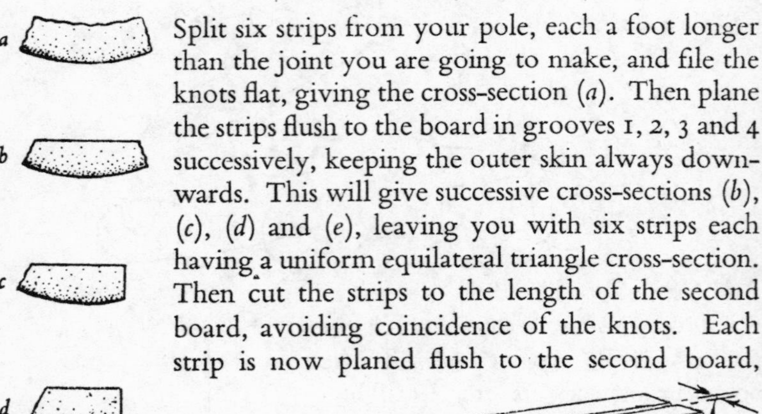

Split six strips from your pole, each a foot longer than the joint you are going to make, and file the knots flat, giving the cross-section (*a*). Then plane the strips flush to the board in grooves 1, 2, 3 and 4 successively, keeping the outer skin always downwards. This will give successive cross-sections (*b*), (*c*), (*d*) and (*e*), leaving you with six strips each having a uniform equilateral triangle cross-section. Then cut the strips to the length of the second board, avoiding coincidence of the knots. Each strip is now planed flush to the second board,

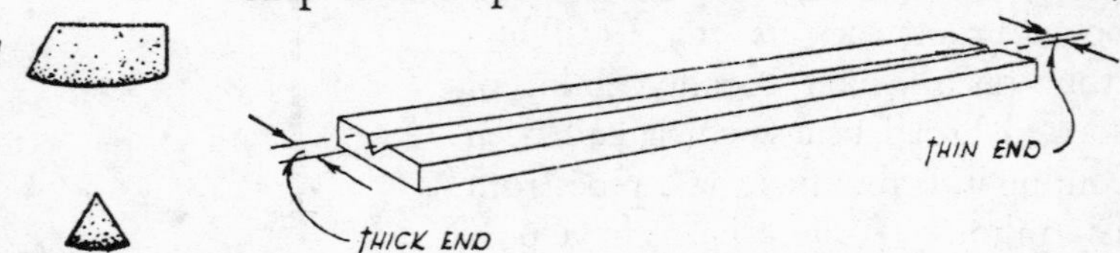

which is about 6 ins. longer than the desired rod-joint and has a groove that tapers from a little larger than the cross-section desired for the thick end of the strip, to a little smaller than the cross-section desired for the thin end. When the six strips are glued together you will have a joint that tapers from too thin to too thick. If your joint is too thin cut some off the thin end and if too thick cut it off the thick end. It is all very easy, especially if you get your boards made for you by a skilled joiner. The angles must be accurate. It is a great advantage to make your own split cane if you are contemplating building many rods, and of course it is a lucrative pastime too if your friends start ordering rods. I make quite a bit at it and hope to make more when I have finished a machine I am making, which will speed up the planing operations considerably.

If you want further information on rod-building or split cane making, never hesitate to write. I am pleased to be able to help when I can.

Sincerely,
RICHARD WALKER

PS. Have you ever tried fly-tying? A highly entertaining pastime, and once you've started you can never pass a stray feather, while a poulterer's takes on quite a different significance!

III

December Letters

Dear Mr. Walker,

I have placed my order for a 'Felton Crosswind' which should be to hand before Christmas, and I hope to get the 'feel' of it by doing a bit of spinning for pike with it during the Christmas holiday.

Your evidence in support of camouflaged casts is overwhelming and I certainly intend to follow your example next year. I will let you know how my results with camouflaged casts compare with previous seasons. You certainly had a most successful year! I have tried all the local shops that might possibly stock 'Dylon' dyes—and several shops in other places—but without success. No one seems to have ever heard of it, though several have offered to order it for me if I can give them the name of the makers, which, of course, I am not able to do. In the circumstances, therefore, I would be most grateful if you would kindly send me some. Perhaps if I can get the maker's name from the packet I shall be able to get the stuff locally in the future.

I have made enquiries about white braided nylon and, as you suggested, Hardy's are able to supply it. This week I have received a new catalogue from Milwards and I see that they are marketing a new line under the name of, I believe, 'Terylene' Polyester Yarn; I wonder if you have seen the catalogue or have any knowledge of this new line. Milwards claim that it has a greater strength-weight ratio than any other braided line, that it is very hard-wearing and non-elastic. I am not sure whether the latter quality is an advantage or not. The slightly elastic properties of braided nylon act to some extent as a shock absorber, but it may be that it is a disadvantage when playing a big fish on a long line. I would appreciate your views on this point, and whether you think this new line would be better than braided nylon for carp and general coarse fishing.

Thanks for your views on baits for carp. Of course, I realize that one cannot generalize on the matter of baits, but I will bear in mind what you say. Can you offer any explanation for the fact that carp at Beechmere will not take worms? I have frequently noticed that fish in different waters react differently to baits, and to some extent it is understandable. I assume that a fish's reaction depends to some extent on its natural food—in one water carp may feed principally on a certain type of grub which happens to abound in that particular water, whereas in another water that grub may be present in only very small numbers and the carp in that water may feed mainly on a different kind of grub. I think it is only logical that a bait which would attract carp in one of these waters would not attract carp in the other water to the same extent. I would have thought that worms find their way into all waters in this country and that where carp are present they are taken as a natural food, though certainly not the staple diet. For that reason I would have assumed that carp would take worms in any water—possibly not as the *best* bait, but at least that they would be taken sometimes. Have you any theory on this phenomenon?

You have certainly taken carp on a variety of baits. Can it be that water-lily seeds form a normal part of a carp's diet? If so, is that the reason why carp can sometimes be taken on green-peas?

Some time ago I had occasion to remove an old tree stump and in the rotten wood I found a grub which struck me as being an ideal bait. It was a large leathery thing, about 1½" long and nearly ½" thick, dirty creamy white in colour, with a dark brown head. Do you know it? Unfortunately, it was too late in the year to try it out, but I intend to hunt for others of the kind next year.

You make rod making (building split cane) sound very easy and I would dearly love to try my hand at it, but as I think I told you in an earlier letter, I have no workshop facilities, and tolerant as my wife may be—a true fisherman's wife!—I suspect that she would 'draw the line' at my making rods and planing, etc., on the kitchen table. When I build my own house, a workshop will be high on the list of essential features.

I have never tried fly-tying, or even fly-fishing. As you no doubt know this county is not blessed with many or very good trout streams. Trout there certainly are, but not in sufficient numbers or of sufficient size to attract much serious attention. I have done a bit of dapping occasionally with moderate results. The two best trout of my career were both taken this year— one 2lb. 5 ozs. on worm, a cannibal which was the record for that particular stream. The other, 3 lb. 1 oz., I took on a minnow—both brown trout. I should add that the latter fish was taken in private water, an old mill pool which receives the overflow water from a trout hatchery. This pool is teeming with small rainbow trout up to about ½ lb. which have escaped somehow from the hatchery (which contains only rainbows for table use) but there is also a small percentage of brown trout (wild) which have been attracted to the pool by the scraps of food escaping from the hatchery. I cannot claim full credit for this fish as it was not in natural conditions, but it gave me a grand fight and was a most beautiful fish, a female, in tip-top condition. Perhaps in a few years' time I may take up fly-fishing seriously—an acquaintance of mine has this year made an artificial lake of about 5 acres which he has stocked up with 1 and 2 year old brown trout and I have a standing invitation to fish when it 'matures'—but in the meantime I remain a coarse fisherman, content merely to fill in the close season by dapping and worming for trout. Please don't think I am belittling the sport—it must be most fascinating—but my opportunities for good trout fishing are so limited that I have never yet been tempted to try my hand at it. Fly-tying I can well imagine to be, as you say, a highly entertaining pastime, but it demands some knowledge of entomology, or at least of standard fly patterns, which I am afraid I do not possess.

Kind regards,

Yours sincerely,

M. H. INGHAM

PS. A friend of mine has just bought a new rod, principally for carp fishing—an Allcocks 'Eclipse'. It is, I think, about 10 ft. 6 ins. long and its taper is approximately the same as that of the carp rod I am making, though it is somewhat lighter. The section measurements compared with the measurements which you gave me are in the ratio of about 3 to 5. Do you think it will be suitable for carp fishing? My friend would value your opinion.

Dear Mr. Ingham,

You will find the 'Felton Crosswind' very nice for pike spinning when you get used to it. I've caught quite a lot on mine during the last two months, but nothing of any size—up to about seven or eight pounds only. I missed several before I realized that the clutch was slipping on the strike, which caused the rather large hooks to fail to penetrate properly. I drop a finger on to the drum as I strike now, which avoids the trouble.

I will send you a selection of 'Dylon' dyes as soon as I can get to the shop where I know they are obtainable, and will also find out who makes them. They really are excellent. I use them for dyeing feathers for fly-tying as well as for casts, etc., and the colours are absolutely permanent.

I had not heard of Milwards' new line, but I can tell you quite definitely that—in my opinion at any rate—the stretching quality of nylon is an important factor which has both advantages and disadvantages. The chief disadvantage is particularly applicable to carp fishing, and it is this; where comparatively large hooks are used, the stretch of the nylon may be such as to nullify the impact of the strike and prevent the hook from going home properly. Resilience in the line is not necessary; the rod ought to provide sufficient to guard against sudden jerks, that is where fairly stout tackle is in use.

'B.B.' and I both found that with the ordinary English braided nylon it was necessary to employ a very long, hard strike to be at all certain of hooking carp on No. 4 Model Perfect hooks. I mean by this a strike right back over the shoulder, stepping back a pace at the same time. My American plaited nylon is not nearly so stretchy—no more so than plaited silk—and with it a normal wristy strike is sufficient. Of course I am referring to fishing a 15 or 20 yard cast. With short casts, or margin-fishing with bread, there should be no difficulty in connecting.

Few fishermen realize how much extra force is needed to fix a big hook. A hook twice as big in the bend and twice as thick in the wire, and twice the distance between point and barb, needs sixteen times the force to get right home (double thickness wire alone means four times as much force, displacement being proportional to *area*). Incidentally, this was another factor which influenced the design of the carp rods—some weight in the tip was provided to help to obtain a firm strike. 'B.B.' and I agreed that this extra weight at the top would help to develop the action in casting lighter baits and give a powerful strike; you will therefore find the rod definitely point-heavy and rather tiring on the wrist for continuous casting, which, fortunately, is not required in carp-fishing. If you use it for spinning you will need two hands after a while! I find mine quite useful for spinning when I don't want to use much lead, as it will throw a light bait much better than my proper spinning rod—as, of course, it was designed to do.

I cannot understand why the Beechmere carp won't take worms. I imagine there are as many worms in the earth surrounding it as anywhere else. I wouldn't say, actually, that they *won't* take worms, only that as far as 'B.B.' and I know, none has ever taken a worm on a fisherman's hook. They eat bread paste well and sometimes five or six fish averaging 4 lb. are caught in one day by one angler. I am not at all sure that *any* of our baits can properly be considered natural foods, in that they could be considered an important part of a carp's diet. I rather fancy that the bulk of a carp's food is the minute organisms which live in the fine upper layer of the mud at the bottom of the pool. This mud is positively seething with minute life, both animal and vegetable, and carp certainly work over it most systematically—hence bubblings. I have watched them routing about in mud and have gone out in a boat and scraped some of the mud out here and there for examination. There has never been anything in it of greater size than what one might describe as microscopic. I have only once done a post-mortem on a carp, but I have often noticed that their excreta is largely mud from the bottom. I fancy they simply swallow mud in the places where it is richest in microscopic life.

If this is generally true, then all our baits are comparatively *unusual*, if not actually *unnatural*, items of diet for carp, and there can be little to guide one in choosing baits. Of course carp are said to consume a great quantity of weed, and I have no doubt that they do eat a lot of the young shoots of suitable weeds. In most waters they get an excellent living and can thrive without ever swallowing anything bigger than a pin's head!

The water-lily seeds I mean are nothing like green peas. After the flower has fallen there is a kind of knob on the flower-stalk, like this:

It eventually disintegrates, and from the inside come a number of sections which originally were arranged like the sections of an orange, but very thin and juiceless. They are shaped thus:

are white in colour, and have blackish seeds inside, along the inner straight edge. I am not sure whether carp actually swallow them, as they do a lot of sucking-in and spitting-out.

They do the same thing with fallen willow leaves in the autumn,

I think they actually eat some of them, but of course it would be hopeless to try them for bait. Carp will usually take floating bread under those circumstances anyway.

I shouldn't like to guess what the grub was that you found in the rotten wood. Quite a number of beetles, in their larva stage, feed on rotten wood, and several moths, also. All the various whitish grubs make useful baits. I expect carp would take withy-bobs where the elm trees or willows overhang their abode. Chub are very fond of them.

I started to write this letter last night, and this morning I passed the shop where the 'Dylon' dyes are sold. Here are what I find the four most useful colours. I make up bottles of each colour, about ½ pint of water to each dye (they have to be boiled). Then I mix colours to get the desired shade. It is quite safe to put the nylon in warm dye—just cool enough to put one's finger in, say 110° F. The dyes will keep a long time in their bottles, if you put a little salt in and keep them well corked.

4 of No. 23 to 1 of No. 24 is a good green.

1 of No. 23 to 1 of No. 28 is a nice pale olive, like rotting weed in its early stages.

No. 28 is a golden straw.

No. 4 is a good brown; with some No. 23 added it is a good dark olive. With some No. 24 it makes a muddy olive.

You can dye quills for floats with these dyes. I think they would even dye celluloid floats.

I am rehabilitating a fair-sized shed for a workshop, as comments from my wife on the undesirability of bamboo dust as an article of diet for small children have become both terse and frequent of late, not even the construction of toys for our small child having appreciably affected them!

The rod you mention sounds as if it would be quite reasonable for carp-fishing. The dimensions are very similar to the 'Hardy-Wallis' rod (now made by Allcocks also and called the 'Wallis-Wizard'); I have had one for many years. It is 11 ft. instead of 10 ft. 6 ins., but the taper is about the same. I have caught a lot of carp on it, including several over 15 lb. and one of 16 lb. 5 oz. The only real difficulty with it when dealing with powerful fish is that, to save the top, one has to hold the rod at a lower angle—to throw most of the strain on to the middle and butt joints—and this of course decreases the *effective* length of the rod. You need plenty of effective length for a good many carp waters, to keep the fish out of the snags which project from the bank. I enclose a picture of a corner of Temple Pool, which shows very well why this is necessary. Incidentally, this photograph shows clearly how muddy the water is, where the carp have stirred it up. The ripples are the result of activity in the keep-net, a 6-pounder. The bush beyond the ripples is an ancient whitethorn which has fallen into the water, a safe haven for any carp which succeeds in reaching it!

Your trout fishing sounds very interesting. Is there a Mayfly season on that water? If so, I'll send you some of my extra-special Mayflies to try. I never take the least notice of standard patterns in fly-tying; I just try to tie something which bears a resemblance to whatever fly the fish are taking. Shop flies are, with few exceptions, terrible. They are mostly tied by women, who have never in their lives seen the thing they're trying to imitate. My own knowledge of entomology is decidedly sketchy, but I *have seen* the various aquatic flies!

You will find J. B. Walker a good chap to deal with and one who is genuinely interested in seeing that his customers get what they want, as long as it is within his power to supply it.

With regard to the wood handle I am going to make for you, it might be better if you sent the butt section of the split cane so that I can bore the beech exactly to size; I could then fit the split cane in and we should be certain of a solid accurate job. I don't mean to imply that you are incapable, but I have lathe facilities here and can get it dead true.

Best wishes for Christmas and the New Year.

Sincerely,

RICHARD WALKER

Dear Mr. Walker,

My belated, but nevertheless sincere, thanks for your letter and contents. I have got the dyes made up and bottled but I have not tried them out yet. I am waiting until I can get some more nylon.

I have just had a most enjoyable day's spinning in Revesby Reservoir and am feeling somewhat drowsy as a result of the fresh air after a very lazy Christmas. Revesby Reservoir, owned by Lady Beryl Groves, is a beautiful stretch of water which serves as an emergency reservoir for the Boston district. It is about 50 acres in extent, surrounded by trees and dotted with little wooded islands, and is teeming with pike, perch, roach and bream—unfortunately no carp or tench so far as I know. I was fishing principally for perch, with a 1½″ Horton Evans 'Vibro' spinner and a 1½″ silver devon. (Have you tried the 'Vibro' spinners? They are most effective.) My bag consisted of about 3 dozen perch up to about 2 lb. and about 2 dozen pike from about 2–8 lb. The 'Felton Crosswind' performed beautifully and I am very pleased with it. It certainly does all that is claimed for it.

Isn't it amazing what a difference a red tag on the hook makes to the attractiveness of a spinner—particularly to perch. On a number of occasions perch followed my spinner right in to the bank, no doubt attracted by the flashing metal, but making deliberate rushes at the red wool on the hook. I am quite certain that the red tag was the 'bait' and that they were not 'coming short' at the spinner itself. I don't know if the red tag makes such a great difference to pike—my catch of pike was not materially affected when I substituted a tasselled hook—but in this particular water it certainly has a great attraction to perch.

I appreciate your points about the advantages and disadvantages of the elastic properties of nylon. Speaking purely on assumption I would say that for the most purposes the disadvantages of the stretching qualities of nylon outweigh the advantages, and that if Milwards' new line is equal to nylon in other respects, but non-elastic, it will be superior. However, the only way to find out is to put it to the test of practice and I have ordered a 6 lb. b.s. line of 'Terylene' yarn. I will let you know in due course how it compares with nylon.

I was most interested in your remarks on striking, as this appears to be a most controversial subject. Some writers say emphatically 'Do not strike—merely tighten.' On checking up,

I find that they are, generally speaking, the 'fish-light' brigade, who use small hooks which do not require a hard strike to drive them home, and whose tackle would not stand up to a hard strike anyway. I have had the mortifying experience of losing a good fish through not having driven the hook in firmly and I am now an ardent believer in sharp striking.

Temple Pool looks *most* attractive. I am not a member of the local angling club and in this respect we differ. I cannot see any attraction in lining the banks of a river when it is possible to fish alone in such beautiful surroundings. It may be that your matches are fished in surroundings which are more attractive than our 'flooded railway cuttings' but, surroundings apart, competitive angling does not appeal to me in the least. The Temple Pool in your photograph is very much like a part of Woldale Lake.

There *is* a Mayfly season on the two rivers where I do my trout fishing and I should be very pleased indeed to try out your special Mayflies, though I should warn you that, as I think I told you before, my fly-fishing experience is limited to dapping and my results may not be a true indication of the excellence of your flies. Nevertheless, I *would* like to try them.

It is extremely kind of you to go to such trouble with the handle for my rod. I have not yet received the cane from J. B. Walker, but when I do I will send the butt section on to you. Many thanks.

Have you any more news of 'B.B.'s' *Confessions of a Carp-Fisher*? I think you said it was to be published in the autumn, but I have not seen any reports on it as yet and I am looking forward to reading it.

My very best wishes for the New Year and may it bring you into even closer contact with the record-breaker in Temple Pool.

Yours sincerely,

M. H. INGHAM

Dear Mr. Ingham,

I should think you *did* have an enjoyable day! That is the best catch of pike and perch I've heard of for years. What a fine christening for the 'Felton Crosswind'? I am glad you like the reel. I am busy trying to invent a neat and reliable ratchet so that it sings out when the clutch slips. Perhaps my desire for this feature is due to habit—listening to the 'angry-bee' noise of my Altex. I miss this in the Felton; I've been used to judging how much line a fish has taken by the pitch and duration of the buzz. If I devise a suitable mechanism I'll get Courtney Williams to see if he cannot fit it as standard. I suppose dyeing the line a different colour every five yards would serve the same purpose!

You will probably think I'm an appalling sceptic if I say are you *sure* that perch are attracted by a *red* tassel? I'm afraid I have formed a habit of believing practically nothing in fishing until I've gone to enormous lengths to find out the truth of the matter. I do not mean to say that I doubt your statement that the perch attacked the red celluloid 'tassel' of the 'Vibro'. I don't doubt it for a moment, because perch always tackle a small fish, or a spinner, by the tail. What I wonder is, was it the *red* that attracted them or would they have struck at the tail just the same if it had been blue, or yellow, or any other colour?

I *think* perch commonly attack from astern because they lack the speed to attack any other way. If they slash the tail of a small fish it will be slowed down, and the perch will catch it easily. They do not rely on surprise tactics, like pike, but hunt their prey down, as doubtless you have seen them doing many a time. There is some doubt whether fish can distinguish between one colour and another. Until I know the answer, I have to assume they can!

You will really have to try your hand at fly-fishing. I would not put it in the same class as carp-fishing, but it has two main recommendations, to my mind; it is the cheapest form of fishing I know as regards tackle, and it takes you out fishing at a delightful time of year, from April 1st onwards. There are a number of other things to commend it, too, which I will not recite now—later, perhaps!

The entomology required is pretty simple; if you know enough to catch fish by dapping, you can catch them with a thrown fly! I think I could put all the entomology of fly-fishing on a couple of these pages—I'll have a shot, just for the fun of it!

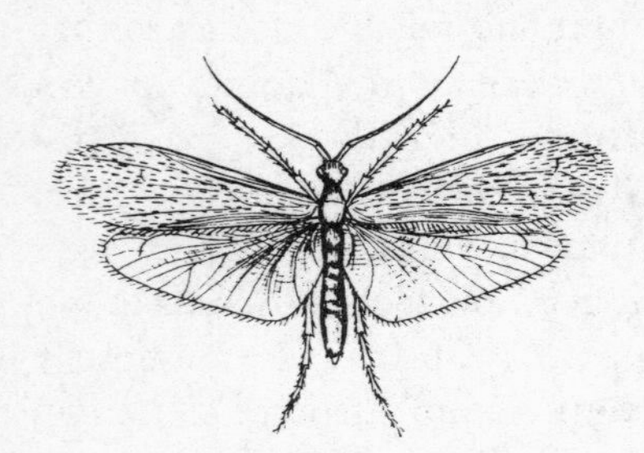

Trichopterae

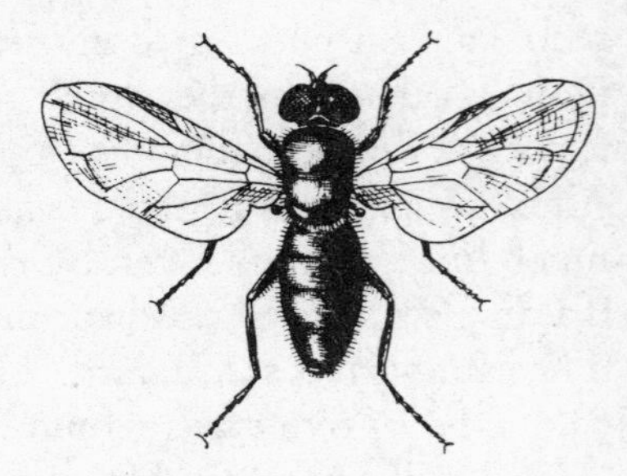

Dipterae

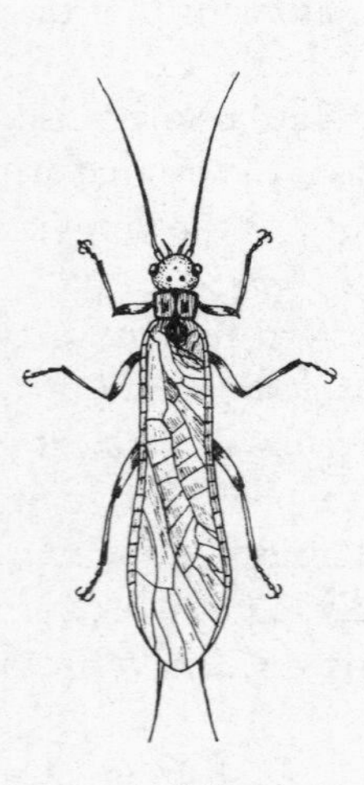

Perlidae

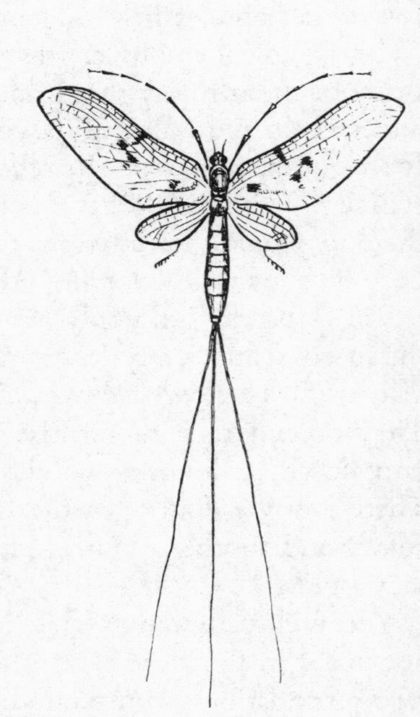

Ephemeridae

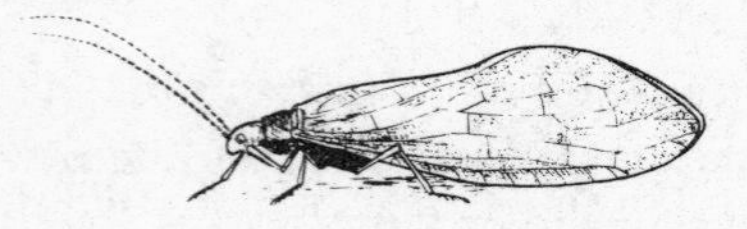

Sialidae

Not counting beetles and ants, there are only five kinds of insects involved. They are:

Ephemeridae. These are the most important to the angler on most waters. Five stages; egg, larva, nymph, dun ('sub-imago') and spinner ('imago'). The last two stages are winged, the dun having coloured semi-translucent veined wings, the spinner having transparent and glassy wings, veined. The species of ephemera which are most common are shown in the table on the following page.

There are other *Ephemeridae*, but these are the main ones. (March Brown only in stony-bottomed rivers.) The male spinners are not much taken by trout; not on the water much, anyway.

Trichopterae. Sedges. These have four *opaque* wings of similar texture to moths, folded like a house roof—*à la* clothes-moth! There are hundreds of species of evening sedges (anglers use various general imitations) which need not be very accurate for evening fishing, e.g. orange sedge, cinnamon sedge, silver sedge, etc. Daytime sedges are *Caperer* (Sericostoma Personatum) very dark chestnut; female has a yellow tail-end and a few white markings on wings; about ½″ long. Also *Grannom* (Brachycentrus subnubilus) rather localized, light fawnish wings, ginger legs, yellowish body, green tail (egg-sac) on female; ⅜″ to ½″ long. All sedges come from *caddis*. None have setae or 'tails'.

Dipterae—housefly-like insects. Examples: Cowdung fly, sits on cow-pats; Bluebottles, etc. *Important one* is *Black Gnat* (Bibio Johannis) which sits on water, in crowds. Female fatter and browner-bodied than male. Dipterae also include gnats proper, e.g. Daddy-longlegs, Mosquito and allied insects of similar shape. None have tails (setae). All have only two *transparent* wings.

Perlidae. Stone-flies. *Four transparent* wings, flat on back. Not much seen on lowland streams. Come from *Creepers*, rather like Ephemera nymphs; the final fly is, however, quite different. Biggest (stone fly) is about 1½″ long. Others are February Red, Early Brown, Yellow Sally, Willow fly, etc. I have never done much with imitations of these. The big stone fly kills in the north, especially the natural. Perlidae have 'tails'.

Common Name	Proper Name	Colour of Dun (Sub-Imago)	Colour of Spinner (Imago)	Number of Tails (Setae)	Size (thorax and abdomen)
MAYFLY (3 species)	Ephemera Danica	Slaty blue-green wings, straw coloured body, brown in markings.	Ivory-white body, Dark brown (nearly) black markings	3	Female $\frac{3}{4}''$–$\frac{7}{8}''$
	Ephemera Vulgata Ephemera Lineata	Browning green wings Body as above			Male $\frac{1}{2}''$–$\frac{5}{8}''$
MARCH BROWN (4 species) ?	Ecdyurus Venosus Ecdyurus Insignis Ecdyurus Volitans	Brown all through Female paler and larger	Bright brown-red ('Great Red Spinner')	2	About $\frac{5}{8}''$
OLIVE DUN (5 species)	Baetis Rhodani Baetis Vernus Baetis Atrebatinus Baetis Tenax Baetis Buceratus	Varying shades of brown-olive and green-olive. Sometimes bluish legs and thorax	Female, brown-red ('Red Spinner'), Male similar but with whitish band round body	2	$\frac{5}{16}''$–$\frac{3}{8}''$
BLUE-WINGED OLIVE	Ephemerella Ignita	Smoky-grey wings Green-olive body	Oat-straw body ("Sherry Spinner")	3	$\frac{5}{16}''$
PALE WATERY (4 species)	Baetis Binoculatus Baetis Scambus Centroptilum Luteolum Centroptilum Pennulatum (larger than others)	Pale watery-yellow Greyish wings	Pale golden body. Male has body-ring as Olive.	2	$\frac{3}{16}''$ (Cent. penn. $\frac{1}{4}''$)
IRON BLUE (2 species)	Baetis Pumilus Baetis Niger	Inky-blue wings Purplish-blue body	Female, crimson body Male, crimson with wide white band ('Jenny Spinner')	2	$\frac{3}{16}''$–$\frac{1}{4}''$

Sialidae. There is only one, the Alder. About ⅝″ long; no setae. *Four semi-transparent veined* wings, brownish; legs dark brown; body dirty purplish brown. Has a great, and in my view totally unjustified, reputation. Shop imitations do not bear the slightest resemblance to the natural insect. You seldom see the fly actually on the water. I have *never* seen a trout eat one.

That is a fly-fisher's entomology on one page! Ants (flying), Beetles, Aphides, and night-flying moths are things which everyone knows about; they are useful at times.

Practically all natural flies have a host of imitations made by anglers and variously named. For example, the Olive dun that comes out in March and April is bluish in cold weather, darkish in any case. Imitations which I can think of offhand are:

Greenwell's Glory
Blue Dun
Blue Upright
Waterhen Bloa
Rough Olive
Heron Blue
Blue Quill
Lunn's Black and Gold Variant

Anyone who likes changing flies can try any of these he owns over a fish eating Baetis Rhodani. My idea is to tie up a fly to imitate Baetis Rhodani, and if the fish doesn't take it, to try another fish. I find the entomology of fishing much simpler and easier to remember than the fly-tyer's bibliography!

I am sending a couple of Mayflies. The one on our stream is Ephemera Danica, with the smoky blue-green wings (sub-imago). If your local May is Vulgata or Lineata, let me know and I will tie some to imitate those. The spent fly will imitate all three. The blue hackle at the tail of the sub-imago imitation is not meant to imitate anything; it is to float that end of the fly and thus maintain a more natural attitude on the water. The spent imitation can be fished—*should* be fished—in the surface film; it represents a dying and drowning fly.

There is quite a history behind the development of these dressings, which are the result of a good deal of experiment. Three or four friends have helped and goodness knows how many different ideas have been tried out. In making realistic imitations we came up against a snag which had us all puzzled for a long time; the patterns which looked best to us, and which also rose fish well, had a shocking record of missed fish. The answer turned out to be collapsibility, by which I mean that anything stiff in the fly, i.e. the rib of the wing feather, the use of bristle for tails, or even detached bodies,

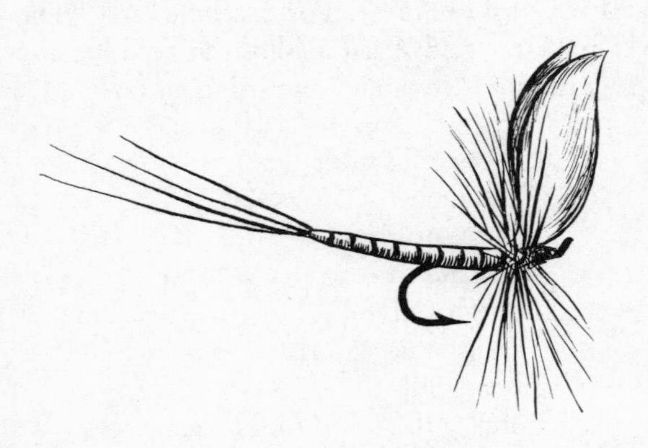

seriously interfered with the necessary sticking of the hook into the fish's mouth. The present dressings are very good; they are soft and gauzy. They killed a great number of fish this season and were in great demand here. They frequently caught fish which had let *literally* dozens of shop Mays pass over their heads the same evening—club water, you see! Another thing is that all the feathers used are easy to get from the local poulterer—in fact, they are all from domestic poultry except three whisks from a cock pheasant's tail.

Also in the box is an imitation of the Pale Watery, tied with long hackles in the style known as 'variant'. I put this in to show you that little flies are easy to tie, too! Never believe anyone who tells you otherwise. I am 6 ft. 2 ins. tall and have hands which are, if anything, too big to be in proportion! If you ever decide to take up fly-fishing, and jib, as I do, at paying from 8*d.* to 1/6*d.* for inferior shop flies, I'll be glad to send you some feathers and things. It is a job that doesn't annoy the womenfolk—in fact my wife has tied some flies herself, better than mine; I wish she would do them all for me!

I don't know what's happened to *Confessions.* 'B.B.' said it would be out in the autumn and that he would send me an author's copy. I'll ask him when I write.

If I gave you the impression that I *enjoy* fishing matches, I didn't mean to. I don't like them a bit, but for divers reasons sometimes participate in them. I wish they had never been invented. I am not exactly a solitary angler; what I like best of all is a day out with one companion. I am glad to say that Temple Pool is unknown to all but a few, and very well concealed; in fact, when I took 'B.B.' he nearly put his foot in it before he realized he had arrived. It doesn't appear on the map, either. One of these days you will have to come and fish it; I would have liked to say this season, but the house will be upside-down, owing to our becoming eligible for family allowance at the beginning of the summer. Next season, anyway, unless you find *cats* unbearable; three Siamese cats own this house, but kindly allow us to live here with them.

Temple Pool is a perfectly delightful place. You never see a soul except very occasionally, a keeper. Tall trees all round, so that the wind has to be very bad to affect the fishing. No eels or perch, in fact nothing but carp, roach, trout and sticklebacks. There are not very many trout. The roach run up to 2 lb.; we've had great fun with them, especially after dark. The carp won't bite at night; the water is nowhere more than 5 to 6 feet deep and mostly only 2 to 3 feet. The trouble is that the carp there are of all sizes from 2 lb. to—well, say 30 lb., and the smaller ones up to 7 or 8 lb. are the only ones that we catch, except on exceptional days. Did I tell you of a gigantic carp in our club water (Arlesey Lake)? It is a perfect monster. The lake is too big, too deep, and too clear for anyone to pursue this fish. There are also perch in this lake, some of which I'm sure must be seven pounders. Everything has been tried to tempt them without success, except a 'Vibro', which I mean to try in the near future; I've bought three in different sizes. A perch of 3 lb. 12 oz. was caught on two maggots and a 14 hook by a roach-fisher in 1945, and one which looked twice as big was seen following it as it was being played. That is the only time a sizeable perch has been caught there as far as I know.

Striking. I think your summary as to the reason for the divers views expressed on striking is sound. I think the best way is to fix up your rod and reel, tie the line to something solid and strike against that, altering the tension of the slipping clutch until you can get a good hard bang without its slipping, but still have the tension light enough to protect the tackle if you happen to overdo it in actual fishing. It is astonishing what you can do with a 12 lb. line on properly-designed tackle. When my first carp-rod was finished I tried it on a hefty springer spaniel, which was given every incentive to go from me to a point 20 yards away. She failed to get there, and she'd do anything for raw meat.

Of course, once a really heavy carp gets properly under way, nothing short of cart-rope would stop it; even then the hook would probably tear out or straighten. Assuming a carp of 20 lb. going at 50 ft. per second, and recollecting that in my youth at Cambridge they said that $s = ut + \frac{1}{2} ft.^{2}$, it would take a strain of about 150 lb. to stop it in a yard. I think if you can hit a carp pretty hard and put on enough pressure to get his head away from danger, the battle is half won. If you are quick you can stop him from getting up speed, except in directions which don't matter. In snaggy waters you have to carry the fight to the fish, so to speak, not waiting to see what he will do, but doing something yourself right from the strike, and being ready to deal with the reaction. They tell me I'm rough on a fish, but I don't get broken very often, certainly far less than those who let a fish go twenty yards into a weed-bed before they start putting on pressure. I would much *prefer* to fish in a water where I could use, say, 3 lb. b.s. tackle and play a fish with my fingers instead of my biceps, but I don't get the chance often. 'B.B.' is setting machinations on foot to obtain permission to fish at Mapperley, so perhaps I might try the light-tackle technique there.

I'll send some more Mayflies as soon as I know which species you have. Actually I am not well acquainted with Vulgata and Lineata, so if you have those you'll have to tell me if I have got the wing colour about right.

Good luck for 1950.

Sincerely,
RICHARD WALKER

IV

January Letters

Dear Mr. Walker,

Your flies are most beautifully tied and I think you are far too modest regarding your skill in this art. To my—admittedly inexpert—eye they are at least the equal, in appearance, of *any* flies I have seen in tackle shops. As to their killing qualities, I hope to be able to report later. Many thanks.

My day's spinning at Revesby was certainly exceptional and the best I have ever had. The weather and water conditions were perfect. I enjoyed myself so much that I went again shortly afterwards, but it was a very dull foggy day, with a light misty rain falling, and my bag was not so good—though I don't complain. 34 perch, up to about 2 lb. and six pike, largest about 9 lb. All the fish, with the exception of two perch, were taken on a 1½″ 'Vibro'; the other two perch I caught on a home-made devon which I made by way of experiment out of an old pipe stem covered with foil wrappings off chocolates—the most colourful and jazzily patterned I could find. The small catch is not a true indication of the efficiency of this home-made spinner as I only tried it out for a few minutes before I packed up. By the way, I was using 100 yards of 5.8 lb. b.s. nylon monofil (.012″, I think) on my 'Felton Crosswind', and in spite of all the reports that I have read to the contrary, I found that it behaved perfectly. There was a slight tendency to 'spring' when I first wound the nylon on the spool, but after the first few casts this disappeared and it laid on the spool beautifully. It is the first time I have tried monofil as a reel line, and—for spinning—I am very impressed. What an amazing difference it makes to the length of one's casts! A pike of something over 14 lb. was taken on live bait while I was there; a beautiful fish (the adjective is not very apt applied to a pike!).

I don't think you are a sceptic at all; on the contrary I appreciate your scientific attitude in not accepting as fact even the most trivial matter until it is amply proved. Nevertheless, I seem to have unwittingly given you a wrong impression when writing in my last letter about 'tasselled' spinners. My intention was to remark upon the difference between a spinner with a 'tassel' and one without, as I had experienced much better results when I changed the hook on my 1½″ Vibro for one with a red woollen tassel. (The 1½″ Vibro as sold is not fitted with the red celluloid tags as are the larger sizes.) I may have referred to a '*red*' tassel, but the object of my remark was the tassel itself and not its colour. I must admit that it had not occurred to me that any other colour might be just as attractive, but I am quite prepared to admit that it might be. Perhaps one day I will experiment with different colours.

Your summary of fly-fishing entomology is most lucid and really valuable to a novice like myself. Next year, perhaps, I might take up fly-fishing seriously, but I will not do so until I know a good deal more about the subject than I do at present. I like to know exactly what I am doing, or attempting to do, and my knowledge, even of local aquatic insect life, is so sketchy that I think I will spend this year in learning all I can and keeping my eyes open. My dapping in the past has been very 'hit and miss' and it has been more by luck than skill that I have caught any fish. During the war I spent some considerable time lecturing, amongst other things, on entomology, but unfortunately my field was restricted to mosquitoes, ticks, sandflies, lice and other 'friends of man'. What a pity my training syllabus didn't include Mayflies and the rest!

I can think of nothing I would like more than to fish in the Temple Pool. It certainly looks and sounds perfectly delightful and I would love to try my hand there with you. I am very fond both of cats and small infants. (Congratulations!)

You mentioned the monster carp in Arlesey Lake in an earlier letter, but not the monster perch. I wish you luck with your 'Vibro'—a 7 lb. perch would create quite a stir in the angling world! The first time I tried a 'Vibro', in fact the very first cast, I caught a perch of 2 lb. 12 oz.—on a 3″ spoon, much to my surprise. Let's hope that a 'Vibro' will prove as tempting to the Arlesey monsters.

Your test of your new rod and 12 lb. line by playing a springer was a drastic one, but I think it amply proves your point. Strangely enough I had, jokingly, suggested the very same test to a friend, but never dreamed that anyone would actually do it. I appreciate your argument on playing carp and carrying the fight to the fish, as you put it. It has always seemed to me to be a sound policy to fish as light as circumstances will permit, but where the only chance of landing a fish depends upon its being kept away from weeds and snags, it is in my opinion sheer folly to use any tackle which is not capable of doing just that (which was the reason why I wrote to you originally). And having equipped myself with adequate tackle it would be even greater folly not to use it for the very purpose for which it was chosen—to keep the fish in open water.

Talking of which reminds me of a little place I know which contains some very fine tench. There are two small ponds, either of which one could cast across with ease, about 12–15 feet deep, with a lot of weed. The only chance of landing a tench there is to play it very hard indeed. The owner told me last year of a catch in 1943 by one rod, in one morning, of five tench which weighed a little under two stones. That may be a 'fishermen's yarn'—I don't know—but I do know from my own experience that there are some grand fish in those two insignificant pools. I should be interested to hear your views on tench fishing some time.

Reverting to flies again for a moment, I'm afraid I cannot tell you which species of Mayflies are to be found on our rivers. I have never before been sufficiently interested to find out—they were just 'Mayflies' to me—but I shall be looking at them and for them with a more critical eye this season, and I will let you know or send you some specimens for identification.

I have tried out the 'Dylon' dyes on some nylon but I am not too happy about the results. Perhaps you can tell me where I have gone wrong. First of all I made up the four basic colours according to the instructions—put the powder into about ½ pint of boiling water, boiled it for a while and then bottled it, after adding about a teaspoon of salt. Before dyeing I mixed up the colours in the proportions you suggested, brought the mixture to the boil, allowed it to cool sufficiently so that I could bear to put my finger into it and then inserted the nylon, using a small bottle, thus: The nylon was left in the dye for 20 minutes, washed and dried, but the resulting colour was very pale. It may be that the result is perfectly satisfactory, but I have the impression that a somewhat deeper colour should result. I have not experimented further, as I did not wish to waste either nylon or dye, when you may be able to put your finger on my mistake. If you can find no flaw in my method I will send you a bit of the nylon I have dyed—no, on second thoughts, I will enclose a bit with this letter.

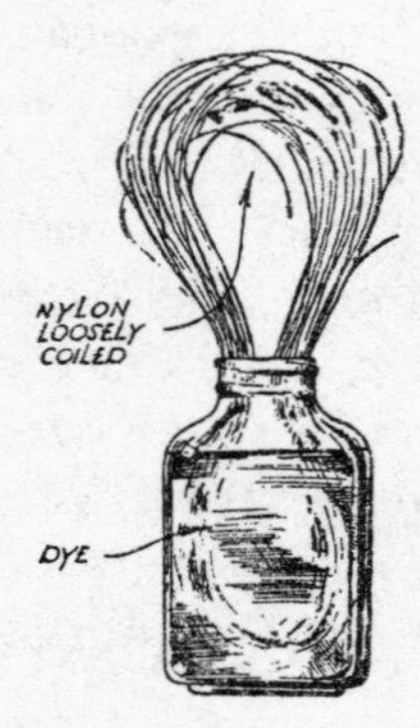

Can you manage a few days fishing up here this summer? You mentioned in an earlier letter that you had made some arrangements, but perhaps they do not preclude a visit to Lincolnshire also.

Yours sincerely,

M. H. INGHAM

Dear Mr. Ingham,

Our correspondence has now reached the stage where I look forward to your letters with much the same pleasant anticipation with which I regard the *Fishing Gazette*! You write extraordinarily well; I think you ought to do some articles for the *Fishing Gazette* or the *Country Sportsman*. You obviously know a great deal about fishing and you have the ability to write about it in an excellent way. What about an article for *Fishing Gazette* about spinning for perch? I only once in my life caught a perch over 2 lb. (2 lb. 13 oz., at Hertford).

If you get a three-pounder, you must stuff it. I did a $4\frac{1}{2}$ lb. trout this year, on the information in the *Fisherman's Bedside Book*, and it worked out all right. I prefer cotton wool to paper, though.

I can catch tench in some waters! Curiously enough my best (5 lb. 10 oz.) was caught quite accidentally, in the middle of the night, on floating crust, 18 lb. b.s. tackle, in the middle of some thick weeds. Of course it hadn't a chance. I felt rather guilty about it, and put it back alive after weighing it. Actually, I was after carp, but all I caught, apart from the tench, was big eels! One thing I do know about tench and that is their fondness for bulrushes. (The tall, dark-green round-section rush, which isn't usually called a bulrush at all.) I always fish close to these if I can, and have found it pays well. Last year when 'B.B.' and I were at Fort Henry on a wild-goose-chase after monster carp, which turned out to be monster bream, we put this to the test; 'B.B.' preferred to fish close to a thick weed-bed and I chose a clump of bulrushes with no weed near. Now I must tell you that 'B.B.' is a very good and experienced tench-fisher, and has caught many big ones by sheer good fishing, yet he had never a touch, while I got a three-pounder and was broken by another fish—2 lb. b.s. line has its limitations. When we changed places, as an additional test, 'B.B.' had two good runs and missed both; of course it was later in the morning and I fancy his fish were just running off holding the end of the worm, as they often do when not very hungry.

I like to use a float for tench, as they are much shyer biters than carp—more delicate is perhaps a better term, as they are, I think, less cunning, but more inclined to play about with the bait, and the float gives one a better chance of knowing what goes on. I usually use a ten-inch porcupine quill, with an orange and black top. I never found a better bait for tench than a medium sized lob or a biggish marsh worm, except where a water is fished heavily; tench will often take paste or breadcrust better then, having been educated to take bread bait by constant ground-baiting. If the bottom is covered with silkweed or soft mud, a composite bait of breadcrust, loaded with just enough paste to make it sink, is sometimes useful, with mashed-up soaked bread as groundbait. A leatherjacket is a good bait, and so are caddis. On the Ouse, many are taken on gentles or paste, but more by luck than deliberate tench-fishing. The old dodge of sinking a bunch of gaudy flowers as 'groundbait' may not be all superstition. I have tried it many times and caught tench, too, but of course I cannot say whether I shouldn't have caught them without the flowers. I have found often that a slow-sinking cloud groundbait, as used in match-fishing, will attract them, and have sometimes managed to get one by laying on towards the end of a match. The tench root about on the bottom, while the roach try to intercept the sinking particles. If I see a stream of what 'B.B.' calls *needle-bubbles*, up goes my float and on goes a red worm! I like my 'Wallis-Avon' rod for tenching, and of course the 'Felton' does nicely. As in carp-fishing, I usually do best fishing in comparatively shallow water, and not too far out. I like tench very much, and I often go after them. Arlesey *pit* (distinct from Arlesey *Lake*) contains some beautiful ones, bright golden sides, white bellies and coral-pink fins. Unfortunately the colouring is environmental and they change colour if transferred to other waters. I never caught one of them over 2 lb., but they are so beautiful that even a small one is a prize to catch. Of course we always put them back. Arlesey pit is a flooded chalkpit. Apart from the tench I don't care for it. It is a bleak-looking place and gives one little scope for watercraft; all pitches look alike.

You shall definitely try Temple Pool and as soon as I can fix it I will do so. I don't know what 'B.B.' is arranging this year, but I expect I shall know soon. He and I usually have a week somewhere, which leaves me with a week to spare; you and I must foregather for an attack on the carp *somewhere* during that week! I can't be very definite yet because I don't know what is going to happen. I would *like* to have a shot at Woldale and it is most kind of you to invite me. As soon as I can see definitely what the programme is, I'll let you know, and we'll catch a carp between us.

'B.B.' and I have had Woldale on our list for some time, and we nearly went there last year, intending also to have a look at Croxby, but we heard that the latter had become a sort of Lido and were rather put off the idea.

I think your dyed nylon is about right. It could perhaps be a little deeper coloured; stronger dye solution is the answer, or probably a second immersion after drying will do the trick. But don't get it *too* dark. The probable reason for the benefit of dyeing was explained to me the other day by a photographer. The nylon is not quite homogeneous; it had a certain capacity for absorbing water. When dyed the interstices are filled with minute particles of the dye, or their sides are coated with it. Some of the best photographic lenses have bubbles in the glass, which give rise to queer effects sometimes, unless blacked out with matt black paint. You will see the parallel; diffusion of light in each case by the double refractive index where there is a space. Dyeing the nylon counteracts any tendency to double refraction and improves invisibility. The actual colour might be of only secondary importance.

I find nylon monofil quite all right on the 'Felton' up to 0.013″; above that it is a nuisance. On the No. 1 'Altex' it is tricky above 0.010″, by reason of the smaller drum. Yes, one can do phenomenal casts with it. I use it a lot for chub.

You can't send Mayfly specimens, except in alcohol, and that obscures the wing colouring. If you put them loose in a box they both shrivel and disintegrate in transit. And I can't tell the difference between Lineata and Vulgata at any time, and can only tell Danica by the wing colour of the sub-imago, and I wouldn't be certain then unless I had both kinds to compare. You must compare the wing colour of your local fly with the artificial and let me know if it errs in shade, and if so in what way. Actually I begin to doubt very much whether trout can distinguish one colour from another, because we dressed some exactly similar in form but with plain black and white wings and a crimson head hackle, and these were taken with equal confidence! I think that the three most important attributes of a dry fly are:

1. Size and shape (which really go together; physical form includes size).
2. Attitude on the water.
3. *Quantity* of light (irrespective of which part of the spectrum is included) *reflected* or *passed through* the translucent feather.

I have done some experiments, and it is most difficult to distinguish the colour of a fly from under the water, even for humans. But one can readily tell the difference in size, shape, attitude or reflected/transferred light. Of course sunk flies are a different matter altogether.

I entirely agree that a tassel on a spinner is important, especially in perch-fishing. I *think* a red tassel is probably preferable, but it *may* not be the best; after all, some of the favourite meals of both perch and pike have plain tails. On the Ouse a gudgeon is by far the best bait for a perch; it has a nondescript brownish tail; and pike like best a biggish dace, whose tail also is a drab colour. Bleak, which the perch hustle around considerably, have practically transparent tails! I usually use a Rhode Island Red hackle for spinner tails, to imitate roach. Possibly a pale buff hackle would be better. It is hard to work out any experiment which would give a worthwhile indication of the best colour.

Your study of entomology is perhaps not so far removed from angling as you think, because one of the most useful imitations I know for all-season work is an imitation of a gnat, which, although not the mosquito which bites us, is almost exactly similar, the only difference I know being in colour, and that but slight and mattering little. It breeds in stagnant puddles, of which every river has a few at its edge, the larva being the well-known bloodworm. The adults fly in clouds over the water, and trout like them greatly.

The entomology of fly-fishing is really extraordinarily simple. You see a fish rising. If it is rising at sub-imago ephemerid flies you can easily tell because they float down with wings cocked up.

Now, Mayfly you can tell at a hundred yards. Other flies are quite easy. Up to June, any fly with darkish grey wings is either Olive or Iron Blue. Olive is thrice the size of Iron Blue to *look at*; and has a greyish-olive body, the Iron Blue has a bluish-purple body. These are the only two you are likely to see *before* the Mayfly. Their spinners are distinguishable by size, and the fact that the Olive (Red) spinner is dead-leaf colour; the Iron Blue spinner (female) has a definite *crimson* tinge.

After the Mayfly, Olives continue, usually lighter in shade than the early ones, but Iron Blue is about finished. Blue-winged Olive then comes in. It has much darker wings than the Olives, and *three* tails, the Olives having only *two*. It is an evening fly, whereas the Oliver is a morning and afternoon insect. The blue-winged Olive *spinner* is a deep golden colour (Sherry Spinner).

The only other one to consider is Pale Watery, which is exactly as its name implies and a fly that no one can mistake; much smaller than Olive or Blue-winged Olive, apart from the colour. If a fish is not rising at upwinged flies (Ephemerids) *in the daytime*, ten to one it is a Black Gnat, Caperer or Grannom. Grannom only comes in April and May and is mousy-coloured with a green posterior (female). Caperer is a plain chocolate chap and may be about any time. Black Gnat is housefly-like. All easy to spot, you see.

In the evening, the rising may be at any kind of sedge-fly, but exact imitation is less important then. Evening rising, which *really is* tricky to spot, is usually at spent small fly, or sedges, but there are few possibles; spent Mayfly you can see, and if it isn't that (and isn't at sedges) it's pretty sure to be at spent Pale Watery or Sherry Spinner (Blue-winged Olive imago).

I forgot to mention March Brown, which comes before Mayfly, but no one can fail to spot that; nearly as big as the Mayfly, and decidedly dark brown, quite a lot darker than the Vulgata and Lineata Mays and an *earthy* brown rather than yellowish or brownish-green. We don't get the March Brown here, which is what made me forget him.

The Big Stonefly is perfectly obvious to anybody, and the smaller Perlidae are of little account.

If fish are feeding on something not included in the above, it is a case in a hundred. The average fly-fisher fishes with a 'somebody's favourite' or 'someone else's glory' and hopes for the best. He is probably familiar with anything from twenty to two hundred fancy artificials, which involve much more trouble to learn than the ten to twenty natural flies. If a man goes out fishing with these imitations there will be few days when he is baffled, and if he knows of any which don't occur on his water he can cut them out.

April to beginning of May (in order of most common first).
Dark Olive and spinner
Iron Blue and spinner
Black Gnat
March Brown and spinner
Grannom

May to June
Mayfly and spent
Black Gnat
Caperer
Stonefly, if present
And half a dozen nondescript Sedges, various sizes, for late evening.

June to September
Medium Olive, Pale Watery, Blue-winged Olive } and spinners
Caperer
Red and black ants
And some odds and ends of sedges for late evening.

Only imitations of *female* spinners are necessary.
In addition, these wet flies are sometimes useful:
Partridge and Orange
Olive nymph
Pale Watery nymph.

If you decide to start fly-fishing I will send you a complete set of artificials, duly labelled, to cope with all the flies in your district, plus the formulae for their dressings. *On no account* go into a shop and buy 'likely-looking flies', or even those which the books say you ought to have. If you have the dressing formulae, you can get flies tied up no dearer than those in the tackle-shop glass cases, or, better still, tie your own. If you keep friendly with one or two poulterers and poultry-keepers and gamekeepers or shooting men, your feathers will cost nothing. The rest of the necessary equipment consists of four 1/– reels of tying silk, one pair hackle pliers (4/–), a vice, which can be home-made, and a few sundries totalling under 2/6*d*. Hooks are under 1*d*. each. It is a fallacy that an expensive tapered line is necessary; any reel will do, the rod can be greenheart and you make your own tapered casts from nylon and stain them yourself.

I shall convince you if I'm not careful!

Sincerely,

RICHARD WALKER

Dear Mr. Walker,

I too look forward to *your* letters with pleasant anticipation. I have learned more from our short correspondence than from all the reading of angling books I have done in the past few years! As for my writing well—I don't know whether I write well or badly, but I do know that I enjoy writing a letter when I have something definite to say, particularly when it is something in which I am interested. I loathe writing 'duty' letters! My masterpiece was a letter which I wrote to my wife when I was in West Africa during the war, which ran to nearly a hundred pages! I had just returned from a hunting trip—but that's another story.

I have fished quite a lot, ever since I was old enough to hold a cane, but I certainly do not know a lot about fishing. Until a year or two ago I had enjoyed fishing as a pleasant way of spending a few hours when I had nothing better to do, but it is only recently that I have begun to take a keener interest in it, and I am appalled, when reading your letter, at how little I do know on the subject. So, no articles in the *Fishing Gazette*—yet.

When I read that article in the *Fisherman's Bedside Book* I decided that I must try my hand at stuffing a fish sometime—in fact, last week-end I looked out two old scalpels and sharpened them up in readiness. I thought I would try a pike first of all; a three or four pounder is a reasonable size, fairly easy to catch and no great loss if I make a mess of it—but the pike I bring home are always immediately appropriated by my wife for cooking.

A tench of 5 lb. 10 oz. is no mean catch, but in the circumstances I can understand your feeling 'rather guilty' about it. Did you see in the *Fishing Gazette* that there were several good ones taken in the Glen last summer, including one over 6 lb.? Thanks for the tip about bulrushes—I'll bear it in mind.

Generally speaking I agree that a large worm is the best bait for tench, in my experience, but I have found one exception. In the two small ponds which I mentioned in my last letter, the tench seem to show a marked preference for bread paste. They are also exceptional in another respect—I have caught several tench there, and missed a few, but not one of them took the bait in the accepted tench fashion. Without any preliminary movement the float disappeared at a steep angle. It has occurred to me that this might have resulted from having too long a length of 'dead' cast lying on the bottom, but I don't think that is the explanation, as I carefully measured the depth when I first fished there. I have discussed this point with a friend of mine who is a very painstaking and observant angler and he has had exactly the same experience in that water. Can you offer any explanation? Could it be that the answer lies in heredity? In confined waters where no new blood is introduced by re-stocking it is, of course, inevitable that a high degree of inter-breeding must take place and the resultant strain will, I suggest, develop certain characteristics, which may become more pronounced in each succeeding generation. This may also be an explanation for the peculiarities of your Beechmere carp! Environment may also enter into it in some mysterious way.

I have read of brightly coloured flowers or an old brass candlestick being used as 'groundbait' for tench, but have never tried it out. I must put it to the test this summer.

I was very interested to read in the *Fishing Gazette* a week or two ago about the use of leeches as bait. You will no doubt remember the article. The particular leeches referred to were called by the local name of 'vamps' and were described as hard, leathery creatures up to about three inches in length. I have tried to identify the 'vamp' and suspect that it is the Horse Leech, but I am not sure as the description given was somewhat vague. Have you had any experience of leeches as bait?

Please don't misunderstand what I said in my last letter about fishing in the Temple Pool. I know only too well what confusion and upheaval is caused by the advent of a new arrival in the family and I wouldn't dream of suggesting that we make it this year. I do sincerely hope, however, that we can, as you say, foregather for an attack on the carp *somewhere* during your second week, provided that this can be arranged without inconvenience to you or to Mrs. Walker. We have booked for our usual fortnight's seaside holiday from 5th to 19th July, which will leave me another week to take more or less when I wish, so I should have no difficulty in fitting in with anything you can arrange. We shall be spending our fortnight's holiday as we did last year in South Devon, at a tiny village near Kingsbridge. It is a charming place, very quiet and remote and (praise be!) completely devoid of trippers. It is about half a mile from the sea, a beautiful sandy bay into which runs the Avon—not, unfortunately, the Hampshire Avon. Last year, our first visit, I took some fishing tackle with me and I had two pleasant days amongst the rudd and pike at Slapton Ley. Rudd do not interest me very much, though, and pike at that time of the year are not very good sport. Do you know that part of the country? Can you suggest anywhere where I might get some carp or tench fishing? I had also thought of writing to the Secretary of the local Angling Club for information.

There were some beautiful salmon running up the Avon last July when we were there. It was most tantalizing to sit and watch the salmon leaping and not be able to do anything about it!

I also tried my hand for the first time at sea fishing—with pike tackle, except for the hooks, which were some I bought locally for the job. Spinning with sand eels from a boat I had some good sport with pollack—sixteen in our trip of about two hours.

You *have* convinced me on the subject of fly-fishing—at least to the extent of beginning in a modest way in April. It must of necessity be a modest beginning, because, apart from the intricacies of entomology and the many other aspects of the art, of which I am completely ignorant, I have never *cast* a fly in my life, so it will be a case of learning as I go. It is most generous of you to offer to send me a complete set of artificial flies, but I really cannot accept it at this stage, as I simply do not know which flies occur on our stream, and which, of the list you gave me, do not occur. I must keep my eyes open and as I identify each fly I will let you know. You have provided the little persuasion that was necessary to make me actively interested in fly-fishing—I have been passively interested for a long time—and now I am looking forward to something completely new to me in the way of angling. Your very lucid précis of the entomological side of the art has contributed in no small measure, as I must admit that I have been somewhat awed by what I have always regarded as a most involved and intricate subject. You suggest that I should do some articles for the *Fishing Gazette*. How about you publishing a book on *Fly-fishing for Beginners*? Do you think it would be frowned upon by the Old Brigade, who seem to revel in making the whole business as obscure and difficult as possible? If so, so much the better! I'm afraid I have no patience with the purists who regard coarse fishing as an inferior branch of the art. I imagine it requires as much skill and patience to catch a carp or tench as to catch a trout with an artificial fly.

Yours sincerely,

MAURICE INGHAM

Dear Mr. Ingham,

You are too modest. In the first place your knowledge of general angling matters is considerable, and in the second, there is no need to be an expert in order to write articles which will please readers and help to pay for your tackle! *No one* is better qualified to instruct an *advanced learner*. (I say this to encourage you, because I myself think you know more than most anglers!) The farther one progresses in any subject the more out of touch with the novice one becomes. The minor details and pitfalls awaiting the beginner are forgotten, and that is the reason why angling text-books are by no means as informative as they might be. I myself try not to overlook the small points by going fishing fairly often with people who are in the early stages of the art; I have often found that, bringing a fresh mind, such people will find a solution to problems which have baffled me for years.

Apart from all this, you can always write a *descriptive* article as opposed to an *instructive* one!

Although the information on fish-stuffing in 'B.B.'s' *The Fisherman's Bedside Book* enabled me to stuff my trout successfully, I found that not all the things suggested were best, and one or two important points were insufficiently emphasized. Firstly, in direct contradiction to 'B.B.', I found the trout needed very little colouring indeed; in fact all I did was to restore the red spots to their original intensity with a little carmine, and whiten the belly. It looks most natural, too. Secondly, I found that fin edges were tattered somewhat. I think it most unlikely that any specimen fish will survive a stout battle, landing and taking home, without damage to fins, especially the tail. The remedy is 'Cellotape' and varnish. You put on the Cellotape, as shown, after the fin has dried, and varnish over with cellulose varnish. When dry, paint in any missing bits of fin-ray with appropriate colour and varnish again. Then clip off surplus Sellotape with scissors and re-varnish. This has made my trout very smart in his fins and I defy anyone to detect the repairs at a greater range than twelve inches, and even then only if they were looking for them.

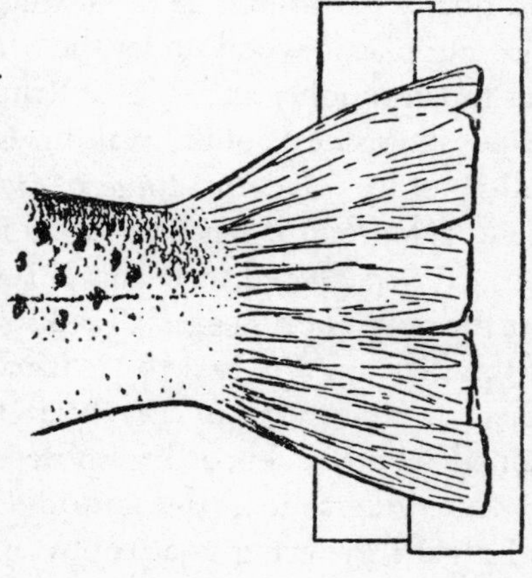

Next, stuffing. It is terribly easy to understuff; I had to soak my fish and re-stuff. The skin shrinks as it dries unless stuffed really tight. It would be quite impossible to make a stuffed fish appear larger than it did in life, and most difficult even to retain the original size. In spite of all my efforts mine has lost two inches in maximum *girth*—I measured it carefully before stuffing and it has gone down from 13″ to 11″. It is also very easy to stuff a fish out to a circular cross-section, when it should be flat on the sides. If I do another I shall cut a rough board out to retain the shape, like this

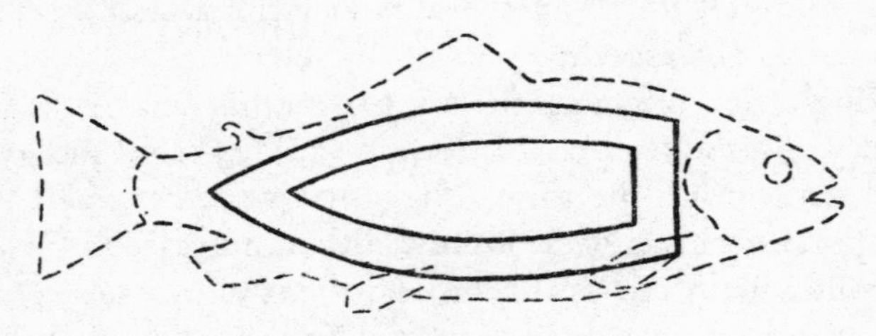

and put it inside before stuffing.

I like cotton-wool better than paper for stuffing, but you need a surprising quantity. I found considerable shrinkage of the head skin and tissue, and although I carefully padded out the cheeks, the top of the head had a very wizened appearance, which I finally got over by filling up the hollows with layers of Cellotape and finally varnishing over. It might be possible to do better by injecting plastic wood under the head skin. The skin everywhere was much tougher and thicker than I had expected and only very serious clumsiness could break it. Against the advice in the book, I did not remove the tongue, but heaped preservative in the mouth; the tongue has now dried nicely and looks quite natural.

I never succeeded in fixing a T-section block to my fish; it is just sewn up like a haggis! Two strings go in and out at each end of the slit, and are used to tie it to the backboard, through four holes. I have not put any background in; I just used a dark-stained wood backboard with details of weight, date and water in white letters along the bottom; I think this more appropriate, as I regard the thing as a trophy and *not* either a decoration or a natural history specimen. I should think a pike of three or four pounds would be ideal for stuffing—big enough to handle easily but not so big as to use an expensive amount of stuffing material, or to take up too much room when finished. I made my trout's eye from perspex; the bought eyes are hemispherical, which is wrong and bulgy-looking—a fish's eye is not as *a*, but as *b*. You need big eyes for trout, perch and pike especially.

I expect tench are like carp in that baits vary in their attractiveness in different waters, and the tench themselves vary in their manner of taking a bait. Float-ledgering is not a very sensitive way of fishing, though. The only way of 'laying-on' I know which *is* fairly sensitive is to put the weights a good way from the hook—say a yard, and use a loading which cocks the float nicely but doesn't sink it. Then plumb accurately and set the float so that the weights are just *off* the bottom, except one small one.

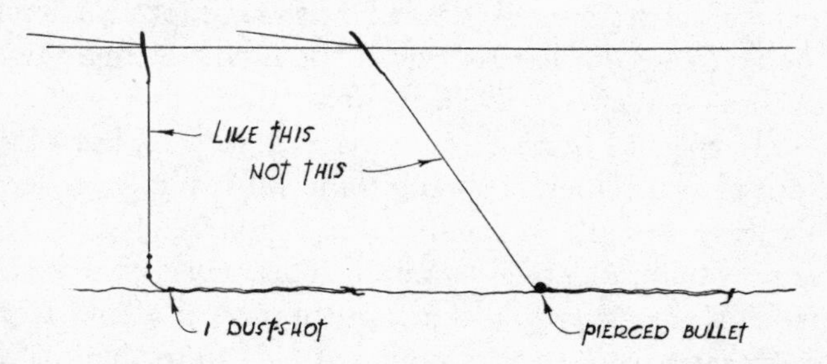

The first method puts no check on a fish to speak of at all, since the float *carries* the weight all the time; a fish has to go a good way before he feels the resistance of the buoyancy of the float. With this tackle the float runs away without going under, at least to begin with. With the other, pierced-bullet, tackle, you see no indication at all if the fish goes towards the lead; and if he goes away he feels the friction of line through lead and the pull of the buoyant float at once. Of course, in the first method the line above the float must be drawn a little, so that as soon as the bait is lifted the little shot tends to swing under the rest and cause the float to tremble.

As regards inheritance, I certainly do agree that extensive inbreeding will take place in most still waters. I don't think it will cause any *new* developments to speak of, but it will result in a high degree of *uniformity* among fish, of a given species, both in appearance and habits. It will, in fact, result in a strain which has concentrated and fixed in it those qualities which, of the available factors present in the original parent fish, were best suited to the environment of the water concerned. I am most dubious about the effect of size-limit regulations for this reason, and also about destruction of such things as herons and kingfishers. I think that preservation of the small fish and removal of large ones will result in a decrease in final adult size in our fish; fortunately the effect on the fish population of anglers and their measures is small, in most waters, compared with natural effects!

I couldn't imagine what 'vamps' were! It never occurred to me that it meant leeches. Of course nearly all fish eat these leeches—I have caught fish which were absolutely stuffed with them. This is exciting—can it be that fish take lobs for leeches? Can it be that carp dig leeches out of the mud? Temple Pool is *full* of leeches—even the sticklebacks gorge themselves with them. I never kill carp, so I don't know if *they* eat leeches, but I intend to find out next summer. I should think those big horse-leeches would be easy enough to catch in horse-ponds. I seem to remember we caught plenty as children. This may turn out to be a fine carp-bait, especially as it is not much used, if at all. It is the first thing that I have come across that *may* fulfil the qualifications of a perfect carp-bait, i.e., a bait that is a normal article of diet for the fish and that will carry a hook of reasonable size and strength. I don't think a lobworm can be said to fall into the first category; no doubt carp do get a lob now and then which falls into the water, but certainly not often enough for it to be considered a normal article of diet for them. I don't know if there are any leeches in Beechmere.

The tail of a lob is very much like a whole, but contracted, leech. I wonder! We may have—or rather *you* may have, got something—summer will tell us. I've never used a leech for a bait, but I know for sure that trout, chub, barbel, perch and ruffes eat them; these are all predatory or semi-predatory fish.

Salmon running up estuaries are *sometimes* taken with a small spoon or reflex devon; the technique is (I am told) continuous casting where the fish are known to be. It might be worth trying when you get the chance. I've never done much sea-fishing myself; I caught a few bass up to 4 lb. at Barry in 1940, on spinners, but I never saw much in it. I expect sea-fishing *can* be very good sport if one knows the ropes, but while it probably needs considerable thought, patience and knowledge, I cannot see the necessity for a high degree of skill; for example, no great accuracy of casting seems to be needed, nor is there any question of skilful playing of fish. All the same, I've often been tempted to try a bit of tope-fishing somewhere.

If you can forget anything you have ever been told about casting a fly, you will learn to cast well enough to catch fish in two or three hours, and well enough to equal most fly-fishermen in one season. This is how to learn. Get a bit of box-rope about ten feet long. Extend it on the ground, and hold one end at shoulder level, with your elbow bent, hand at shoulder, and the rope behind you. Now smartly bring your hand and forearm forward until your elbow makes a right-angle. You will find that the rope goes forward like this:

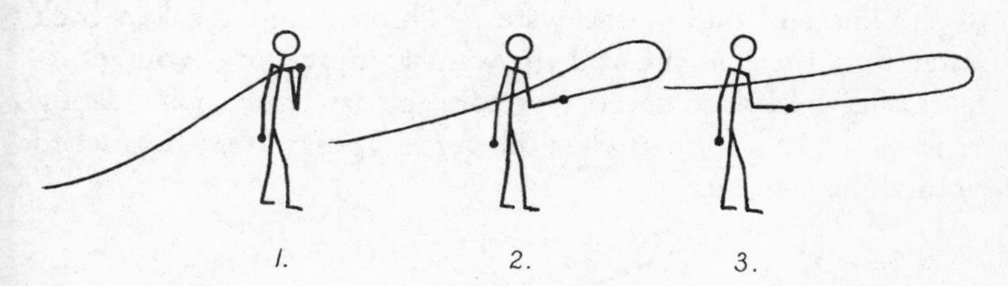

eventually straightening, more or less, in front of you. (You will immediately get the impression that, had the rope been lying at shoulder-level instead of on the ground, it would have gone forward even better.) The important conclusion that this little experiment leads to is that, in an unweighted line, a loop forms, at the point of applied propulsion, which unrolls in a forward direction until the line is straight ahead. Whereas, in a *weighted* line, the *weight* flies, trailing the line, in an *unweighted* line the part of the line nearest the point of propulsion leads the movement, passing its energy on up the line until the end is reached.

This is how a fly is thrown. Don't attempt to throw the *fly*. Concentrate on getting the *part of the line nearest the rod-point* on the move, and the rest will follow. Start with your line (with cast and a big fly, preferably with the hook broken off at the bend, attached) out in front—you can let the stream extend it. Don't start with less than twenty feet of reel-line out; it takes some weight of line to develop the action of the rod. Your rod should incline about like this:

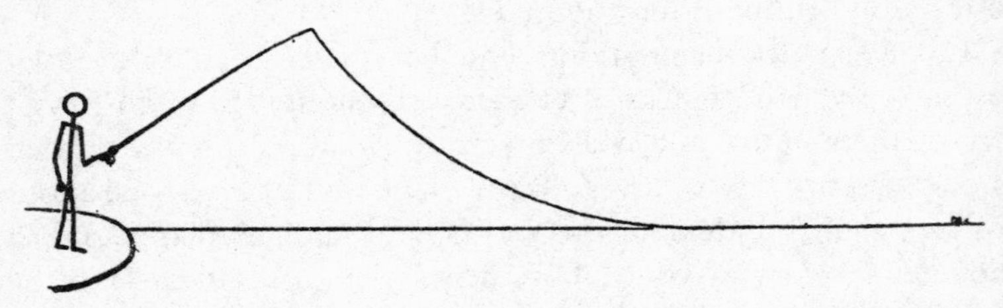

Starting slowly, and with *ever-increasing speed*, bring the rod up to *vertical* and there *stop suddenly*. As soon as your upward movement commences, the rod will take on a bend, due to the weight of the line and pull of the water. The rod-butt is taken back faster than the line and rod tip want to move, and your ever-increasing backward speed therefore imparts an ever-increasing bend to the rod, so that when the vertical position is just reached your rod is like this:

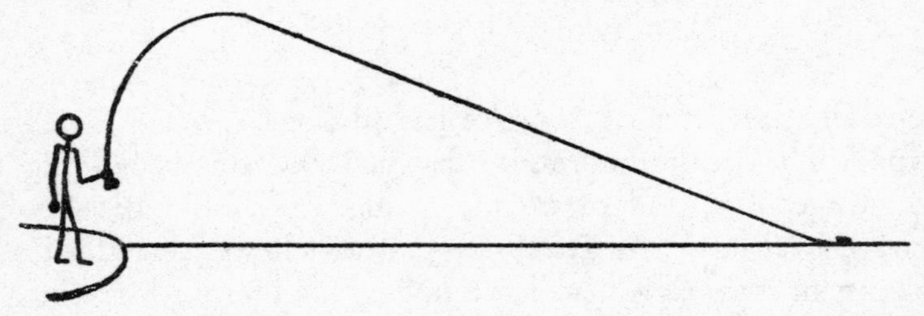

Now you stop suddenly. The rod straightens and over-springs to this position:

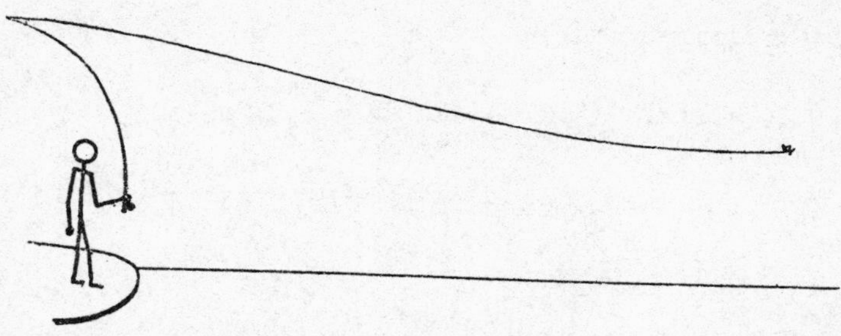

Now pause, turn your head, and watch the line. You'll see it unroll in the air behind just as the box-rope did forwards in your initial experiment. While it is doing this, try to keep feeling the line by very lightly holding the rod, so that it is pulled a little backwards by the line.

When the line is about two-thirds unrolled behind, like this:

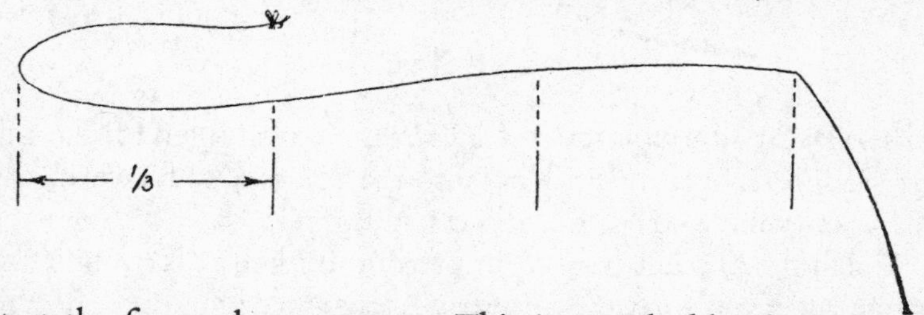

start the forward movement. This is exactly like the back cast reversed—slowly at first, with ever-increasing speed, then stop suddenly. In the case of the forward cast, the finish is at about this angle, before the stop:

and after stopping, this

Observe that although the rod *appears* to be well tilted forward in the second diagram, this is because the rod is *bent* forward; the butt is only inclined a little, about ten degrees.

Watch the line unroll in front of you; just before it straightens, let the rod drop forward to nearly horizontal, when the fly will drop lightly on the water.

Always understand the *mechanism* which drives the fly and try to make that mechanism work. Watch the line in the air at first and get those loops rolling.

Of course with a rod your *wrist* is the pivot instead of your elbow, as in the case of the box-rope experiment, in which your forearm was used as a rod, your wrist (unconsciously) acting as the rod's spring.

Don't worry about accuracy too much; you will find that very easy to obtain once you've got the hang of the unrolling loops.

If you find your line catches the ground behind, it can be remedied by using more force on the back cast or 'stopping suddenly' sooner, or both. If the fly hits the water with a smack, stop sooner on the forward movement.

Make sure you use a heavy enough line—size C or D. It needn't be tapered, but it must have weight. You can't hope to learn casting with a light line, and even an expert will never be happy with one. And if in doubt, choose a heavier line. Don't start with a nylon cast of more than two yards. I suggest a nylon cast, tapered thus:

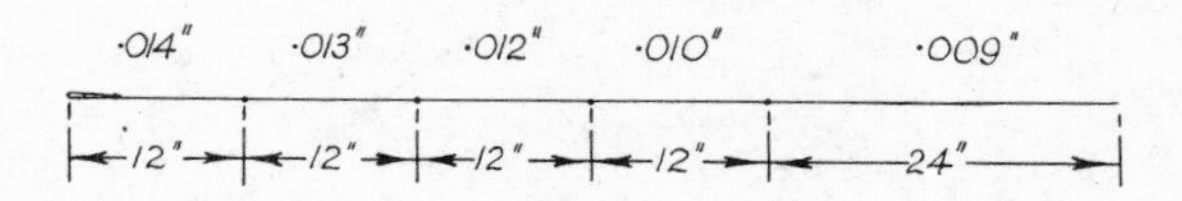

When you become proficient, you can use 2½ yards:

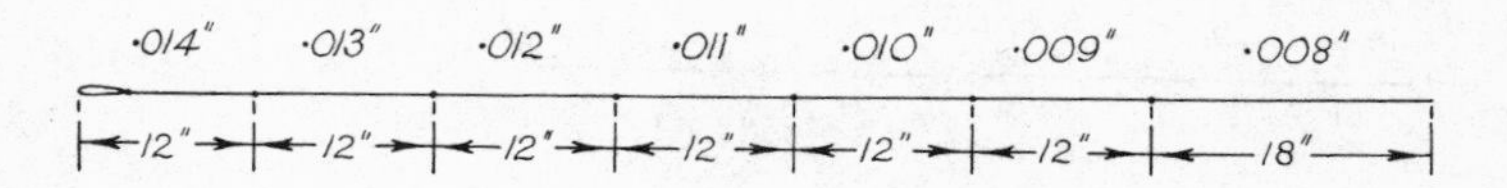

And do use a big fly, like a May, for practising. It acts like the tail of a kite and helps you keep in touch with your line when it's in the air. It's surprising how easy it is to learn to cast. I've taught dozens in very quick time. When you've learned this simple overhead cast you must try doing the same movements with your rod semi-horizontal, your back cast going to your right and forward cast to your left:

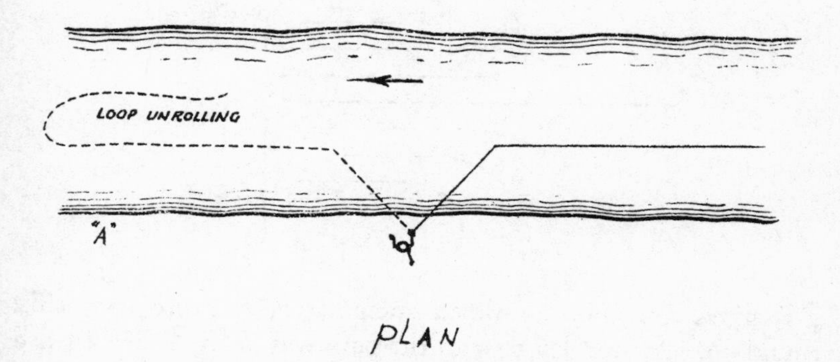

VIEW FROM "A"

This is useful for upstream fishing under your own bank and also enables you to use a little trick. As the loop unrolls in a partially *horizontal* plane, as it does in this cast, it is possible, by dropping the rod-point at the right moment, to cause the cast to fall in any of the following positions:

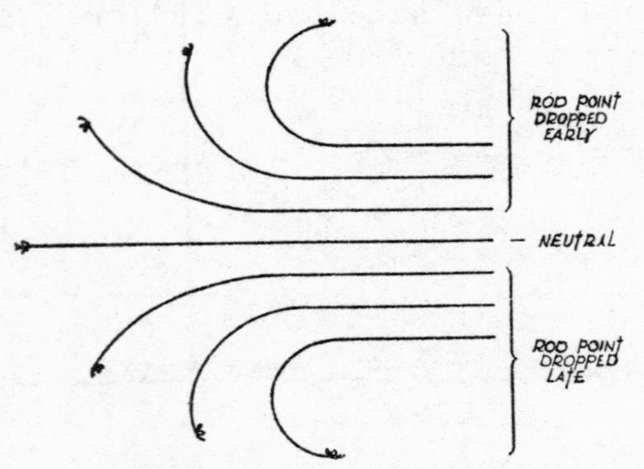

This gives you some terrific advantages; you can throw your fly round corners, and lay it with the gut away from a feeding fish where they are shy of having it over their heads. It is much easier than you might suppose.

Just consider this set-up

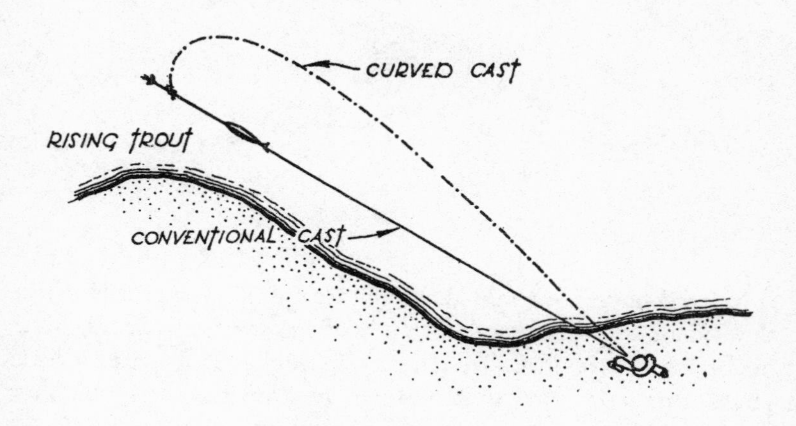

or this, which is a spot I know well!

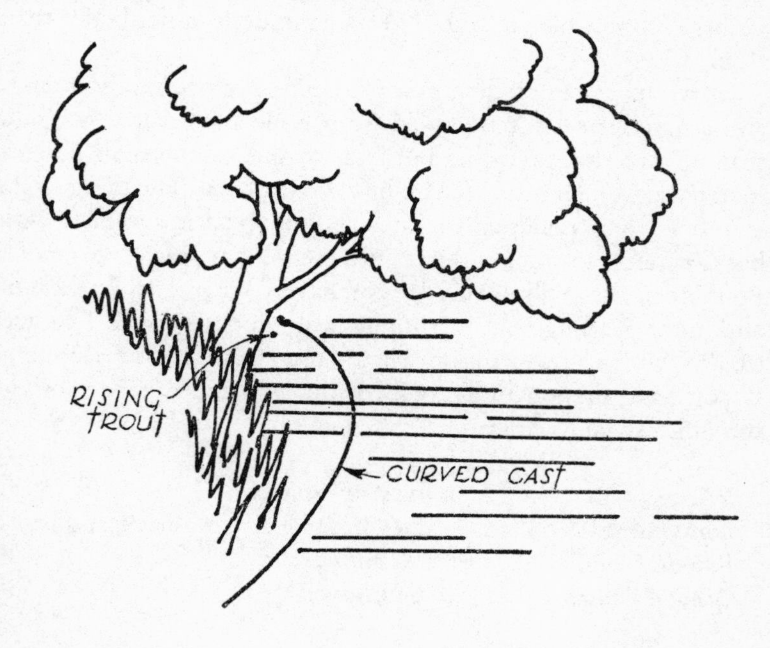

or this, common in water meadows

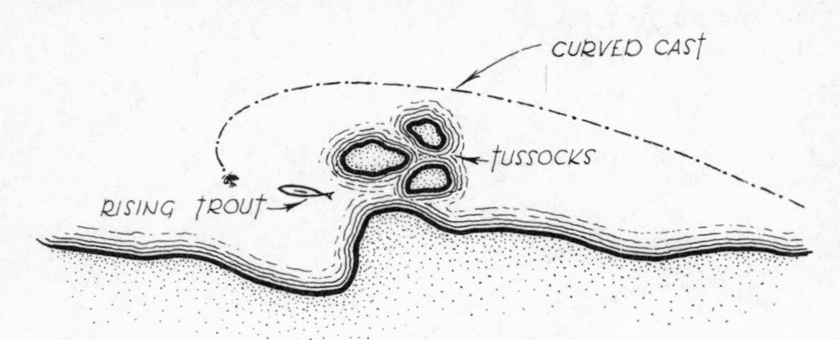

Now, I have no doubt that you are thinking that this is like the Indian rope trick and that it is the cast of an expert, quite beyond ordinary mortals! It isn't, though. It requires a little practice to judge the right moment to drop the rod-point, but anyone can learn it in a couple of outings, *always provided the mechanism which brings it about is understood.* A new member of our club bet me last spring that I couldn't throw a fly round a corner—impossible, he said. Now he can do it rather better than I can!

I have just been reading a book which says that only interest and amusement can be derived from tying one's own flies, and that no financial saving is possible, owing to the high cost of materials. Which is true if you buy the feathers. The thing to do is to beg from friends all the cock's heads you can, complete with hackles, and to pluck them into envelopes and save them. Poulterers, also, will usually let you have your pick of feathers of all kinds. Starlings can be caught easily in the garden, I should think. My cats keep me supplied. Don't buy exotic plumage. If you have these natural cock hackles you can dye to most of the other shades necessary:

White	dyes any shade
Light Sussex ('Badger')	dyes any shade, with black middle
Rhode Island Red	use undyed
Golden Ginger	use undyed

Rhode Island crossed with Black Leghorn	use undyed
('Furnace' and 'coch-y-bondhu')	'Furnace' has black centre, red outer. 'coch-y-bondhu' is the same but tipped with black on each fibre as well.

Hen hackles of the same colours should also be saved, also *wing* feathers of ginger and Rhode Islands; these are used for winging sedges.

Speckled breast and back feathers from the partridge are useful, and the rich brown tail feathers. The pheasant gives some useful, but not essential, feathers.

Flight feathers from goose, swan and others are useful; you use one or two strands of feather-fibre for bodies, wound round the hook shank. They can be dyed any colour. Heron feathers dyed in yellow dye make a fine olive body; I can always let you have some. One feather makes a lot of bodies!

There are dozens of common feathers which one finds useful, especially when you've had a bit of experience in fly-tying; you see a dead bird in the hedge in quite a new light!

I'll send you some flies presently, and some materials as soon as you start tying. As you say, it would be better to wait until we know exactly what flies you have before I send the bulk, but some are certain to be there and I'll send feathers for those.

Don't buy an expensive vice. Get a bit of $\frac{3}{8}''$ steel rod and have it bored and shaped like this:

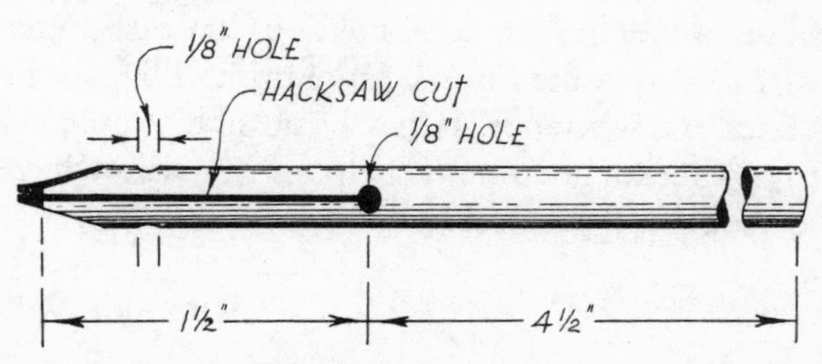

Then get a $\frac{1}{8}''$ bolt and wing nut for the hole nearest the end. This makes an excellent vice. You can use what method you like for clamping to the table. I used a vice like this for years, and just clamped it in an ordinary small table-vice. I have a smarter-looking job now, but the resultant flies are no better! About the only things you *have* to buy are hackle-pliers and silks.

You'll need black, olive, crimson and yellow in tying silks. You can also get one or two promising-looking colours in 'Sylko' from Woolworths—browns and oranges chiefly, and perhaps some pale watery-yellow. There should be plenty of change out of a pound when you've got all you want for tying trout-flies. 'Dylon' dyes do feathers admirably; with a few natural colours and about four shades of dye you can get a great range of shades and colours. When dyeing feathers, use filthy water. If necessary, put a handful of mud and dead leaves in, boil and strain. You'll then get soft subdued shades instead of harsh glaring colours, which are not wanted for trout flies. Salmon and sea-trout flies are, of course, studies in folklore and require different treatment, though I must admit that one of my friends always recites 'Double, double, toil and trouble, fire burn and cauldron bubble' when we have a dyeing-session, which reminds me, he gave me some teal plumage not long ago. If you get any, treasure it, also mallard plumage, breast and wings.

My split-cane machine is finished and awaiting installation. Soon I hope to commence production, whereupon I'll send you the split-cane for a fly-rod. Mustn't miss a convert if we can help it!

I have done an article on fly-tying for *Fishing Gazette* but the illustrations are not quite finished.

We will definitely have a 'combined ops' on carp somewhere. As soon as I can straighten out a programme I'll let you know when I'm fixed and when not. It may be possible to attack Temple Pool; I am getting some domestic help for my wife which ought to ease the problem considerably.

Sincerely,

RICHARD WALKER

PS. I have read many attacks on the Dry Fly Purist in fishing books and periodicals. I expect such people must exist somewhere.

I've never yet met an angler who was at all snobbish about trouting or fly-fishing. One gets the *impression* that anglers with a superior attitude about these things *do* exist, but I wonder if they *really* do? The only snobbery in respect of trout and coarse fishing I have ever come across has been from *non-anglers*. At one time I was very vehement against 'purism', but have since wondered if I wasn't flogging a dead horse. I think that most fishermen find eventually that there is more *fun* in catching a trout on an artificial fly (especially of their own manufacture) than on a worm; and for that reason they prefer to use the fly. It's a matter for the individual to decide for himself, not for arbitrary rules or expressions of 'public opinions'. I might go as far as to suggest that no one ought to catch a trout on a fly-fishable stream on bait until he has *tried* fly-fishing and is sure that he will get more *fun*, for his own delight, with bait than with fly. My point is not that I am sorry for a worm-caught *trout*, but I *might* be sorry for the *catcher*, if I thought he had missed the often greater pleasure of getting the fish on a fly. Trout are the easiest fish to catch that I know of, and where they are numerous, bait-fishing becomes a bit boring! (as does any too-easy form of angling!).

R. W.

Dear Mr. Ingham,

Here are a few flies—more later. The two Sedges are more or less nondescripts and imitate quite a number of insects. The speckle kills best before sunset, the grey at last light.

The *Red Ant* will kill after a flight has crossed and for several days after.

The little *Black Gnat* is for smutting fish—you'll see he has an irridescent body. He is almost always taken, but as he is so small, he often comes adrift!

'*Catamaran*' *Gnat*. This is one of my concoctions. It tries to imitate a drowning mosquito or 'some such similar sort of animile'.

Orange Partridge. This is a most ancient fly. These are William Lunn's version. Fish take it for a hatching nymph, or for a dead and drowned Red Spinner. Fish it awash or sunk. My best trout took one of these.

'*Cussy's favourite.*' Another of my concoctions. It resembles so many small flies that it becomes useful to try on a fish whose diet you can't ascertain. If I haven't an imitation of the fly the fish are 'on' I use an appropriate size of Cussy's, and more often than not it passes muster. Dressed much bigger it serves for Mayfly very well indeed.

Iron Blue. There are many dressings. I use a rather lurid purple body; it attracts quite well.

Red Spinner. This is what is called a detached body. I doubt if it makes any difference in practice, but it looks realistic on the water.

The *Blue-winged Olive* varies in body colour a lot and this example is a dark one (some are very light green-olive). This dressing with dark body also does for early dark olive dun (Rhodani).

The *Sherry Spinner*, its transformation; I've dressed spent; this is a useful shape for spent spinners, as it is not only realistic but it always falls and fishes in a realistic attitude. Trout love spent fly, and if in doubt, always try a spent imitation.

The ordinary *Olive* is a straightforward copy of the summer variety.

I send these for you to observe the simplicity of most dressings and the common feathers used. I have lots of materials and will gladly send some as soon as you want them. I hope you *will* have a shot, because it really is a pleasant pastime and one which you can take up and put away very easily. I dress flies at all sorts of odd moments. Don't ever believe it's difficult.

Sincerely,

RICHARD WALKER

Dear Mr. Walker,

Before I forget—there is a point in connection with carp fishing that I have been meaning for some time to raise. It is the question of landing nets. You did, in an earlier letter, give me a description of the net which you have made for your own use, but I gathered from what you said that you are not entirely satisfied with it. As I see it, the difficulty is to get a net which is large enough and strong enough to accommodate even the monster carp of one's dreams, and at the same time is light enough to use in one hand. I agree entirely with your sentiments on gaffing carp and the landing net is, as far as I know, the only alternative—but what size, shape and construction? It appears to me that a round net ring is the most effective shape, and that provided the net is deep enough great strength is unnecessary. If the net is sufficiently deep a fish can be completely enclosed without even raising the ring above the surface of the water, and in such circumstances only tensile strength is required to *pull* it—as distinct from *lifting* it—on to the bank. The only net I possess of sufficient size for carp is a most unwieldy improvised affair, and I intend to equip myself more efficiently before next June. I would appreciate any hints or suggestions you can give me on this subject. The factor that I consider to be of supreme importance is size. I always fish with the hope that one day I may contact a *really* big fish and it would be the height of folly not to be prepared for the big fellow when it does come my way.

There is a size limit beyond which a landing net becomes so difficult to manage that it ceases to be an effective instrument. Is the gaff the only alternative once that limit is reached? There appears to be scope for inventive genius here!

It had not occurred to me to write a descriptive article and I must confess that it appeals to me more than the idea of writing an instructive one. I have two or three days' holiday due to me in the near future, which I hope to spend at Revesby Reservoir. Perhaps after that holiday I shall have something worth writing about! We'll see.

Thanks for the tips on fish-stuffing. I'll bear them in mind when I try my hand at it, which I hope to do before long.

This subject of leeches is interesting, isn't it? As you say, we may be 'on' to something. I am following it up and trying to learn as much as I can about the leeches themselves—what varieties are available, where they are to be found and when, and so on—

before June, when I intend to try them out as bait. It will be interesting to compare results.

I think this subject of natural baits would bear careful investigation. The fly-fisher goes to great lengths to imitate as closely as possible the actual flies upon which his quarry feeds, but the vast majority of coarse fishermen seem content to fish with worms, maggots or paste. Some of the less widely used baits—I am thinking particularly of hemp—*may* resemble natural foods, but as far as I know no one has seriously investigated the possibilities of using the natural insect life of our ponds and rivers as bait. I may be wrong here—it may be that the subject has been gone into carefully and dropped—but I have not heard ot it. Caddis, we know, are a deadly bait. I have caught trout whose stomachs were distended with water-beetles and nothing else, and as you suggest, fish may take lobs for leeches. I have no doubt that the availability of worms, maggots, etc., is a great contributory factor to their popularity and it cannot be disputed that in most waters they are effective. But to me it seems only logical that a more natural bait would be more acceptable and less likely to arouse suspicion. No doubt many of the natural baits would be more difficult to obtain, but patience is one of my few virtues, and I think I will not confine my investigations and experiments to leeches alone.

For me the attraction of sea-fishing lies in its novelty. I enjoyed my first attempt last year and I shall certainly have another go when I visit Devon again this summer, but I do admit that no great skill is required. I don't know enough about the subject to be able to exhibit much skill in the actual method of sea-fishing and once a fish is hooked, provided one's line is long enough, it is only a question of time before it is in the net.

Now to fly-fishing. Your description of casting could not be more clear and explicit. I appreciate the principle underlying the art of casting. When I was a lad my brother and I were very fond of playing 'cowboys'. A favourite game was for one to lasso the other and then while the victim tried to escape the lasso-er tied him up even more by throwing half-hitches along the rope on to his arms and legs and round his neck. We became quite proficient at it! I expect you have seen the same thing done at circuses, which was where we got the idea.

I had not realized that *such* a heavy line is required. Somehow I had got the impression that a fly-line was a gossamer thing, though, of course, when one thinks for a moment it is obvious that a fine line could not be cast very far. I assume that the grading of fly-lines by letters refers to the weight of the line and not to its strength—I am led to this conclusion by Allcock's catalogue, which gives a size 'E' line of one quality as 16 lb. b.s. and one of the same size in another quality as 28 lb. Allcock's do not give a size 'C' line in their catalogue and the one size 'D' quoted is 36 lb. b.s. I am not questioning your advice on this point—I assume the conspicuousness of the actual line is not of any consequence provided the cast is of sufficient length and tapered to a sufficiently fine point.

There is one other detail in connection with casting that puzzles me. You say that the forward cast is commenced when the line on the backward movement has unrolled to about two-thirds of its length. There would appear to be a tendency, by so doing, to 'crack' the line like a whip and to flick off the fly. You will no doubt have noticed that the section in Allcock's catalogue on fly-casting also makes this point. Is your answer to this that the forward movement is commenced slowly? Once again, please don't think I am offering criticism—I am genuinely seeking knowledge.

I take it that all your remarks refer to a right-handed angler. I am, in most things, ambidextrous, but when fishing always hold my rod in my left hand. I take it then, that when casting in a semi-horizontal plane my back cast will go to the left and the forward cast to the right. I can quite see that this method of casting does give you terrific advantages, but does it not make striking slower?

Your package of flies arrived to-day—they are magnificent. The little red ant particularly is a masterpiece of imitation. I can't begin to thank you for your kindness and generosity—I only wish there was some way I could return it.

I can well understand anyone making a collection of flies just as some people collect stamps. They are most fascinating. I really must try my hand at it and see if it is as easy as you say it is. I should have no difficulty in getting a supply of the commoner feathers fairly quickly and the less common ones will no doubt turn up from time to time. I can get a vice made up at my garage, silks I can get locally, and hackle pliers I have ordered. Hooks will present no difficulty—16, 14, and 12 appear to be the usual sizes and a few smaller ones for the smaller flies. I think that only leaves the actual method of tying, and here again I must plead absolute ignorance. Can you recommend a text-book which explains the *method* of tying flies as distinct from the dressing formulae? If so, this would save you an awful lot of trouble and writing. Being ambidextrous may prove an asset in fly-tying as it has proved in many things.

For the offer of split-cane for a fly-rod again I can only offer my most sincere and grateful thanks. I hope the machine proves a great success.

Your argument on bait versus fly-fishing is unassailable. Assuming that one fishes for pleasure and not for the sole purpose of catching fish, it is I think only logical that one should try all the accepted methods before deciding upon a particular one. Then one has the satisfaction of knowing that, whatever anyone else may do or say about that particular method, it is the one from which the individual derives the most pleasure and satisfaction. You say that any too-easy form of angling becomes boring—I couldn't agree more. I think I have mentioned the Mill Pool at Thimbleby—it simply teems with trout and on worm it is possible to catch them as quickly as one can pull them them out. It was to escape this that I used a live minnow with which I caught my largest trout. I also know a small pond a few miles from here—a beautiful spot which is very little fished—which is *full* of rudd. Here again, with a slowly sinking maggot it is possible to catch huge quantities of fish. It is so easy and the small ones are so difficult to avoid, that I have stopped fishing there. With regard to Thimbleby, I have no doubt that with a fly I would catch fewer fish, but I would derive more pleasure from it. It may be significant that the best fish ever caught there

—a brown trout of something over 4 lb.—was taken on a fly last season.

That particular argument cannot be applied to the great majority of our streams, where trout are *not* plentiful (Thimbleby is exceptional for reasons I have explained) and where the capture of a trout on either bait or fly is something of an occasion. Nevertheless, I think your main argument holds.

I must admit that I have never *met* anyone who was at all snobbish about fly-fishing, and, as *you* were, I may be flogging a dead horse, but I have no doubt that such people do exist, though perhaps, happily, not in great numbers. I feel sure that there are ardent fly-enthusiasts who, not being so generous and open-minded as yourself, derive such pleasure from their fly-fishing that they inevitably tend to despise bait-fishing, which they regard as being so much an inferior sport. It must be hard to keep an open mind in such circumstances—I must watch myself! But I will flog this horse no more.

Thanks for everything.

Yours sincerely,
MAURICE INGHAM

V

February Letters

Dear Mr. Walker,

I see from the local paper that a club has been formed and has acquired the fishing rights of Croxby Pond. It is a coincidence that this should happen so soon after I had said that I would explore the possibilities of Croxby, and I think the action of the twenty-odd members of the newly formed Croxby Angling Club is most praiseworthy. I have spoken to the secretary of the

Club by telephone to-day and he tells me that it is proposed to limit membership to about 30; there are still some vacancies and I have asked for my name to be put forward. I understand the club proposes to carry out some work to improve the condition of the Pond and the annual subscription—for this year at least—is high—six guineas. The secretary tells me that he caught several carp up to about 8 lb. last season and that there are many big fish in the pond. So it looks as if we may get some fishing at Croxby after all!

Could you possibly tell me the dimensions of the split cane which you have so kindly offered to send me for a trout fly-rod? Please don't think that I am trying to hustle you, but as you may well imagine, I am anxious to get the rod into action as soon as possible after the 1st April, and as J. B. Walker's deliveries are delayed about three weeks after the placing of an order at present, I don't want to be kicking my heels for three weeks after I receive the cane from you while I am waiting for ferrules, etc., to arrive.

Weather permitting, I hope to have another day at Revesby Reservoir on Saturday. If I get a pike of suitable size I will have a shot at stuffing it.

I make no apology for this short note—I just thought you might be interested in the news about Croxby.

Yours sincerely,

MAURICE INGHAM

Dear Mr. Ingham,

Landing nets *are* a problem. Mine is much too heavy and I have been thinking how to make a better one. I agree that the problem of lifting a fish hardly arises, as even a ten-pounder is almost impossible to lift at the end of a four-foot shaft. I always *drag* the fish to the water's edge, and then take the 'neck' of the net in one hand and the middle of the cord which joins the arms in the other. This causes the arms (which are flexible) to close up; then I just lift. But I think a proper ring is much better than the arms and cord idea. Perhaps a strong light ring could be made from bamboo strip. If a couple of strips were planed up and glued together, skin side outwards, and then heated and bent to shape, they should result in a very effective pear-shaped net. A net for carp should be both big *and* deep. A completely 'whacked' carp, especially a big one, lies on its side and is very difficult to get into a small net; it always turns out that the fish is lying at the worst possible angle for netting! I remember during the war seeing a most ingenious device for dealing with tench which had to be fished for over a bank of weeds about ten feet wide, on the Basingstoke canal. An old fellow there was fishing with a twenty-foot roach pole, and on the lower four joints of a similar, but older and more weather-beaten pole, he had a landing net with a ring made of light basket-cane. The net was deep and had a cord threaded in its meshes to make a second ring about a foot below the proper one, the end of the cord being tied to the end of the pole on the bank. He kept the net pushed out over the weeds all the time. The theory was that having netted his fish he pulled the cord and closed the bag, obviating accidents while the fish was being dragged over the weed, which was done by the cord, not the pole to which the net was attached. I never saw the thing used, but it looked very effective, and there were three tench in the old chap's keep net, all between 2 lb. and 3 lb.

I cannot find any information on leeches except the usual vague encyclopedia stuff, which says that there are twenty species in this country and that they are common in ponds and streams. The ones I know are the big brown ones (horse leech, so called because it has nothing whatever to do with horses?), a medium sized jet black one which is common in chalk-streams, and a small greyish-white one about the size of a fat gentle—another possible connection here.

Actually, I have done a little in the way of trying natural baits, though not, so far, leeches. One might imagine that dragonflies or their larvae would catch fish, but I have tried both many times and never had a touch. I know a chub-hole on the Ouse where in summer you can catch 2-pound chub on almost anything, dapped; I have even had them on cigarette-ends. They bask in a tight-packed shoal, and each knows that if he hesitates, the next chap will have the bait. But they will not touch a dragonfly or larva. Trout and chub will take frog or newt tadpoles. Many fish will take water snails. I once caught a good trout ($6\frac{1}{4}$ lb.) on an imitation water-rat. Water-boatmen are eaten by fish and I expect water beetles of *all* kinds are, too, but all these are hard to get in sufficient quantities, except at the weed-cutting. Of course Mayfly nymphs are a deadly bait for all coarse fish. These nymphs live in gravelly mud; they make burrows like rabbits, and they can stand dirtier water than any other ephemerid. Very few coarse fishermen know they exist, because the fly itself is finished in most places before June 16th. Nymphs from eggs of the previous year are half-grown and if you dig them out of the mud you can soon collect enough for a day's fishing; but they must have running water if they are to be kept. They're like this:

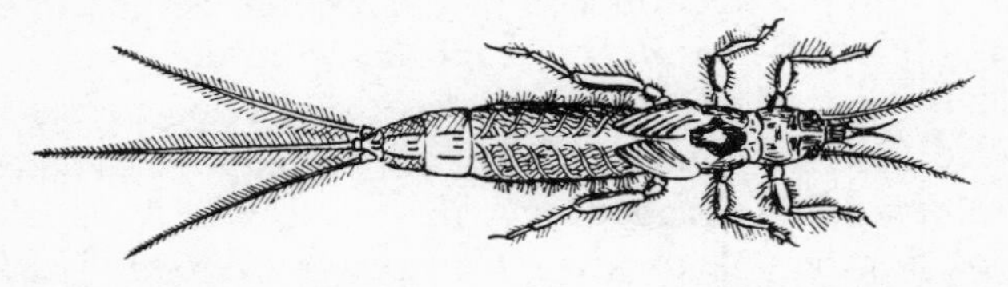

I have some dried ones and some more in spirits. All ephemerid nymphs follow the same general layout. March Browns are flatter and live under stones; some of the Olives live in weeds, and Blue-winged Olives coat themselves with mud and filth and live in tributary ditches and like places. I should think they would all make good baits on suitable tackle. The fly-fishermen's artificial nymph imitates the nymph about to hatch, as do several flies which are not specifically described as nymphs; Hackle Blue-wing and Orange Partridge for example, unnatural-looking but effective.

Fly-fishing. Your line *must* be heavy, and it must be flexible, and oil-dressed. Size C is .0375″, D is .0335″. I use an HCH line on an 8 ft. s.c. rod mostly—this is the No. 2 Kingfisher. A heavy line helps greatly in defeating wind. Do not get lighter than D. I cannot throw HEH well on any of my rods, but I can throw level E on my lightest and whippiest. I would advise D if you average 10–15 yard casts, C if 15–20 yard casts. You attach your cast to a level line thus; clean off the dressing from the end inch by soaking in cellulose thinners and then scraping. Fray $\frac{1}{8}$″ of the end and clip to taper. Pass a bit of nylon monofil, say .016″ or so, through the hole, flatten one end with hot pliers, and whip with fly-tying silk like this:

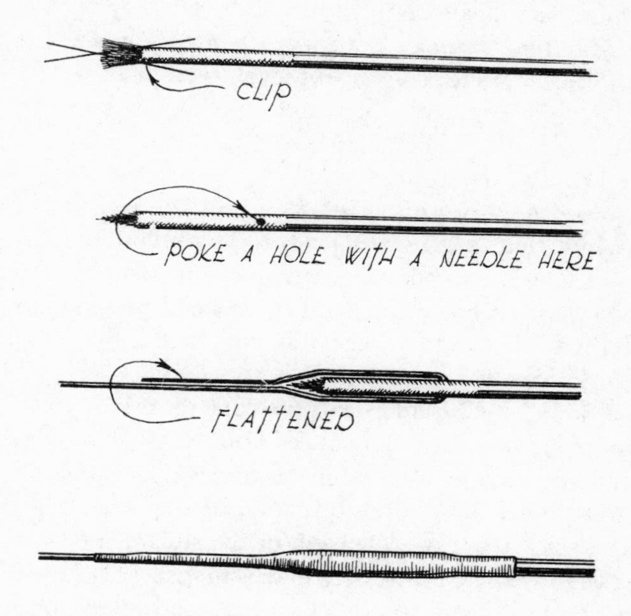

Give two or three coats slow-drying best quality copal. Let the nylon be 18″ long or so, with a neat loop at the end, to which your cast proper can be readily looped and detached.

The fly-line is greased and alights with no disturbance if properly thrown. This junction of line and nylon extension is not very strong, as you may already be thinking; but it is a good deal stronger than the point of your tapered cast, which will not exceed 0.010″ in trout-fishing. I use .008″ for Mayfly and .006″ for small flies, as a rule, but .006″ is a bit fine for heavy fish if there is much weed.

You've guessed right about the reason for starting the forward cast before the back-cast has finished. My estimate of 2/3rds was only a guess; there is a fairly wide latitude in the timing, but the slow start of the forward motion is the secret. I say slow, but it is only slow compared with the ultimate speed. The whole motion must be a smooth acceleration; not a sudden jerk or flick like one uses in casting a weight from a fixed-spool reel. You kind of *pull* the line out of the air behind you! If you wait until the line has straightened *completely* behind you, it will begin to *fall*, and by the time the action of the forward cast has made itself felt, the fly will be at a nice convenient level to embed itself firmly in your ear! You must also be careful to throw your back-cast both behind and *up*, for the same reason. You do not let the fly alight on every forward cast, you sling it back and forth once or twice, measuring your distance. You hold the reel line between reel and butt ring in the spare hand, and by pulling line from the reel and feeding it to the ring as the line is *about* to straighten, either forward or backward, you can extend your range. You should always let a little line go as you let the fly fall; it helps it to fall lightly.

But as long as you understand the rope idea, you will soon be able to overcome any difficulties you may encounter. The horizontal cast can be used forehand or backhand, but it is much easier to throw a curve forehand. You, as a left-hander, will find it easier to fish from the left bank of the stream.

You seldom strike too slowly in dry-fly fishing! Far more fish are lost through being too quick. Often and often you have to throw a slack line to avoid drag, but even with all the slack you can get on the water, you seldom connect too late. When I see a rise, I pick up the slack with a quick lift—a sort of half-hearted back-cast, without any hurry.

I'm glad you liked the flies. The ant is one of those humbugs, whereby you can impress people with your skill in tying, when actually it is the easiest thing to tie there is, much easier than the drab and unexciting Iron Blue, for example. To tie the ant, take a hook and wind hot-orange silk round it firmly to make two piles, thus: Give this two or three coats of cellulose. Then take two pale cream cock hackles, and strip off all except the point fibres, of which leave enough to imitate the ant's wing. Lay these on the front hump and bind down; again varnish—be careful not to get varnish on the feather. Then

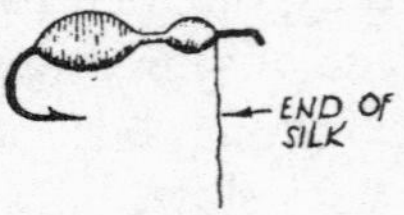

END OF SILK

take a suitable ginger hackle, and strip off the fluffy base fibres; you will need to remove about half the total. Tie down the stalk end ahead of the front hump, thus:

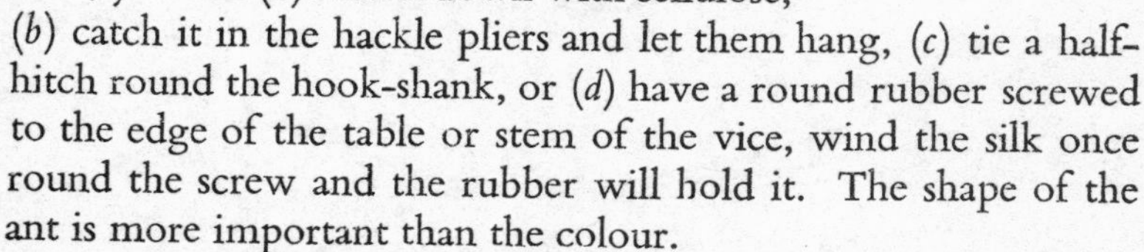

Cut off surplus stalk. Catch tip of hackle in hackle pliers and wind round and round hook until it is all used up. Tie down the end and finish with two or three half hitches, or better still, a whip-finish. Varnish the head with cellulose.

If you want to let go the tying silk at any time, you can (*a*) stick it down with cellulose, (*b*) catch it in the hackle pliers and let them hang, (*c*) tie a half-hitch round the hook-shank, or (*d*) have a round rubber screwed to the edge of the table or stem of the vice, wind the silk once round the screw and the rubber will hold it. The shape of the ant is more important than the colour.

For upright-winged flies with hackle-point wings (hen hackles for the sub-imago, cock hackles for the imago or spinner, generally speaking) tie on the wings before making the body. Put your two 'wings' shiny sides together, lay stalks along the hook (cellulose it first and let dry) and bind down, like *fig. a.* (*page 108*). Cut the stalks at about half-way down shank, but leave the wings as they are until you've finished the body. Then tie in the tails, which are usually fibres from a big cock's hackle, for small flies, *fig. b.* Now tie in the body material; a hackle-stalk, say, stripped of all its fibres; this makes a good body for many flies, and can be used natural or dyed. Tie in the thin end like *fig. c.* Half-hitch the silk or otherwise prevent it unwinding. Then wind your body material back to the wings and bind down the end with the silk, cutting off the surplus body material. Your fly now looks like *fig. d.* (If the body is to have rib, to wind over the body material, this is tied in last and wound back over the body—by last I mean after tying in the body material—and tied down by the silk.) Now attach your hackle as in the ant; tie down the stalk. The stalk can either go *between* the wings or *underneath*; between for divided or spent wings. Before winding the hackle, take several turns of silk in front of the wings, holding them up between finger and thumb. You can set them up at any angle you like by putting more turns behind or in front. Now your fly is like *fig. e.* Now wind the hackle and tie down. Easy! The hackle can have some turns behind and some in front of wings, or be placed as seems desirable.

For spent wings, set the wings vertical *first*, then separate and

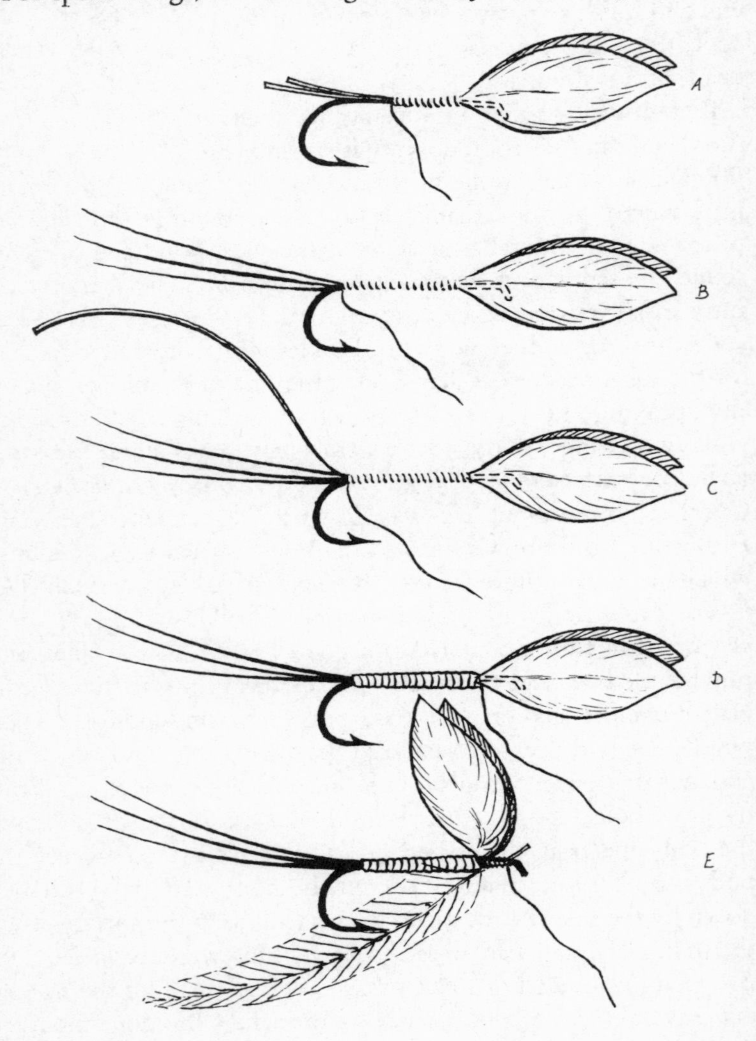

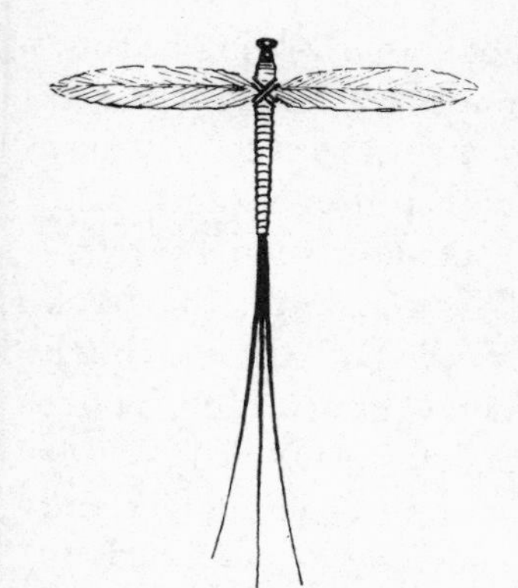

set horizontal by a figure-of-eight binding (*left*). I say to myself 'under straight, over diagonal, under straight' and so on. One important point—always leave room between wings or hackle and eye to finish. A tiny wire ring on a handle pushed over the eye of the fly will keep the feathers out of the way while you finish (*below*).

Sedges ought to be tied with opaque wings, usually solid feather. These are hard to do, and really do need practice to put on well. You put two slips between finger and thumb, with a loop of silk, and pull the loop tight with the thumb and finger pressed together (*left*). Solid feather wings are also used on ephemerid imitations, but the hackle-point wings are in every way as effective and easier to tie. They are much *better* for spinners and spent. You can get over the difficulty with the solid feather wings (which are normally made from the web of flight feathers, a piece being cut from a left and a right hand feather to make the two wings) (*right*), when tying sedges by using the tip of a feather, as in the speckle sedge I sent you. The solid web method is quite quick and easy when you've got the knack, but it takes a lot of practice.

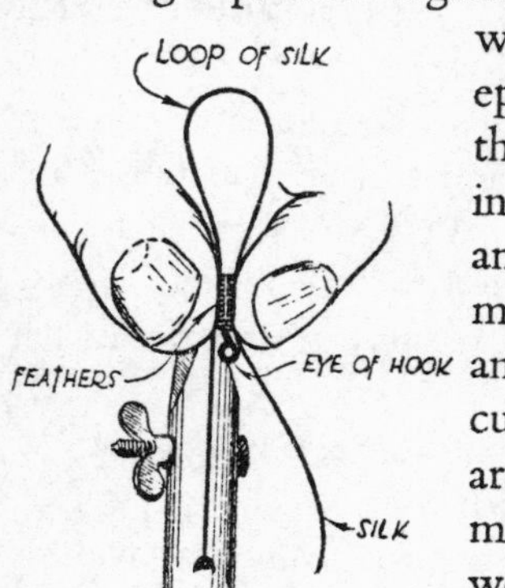

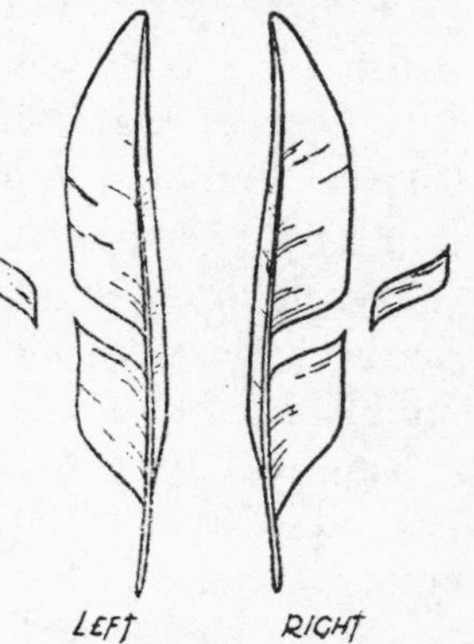

You will not learn a great deal from books on fly-tying because each writer has his own methods and none is best. I am reluctant to advise any one of them, because you may be tempted to follow their dressing formulae, instead of working out your own by reference to the natural insects! Still, the book by Roger Woolley (*Fishing Gazette* book service) contains useful information about materials. One book I like very much, which has little to say about manual technique in dressing but much about flies and fishing with them, is J. W. Hills's *River Keeper*, published by Geoffrey Bles. It is the life and work of William Lunn, River Keeper to the Houghton Club. Of all fly dressers I admire Lunn the most, but I differ from him on one point—he often uses two or even three hackles on one fly where one would do, e.g. his Caperer has one black and one red hackle in front of the wings; I use a red hackle with black centre, which kills quite as well as the two. But read this book if you can; it has quantities of useful information on all aspects of fly-fishing for trout in chalk-streams.

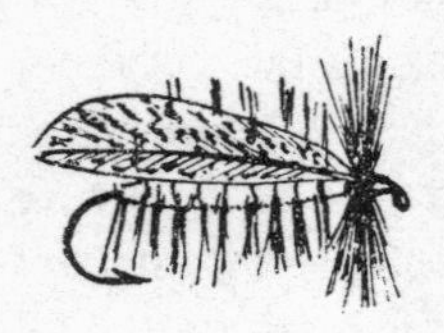

Fly-dressing, like many other pastimes, has acquired certain conventions which I violate with glee and I hope you will, too.

Never hesitate to used dyed feathers to get the right shade.

Never hesitate to clip wings or hackle if they need it.

Let your hackling be *sparse* rather than *bushy*, and better *too long* than *too short*.

Don't hesitate to try unconventional ideas; always try to visualize how a fly will appear to the fish.

Remember that hackles on dry flies are for *floatant* as well as *imitative* purposes, and you very often have to strike a compromise for the best result.

To help dry flies to float, oil with medicinal paraffin and dry off surplus with rag or blotting-paper. If wet flies insist on floating, use glycerine on them.

You will have to get proper fly-tying silk for small flies. Pearsall's Gossamer is the best I know. I only use black, crimson, amber and olive.

Poultry hackles will do for nearly *all* your feathers. Always get all the *whites* you can, as you can dye these any colour you want.

I don't know whether I ever explained that which you probably already know, that a 'spent' fly is an ephemerid which has laid its eggs and died. The live fly has its wings up and together like (*a*), but when spent they fall flat like (*b*).

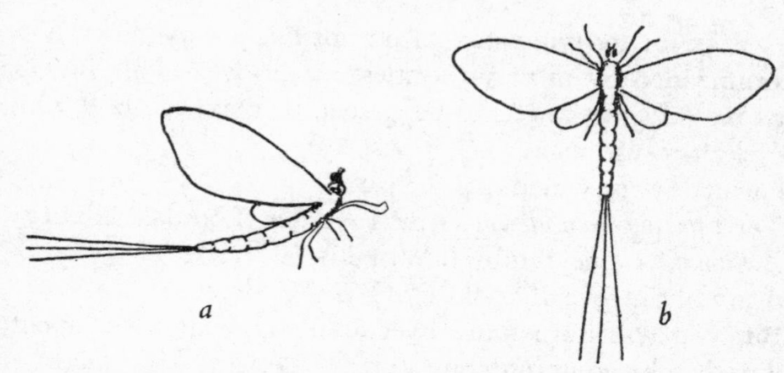

Trout are very fond of spent fly: a fly taking fish at all times is what we all hope to design and if it ever happens I dare bet it would be a spent imitation. Trout usually ignore fresh flies when they are on spent, but very often they will take a spent copy when they are on fresh fly. Always dress spent fly with a glassy wing—a clear hackle. Never opaque feather.

Your second letter just arrived. Good luck to the Croxby Club: may it prosper exceedingly. If you have any say in rule formation, I should say these would be desirable:

No gaffs allowed.

Use of boats prohibited during carp season, unless their use is essential (June to October).

No fish to be removed under 15 lb., and then only on payment of £? to club restocking fund (unless there are very large numbers of fish in the water).

In the 'deep and weedy clay-pit' we had a large wire-netting cage, about 6 ft. × 6 ft., with string-net cover, into which anglers could put carp pending official weighing. The wire should be covered with cabbage-sacking to prevent injury to the fish.

I can't say yet what size the s.c. for the fly rod will be, but I will get the ferrule and corks as soon as I know the sizes needed.

I am enclosing a few assorted feathers for you to try your hand on.

Sincerely,
RICHARD WALKER

PS. Wax for fly-tying silk. I do not like a very sticky wax as recommended by most authorities; candle wax alone isn't bad, but I use 80% beeswax and 20% suet. It makes a good whitish and clean-to-use wax.

Further books which may help are:

Trout fishing from all angles by Taverner (Lonsdale Library).

A Summer on the Test by J. W. Hills

and any of the several books by G. E. M. Skues.

But you will learn more by employing your own inventive ability than by anything you can read. Perhaps this thought may help—a good caricature of Churchill is more readily recognizable than a *bad photograph* of him!

R. W.

Dear Mr. Walker,

I have at last received my cane from J. B. Walker and am forwarding the butt joint with this letter. There is no great urgency —I know you are a very busy man, and there is quite a long time yet before 16th June—so please don't inconvenience yourself. I am most grateful for your assistance and am only too pleased to await your convenience.

Strange that you should suggest a built cane landing net ring. I have been toying with the idea of making one as illustrated on the following page.

I want the efficiency of a round net with the strength of a pear-shaped one. The cane supports in my sketch would, I think, make the net more rigid and would strengthen the ring at the points where the joints come. The triangular area between the supports and the ring is a potential source of danger, but this could possibly be overcome by stretching netting over—otherwise

I have visions of a fish slipping between the supports and the shaft. A pear-shaped net would be much easier to make, of course, but I am particularly keen on having a round net—I think it is a great advantage to be able to net a fish at whatever angle it may present itself, without any preliminary manoeuvring. I should be pleased to know what you think of the idea.

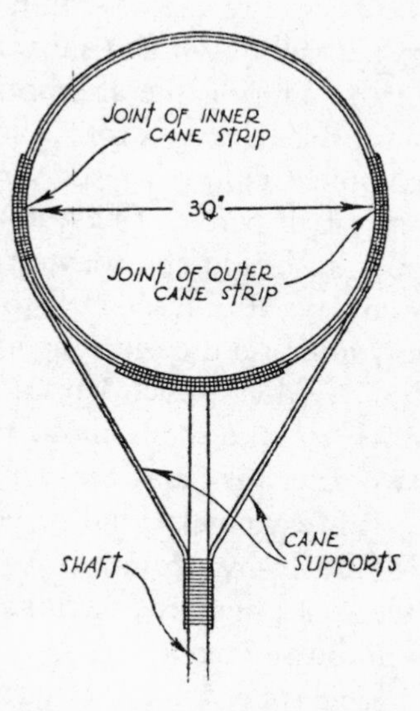

Have you ever done any net-weaving? I think it would be far simpler to make one's own net to one's own requirements than to have one specially made. If you include net-weaving amongst your many and varied activities perhaps you could give me some tips on how to set about it.

I have no more information about leeches—at least nothing of practical interest—but I am still trying.

As there are likely to be very few occasions when I shall require to cast more than 15 yds. I intend to get a size D line. Do you recommend any particular make or type?

I have spent some time examining the flies you sent me and from them and from your description of the method I think I have learned quite a lot. I gather that the object and the difficulty in tying solid feather wings is to compress the fibres vertically.

As soon as my vice is finished, which it should be in the next day or so, I shall be equipped with all the basic necessities for fly-tying and I hope to have a go one night this week. I think for the present it would be as well if I confined myself to mastering the manual technique, which I shall try to do by copying some of your larger flies. As soon as I produce any which I think are worthy of notice I will send them for your criticism.

You mention an encounter with an old fellow on the Basingstoke Canal. I know it well, and have spent many happy hours punting on it. I was stationed close by the canal for some time during the war and I deeply regret that I did not avail myself of the opportunity to fish. I see it was reported in the *Fishing Gazette* recently that the canal has changed ownership and that the fishing is to be preserved.

My latest outing to Revesby Reservoir was not a great success. There had been several days of very rough, stormy weather and the day of my visit was dull, with a gale of wind. The pike seemed to be well down and showed little interest in anything I offered them. During the afternoon the wind dropped a little and the sun broke through for a short time and the day was saved from complete failure by six small pike—largest about 3 lb.—and a few small perch. I have found repeatedly that the best time for pike is a bright clear day, preferably with a gentle breeze, coming two days after a spell of stormy weather. I have never yet done any good on the morning after a stormy night. I have a few days holiday due, which I must take before the end of March, and I hope to take them about the 16th, so that I can have a day or two after pike and the remainder after trout.

It is extremely kind of you to offer to order the ferrules, etc., for the fly-rod from J. B. Walker for me. It will save a lot of time. Please let me have the invoice so that I can pay J. B. Walker, or reimburse you.

One more query about flies. I notice in the ones you sent me that the bodies differ very considerably. How is the ribbed effect obtained? Is it done by over-wrapping with silk after the body material has been tied in? The body of the cowdung fly appears to require a different technique. Is this what, I believe, is known as a dubbed body—made with fur?

No more news yet about membership of Croxby Angling Club. I understand there will be a meeting in about a fortnight's time and that I stand a good chance of being one of the lucky 30. I've got a copy of the rules, which contain no equivalent to the suggestions you made. When I see the Secretary, as I hope to do some time this week, I will certainly mention the points you raise. I think they are most important. Another thing I intend to mention, which has been bothering me a good deal—I understand the Pond has a deep side and a shallow side and that there is a scheme afoot to dredge out and deepen the shallow side. I don't know just how shallow the so-called shallow side is, or how much it is proposed to deepen it, but I think you will agree that unless this question has been very carefully considered it may be detrimental or definitely harmful to fishing.

Yours sincerely,
MAURICE INGHAM

Dear Mr. Ingham,

I like the idea of your reinforced net, but wouldn't it be better like this: This would give extra strength in the side arms.

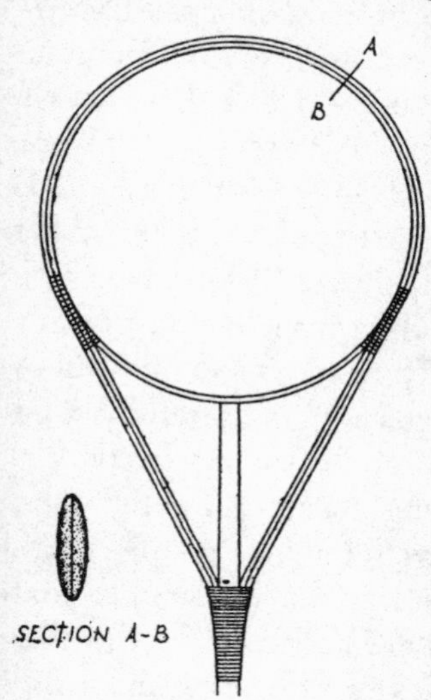

Make sure the hard part of the bamboo is outwards and that you use good water-proof cement.

I know the theory of net-making, but it is like knitting, very slow and tedious until one becomes expert by practice, which I have never done. One can get nets made to order so cheaply that I've never troubled to make my own. It pays to dress nets; warm some raw linseed oil and stir in a little dehydrated lime, let it settle and pour off the oil. This removes any acidity from the oil. Then thoroughly soak the net and hang it up, well spread, to dry, which takes 2–3 months according to the weather. The net will then last almost indefinitely. Twisted flax is as good as anything for nets.

I can't recommend any particular make of fly-line; it must be oil-dressed and ought to be perfectly smooth and supple—not stiff or in any way whiskery or rough. Twenty yards, plus 30 yards flax backing, will be plenty. Like most things, the best is the most expensive.

I'm not very good at dubbed bodies and hardly ever use them, though they are supposed to be very effective, especially for wet flies. The cowdung flies are bodied with dyed fibres from the secondary wing quill of a swan. The ribs on bodies can be obtained by silk or other material in open turns, or by using a material which provides its own rib; for example, a fibre from a peacock eye feather, stripped of its fluff with a scraper, has this appearance:

(size exaggerated). The dark stripe down the side makes a natural rib (see Cussy's favourite). Hackle-stalks from coloured hackles have a natural white rib. You can get various effects in this material, for example, the Houghton Ruby, which imitates a spent female Iron Blue, has a body of Rhode Island cock hackle-stalk, stripped of its fibres and dyed crimson, giving alternate chestnut and crimson bands round the body. I like these hackle stalk bodies as they have a realistic taper and are very buoyant (see Pale Watery I sent). Their only disadvantage is that they lack translucence. J. W. Dunne invented some excellent bodies, made of artificial silk on a white-painted hook-shank. These have a fine translucent effect when oiled or celluloid-varnished; you mustn't use wax on your tying-silk for these. They are not so buoyant as the hackle-stalk bodies, but they float well enough if carefully oiled and well-dried by false casting before allowing them to settle.

I prefer the softer hackles from young cockerels for dry flies, because, although they don't float as well, they are more collapsible and more likely to go in a trout's mouth; the old idea that hackles from a cock of three years old are necessary for dry flies ought to be exploded. These stiff hackles often prevent a fish from sucking-in a fly.

Yes, you've spotted the difficulty in using solid feather for the wings. The secret is to grip wings and silk loop quite tightly between finger and thumb while pulling the loop tight. But don't worry about these wings; you can always use a feather with a stalk, either hackle-point or small wing-covert, instead. Let the natural be your guide, then you can't go far wrong.

It is very useful to have a selection of under-water 'flies'—imitations of caddis and nymphs. You can make an excellent artificial caddis with body of swan fibre, dyed yellow or

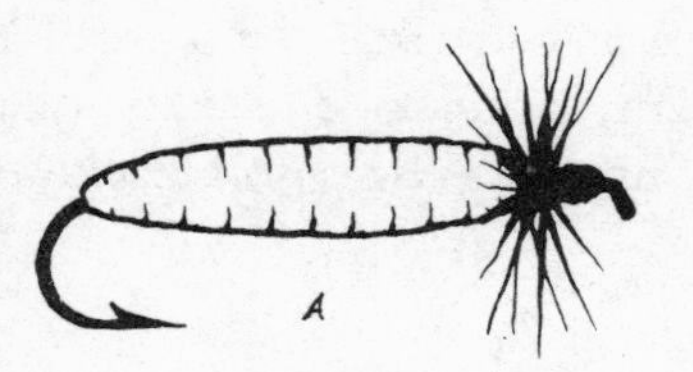

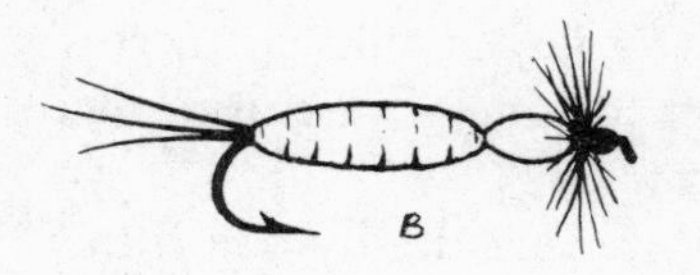

green, and a short hackle of grouse feather (*a*). Nymphs can be done in a similar way, but with a sort of double body (*b*). If you tie two hackles, each stripped of its fibres on one side of the stalk, in at the tail, like this (*c*), tie in at the waist, thus (*d*) then cut short (*e*) and finish with head hackle, it makes for greater realism.

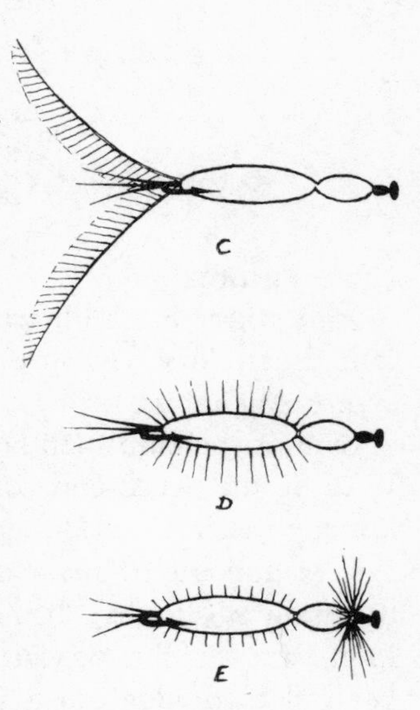

Nymph fishing is good fun; you grease the gut cast to within the right distance of the nymph, according to the depth you want to fish, and use the greased gut as a float. Dip the nymph in glycerine to make it sink easily.

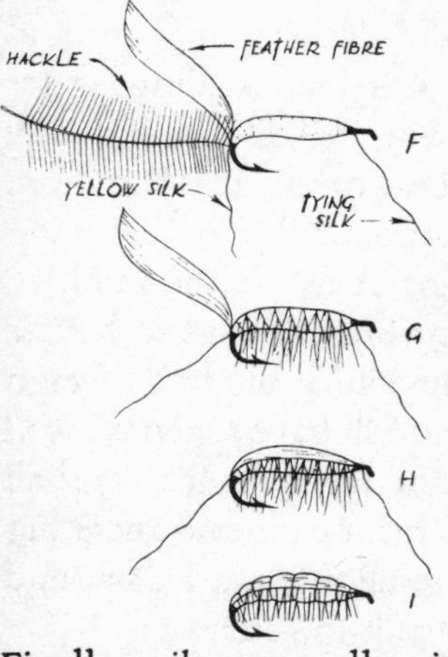

Imitation freshwater shrimps are easy. Take a fair-sized hook—say size 8, old scale, and make a body of ginger wool to nearly half-way round the bend. Tie in at the tail end a buff hackle by the point, a strip of buff feather fibre and a bit of yellow silk, thus (*f*). Then wind the hackle back to head in open turns. Stroke it down so that its fibres point downwards like this (*g*). Now bring the feather fibre over the back and tie down at the head, like this (*h*). Finally, rib over all with the yellow silk, which gives this effect (*i*). Finish at head and clip hackle to length if necessary.

This makes a deadly shrimp. If you can cast it on a weed-bed and bring it out and across stream in quick jerks you usually get an offer if a fish is there. Purism? Use a soft hackle for this 'fly'.

Another deadly one is this

More Purism.

And where big, old, crafty cannibals exist, try this—a rabbit's tail, fished 'dry', in short jerks, on a treble hook, imitates a swimming mouse!

One of the club members caught a perch of 3½ lb. at Arlesey Lake at the week-end, on lob-tail. I hope to go myself on Sunday next.

It is difficult to make any comments on the desirability of dredging at Croxby. If there is a wide expanse of reeds standing in just a few inches of water, as is the case in many lakes, it might be well to dredge out a series of bays three or four feet deep. But if the shallows are clear of reeds and deep enough to hold fish, they are better left alone, I think. Carp like shallow water and it encourages surface feeding, which makes floating-crust fishing profitable. I like this method best of all; it is far more exciting than bottom fishing. On no account do any dredging before May, otherwise you'll cut up a lot of fish in the mud.

I went up to the trout stream here last Sunday, just to have a look round, and saw a tremendous trout which ought to weigh close on 10 lb., if in good condition. The fish have spawned well this season, and if the herons will give the fry a chance we shall not need to do much re-stocking. The main danger is these big old cannibals, which think nothing of swallowing a half-pound fish, and they are very cunning and difficult to catch out.

I have sent your butt joint off. I have put some corks on at the join, as it is better to do so while the cement is still wet. The extreme butt-end is bored 7/16" for lightness and to allow clearance for the screw of the rubber knob.

The wood is beech and has been stored under a glass roof since 1932, so it ought to be seasoned pretty well by now.

It is not likely that you will get the ferrules set on dead straight; it doesn't matter anyway. Let the rings be put on so that in use the natural hang-over of the rod counteracts any error in fitting the ferrules.

Fitting the ferrules is the most important thing of all—work slowly and make sure of a *dead tight fit.*

Don't forget to thin the splints before finally setting the ferrule on.

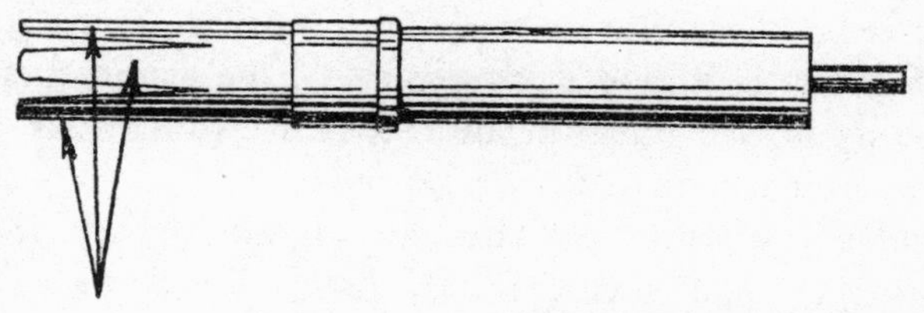

Sincerely,
RICHARD WALKER

Dear Mr. Walker,

Many thanks for the butt-joint which arrived safely yesterday. All the corks are now in position, as also are the cane wedges over which the ferrules will eventually go. I've got the male ferrule fixed on the top joint and am very pleased with it. I was a bit apprehensive at first, but a micrometer and a little careful work with some fine sand-paper made a sound job of it and I sincerely hope I never have to remove it. Now that I have taken the plunge I feel more confident and whilst the finished job may not be up to your standard I shall not be ashamed to have you inspect it.

Your suggestion for the landing net is, of course, far better, and when I've got this rod out of the way I'm going to have a shot at making it. A few days after writing my last letter I was given a copy of the American magazine *Field and Stream* and by a strange coincidence it contained an illustrated article on net-making, landing and keep-nets. It is extremely simple—I've had a trial 'go' and find it quite quick to do. My new landing net will be, I hope, a completely home-made affair. Thanks for the tip about oil-dressing nets. What mesh do you suggest? A very small mesh is unnecessary, but a very large mesh will not distribute the weight of a large fish—I thought perhaps 3″.

I like the description of your artificial nymphs, caddis and freshwater shrimp very much. When I get time to have a shot at fly-tying—which I hope to do this week—they will be amongst the first that I tie. I appreciate the value of having some underwater 'flies' and as the majority of the ones you sent me are dry flies I think some imitation nymphs, etc., may be of more immediate value than my own copies of your flies. Have you got a formula for an imitation dock grub? I have found these grubs most deadly in our streams, but as they are so difficult to come by one cannot use them very extensively.

I wonder how you have fared amongst the perch at Arlesey Lake to-day. You have certainly had a lovely day for your outing. I got several nice perch at Revesby last Monday afternoon. I managed to combine business with pleasure to the extent of getting nearly three hours' fishing, during which I caught 15 small pike up to about 2½ lb. and about a dozen perch, the largest of which was also about 2½ lb. It was a lovely bright afternoon, but cold—there had been a sharp frost the night before and the margin of the lake was still frozen in the shade when I was fishing—and the big pike were conspicuous by their absence. I find that perch are particularly susceptible to a kind of 'sink and draw' method of recovery. Using a 1½″ Vibro I recover fairly rapidly for 6–8 turns of the reel, at the same time raising the rod point. Then I lower the rod point and wind in much more slowly for 4–6 turns. On Monday I found repeatedly that perch took the spinner during the 'sinking' stage. I suspect that this method would be deadly using a small plug and a weighted cast in place of a spinner. Next week, when I am taking the remnant of last year's holiday, I hope to put it to the test.

That large trout you saw sounds a very attractive quarry. I hope you make his closer acquaintance.

Reverting to flies again for a moment; can you suggest a really good and efficient method of storing flies at home and of carrying them in the field?

And one more question; what knot do you recommend for joining the sections of your casts?

That copy of *Field and Stream* contained another article which interested me immensely. As a veteran rod-maker the subject is no doubt well known to you, but to me it is new. In the article the relative merits of 5- 6- and 7-strip construction in the building of split cane rods were discussed. It appears that rods of five-strip construction have been in use in America for some time and it is suggested that seven-strip construction is superior to five. The argument used against hexagonal construction is that by having an arrangement of flat opposing flat, the rod has an apparent tendency to act through preferred planes. For practical purposes, whatever may be the direction of the strain applied on the rod, it can only bend in three planes. Arising out of this is the fact that by neglecting to utilize the increased resilience of corner to flat construction a hexagonal-section rod is less effective than a five- or seven-strip rod of equal size or weight. It is also pointed out that the shearing strain (I don't know if this is the correct engineering term!) coincides with the joint between the segments of a hexagonal rod, thus tending to cause the two halves of the rod to separate.

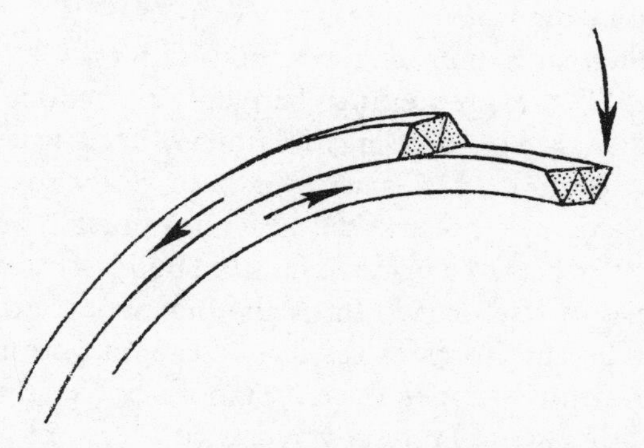

In odd-sided rods it is claimed that this stress is off-centre and the possibility of the sections separating is more remote. Most of these so-called advantages in odd-sided construction appear to me to be technical rather than practical, but there *may* be some real advantages.

(1) Greater resiliency (2) Greater strength-weight ratio (3) Greater accuracy in casting—the bend of the rod following the direction of the cast instead of, as may appear to be possible in a hexagonal rod, being deflected from it by bending in a preferred plane.

The increased resiliency and 'punch' of a seven-strip or five-strip rod will, of course, be appreciated by the Americans, as I understand that most of their fishing involves casting artificial lures in infinite variety, but it *may* be useful here as a spinning rod.

I frankly admit that I don't fully appreciate the mechanics involved and I should be interested to hear your views.

Yours sincerely,

MAURICE INGHAM

Dear Mr. Ingham,

I have no doubt at all that you will make a success of the carp rod. If you can fit the ferrules successfully the rest is easy. The whippings are simple. The best plan is to mark the position of the rings and put a bit of sticky tape round where the ring-whippings are to go. Then do the *intermediate whippings* (if any) before putting on the rings; the rod turns round and round much more easily without the rings.

My landing net is one inch mesh, but I don't think it need be as fine as that. Two inch ought to be plenty fine enough.

I have tried several dressings to imitate dock grubs and rush grubs, but I cannot say I have ever been really successful with them. Perhaps it is because the imitation doesn't *smell* like the real thing. The best I've made so far has a body of cream knitting-wool, a head of one or two turns chestnut wool, and a reddish-brown hackle, cut short, for the legs. I caught a trout on a grub made from a pipe-cleaner once. Smooth-bodied grubs can be imitated with a wool body covered with a strip of fine surgical india-rubber wound over it. This makes a good Mayfly body, also, but not a lasting one.

I've just found an infallible test to distinguish *Ephemera Danica* from *Ephemera Vulgata*

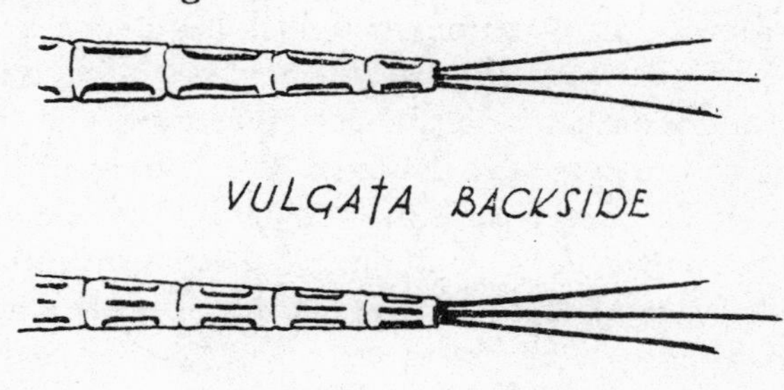

I didn't go to Arlesey after all; I had orders to complete the cattery, as five kittens have appeared and the plan is to keep them outside this time, owing to the repairs to furniture costing more than was received from the sale of the last batch of kittens!

One of the easiest ways I know to carry flies is to glue one or two corks rings on to a bit of dowel, then fix the end of the dowel to a tin-lid. Let the corks be nice and oily, or your hooks will go rusty.

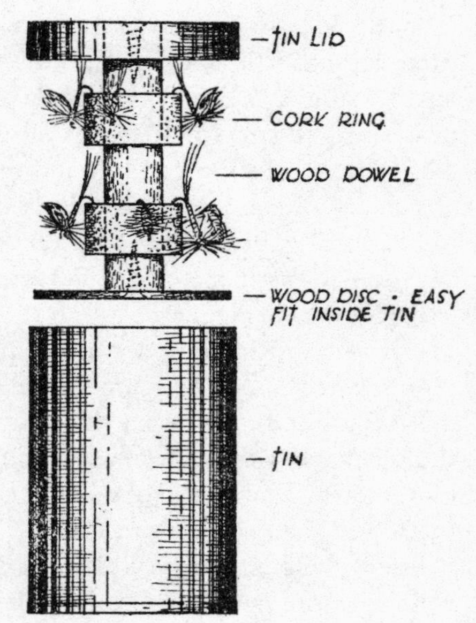

I generally find I am carrying three or four tobacco tins about during the trout season, each containing a jumbled mass of flies in various stages of decrepitude. The best thing to keep materials in is the cubical variety of biscuit tin, about 12″ × 12″ × 12″. These are moth-proof unless they get bent.

I don't believe that five- or seven-strip split cane has any advantage over six-strip. If a hexagonal rod has preferred planes of action, which I doubt, one doesn't notice it in practice. Hardy's tried various numbers of section and eventually went back to the hexagonal form. I have a square-section rod which has a very nice action; it is made of just two flat strips! In practice, of course, a good split cane rod is not really hexagonal, especially at the butt. The 'flats' are decidedly convex. This idea of odd-polygonal rods is a perennial—it has been debated in the *Fishing Gazette* almost since split-cane was invented, on and off. If there were real practical advantages I should think rods would be all made that way by now; it is easier to make a 5-strip rod than a 6-strip, and a 7-strip is not much more trouble.

I've been trying for some time to get hold of one of the new American Fiberglass rods which are supposed to be the last word in strength and lightness. It is difficult to get American stuff these days, though.

Actually it will have to be an exceptional material to better the ordinary built cane; a good built cane rod is practically everlasting and will go on standing the most tremendous shocks for years and years. I have a little 8 ft. fly-rod which had its 21st birthday last year, being my first split-cane rod and a birthday present. It has been in constant use all that time and has caught some biggish fish; a 14 lb. pike, a 12 lb. carp and a 9½ lb. salmon among others. The cork handle wore out beyond repair last year and I re-corked it; that is all the repairing it has ever had, except for a new set of rings and re-whipping. Of course there are plenty of split cane rods about which are fifty or sixty years old and still going strong. Like most fishermen I have often had occasion to wish my rod different, but I've never felt that the material was inadequate.

I have been thinking about the possibility of long-range dapping for carp when they are on the surface. At the Temple Pool there is a good Mayfly hatch (the pool is chalk-stream fed) and the carp take Mayflies well. Of course the Mayfly is almost over by June 16th, but I have often noticed carp taking insects from the surface all through the summer.

Long-range dapping (which is also useful for chub and trout) is done as outlined in the following diagram. You throw so that

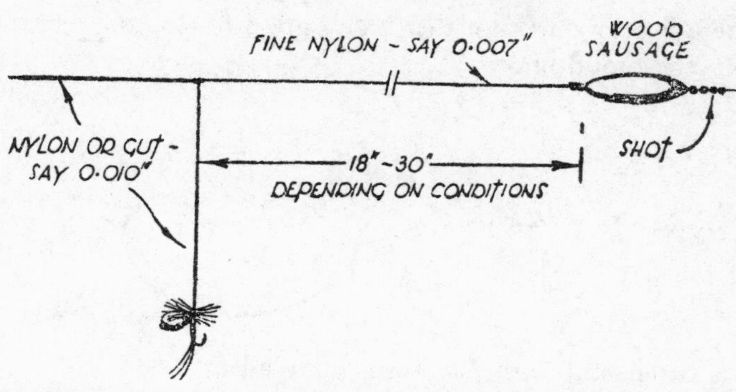

the loaded wooden sausage (which is chosen to carry enough shot for handy casting) lodges somewhere convenient, such as in a weed-bed, on the opposite bank or in the reeds. The fly is oiled to float. As soon as the sausage has been successfully lodged, the slack is taken up and the rod put in a rest so that it is almost upright:

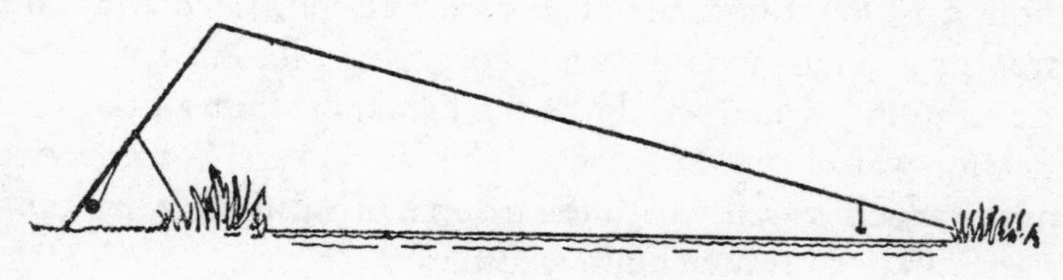

This lifts the fly clear of the surface, the lengths of gut or nylon being chosen to facilitate this. You then wait until a suitable opportunity occurs, when you tilt the rod forwards enough to let the fly dibble on the surface. If it is taken and a fish hooked, either the sausage comes clear from its resting-place, or the fine gut breaks, leaving you still attached to the fish. There are two advantages over conventional fly-fishing, and two disadvantages. The advantages are that you can plant the trap in situations where a fly could not be thrown, and that you can wait, irrespective of current or wind, with your fly ready to drop at any moment. The disadvantages are that the sausage, if it falls in the water by accident, will scare the fish, and you are dependent on a suitable lodging-place for it. I have an idea that the legality of all this is not quite beyond question!

There is only one knot that is any good for joining lengths of nylon: the blood knot:

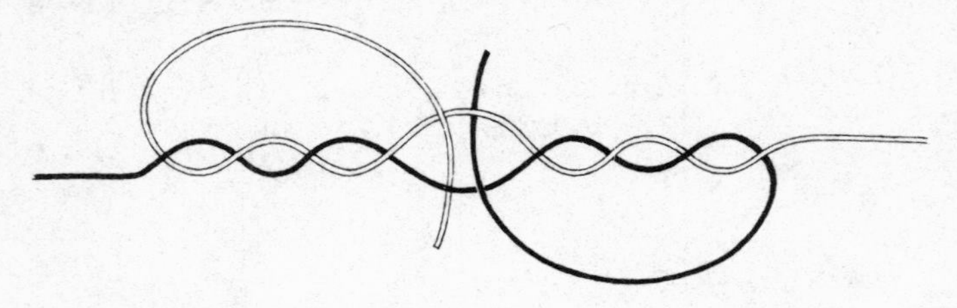

It is better still with *four* turns each side.

Messrs. I.C.I. say that there is no advantage in varnishing knots in nylon; they say the knots recommended will not slip. They apparently have overlooked the fact that nylon loses about 15% of its strength when thoroughly soaked. Take a cast of 3.2 lb. nylon; this will be about 2.7 lb. b.s. when wet. The knots have a strength of about 80%; our 3.2 lb. cast, if knotted would when wet break at about 2.18 lb. But if the *knot* were well-varnished and didn't *get* wet, its strength would be not 80% of 2.7 lb. but 80% of 3.2 lb., i.e. 2.56 lb., which would be the breaking strain of the varnished-knot-wet-elsewhere cast. This is a 17.4% increase in strength, which is well worth the trouble of varnishing the knots.

I use this knot for attaching eyed flies:

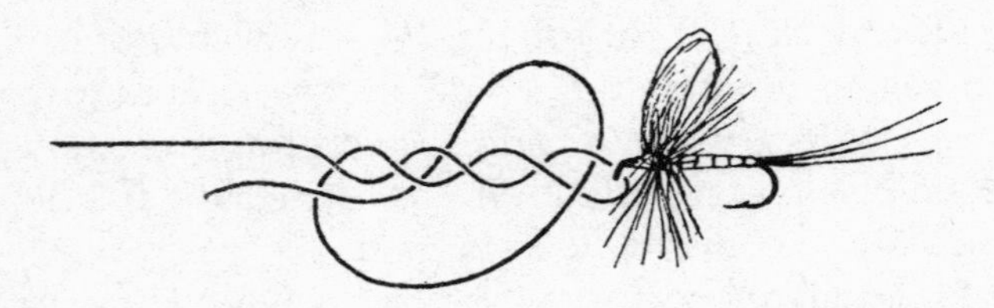

And I take care to oil the knot as well as the fly, to keep water out—in pursuance of that 17.4% advantage!

I find wet-fly fishing much more difficult than dry. I can manage the nymph technique—gut greased to within a few inches of the nymph—but when the conventional wet-fly technique, with all the cast and most of the running-line sunk, is used, I miss nine rises in ten! I found a useful idea for fishing Mayfly nymph last year. The nymphs usually emerge from their burrows in late evening, that is, for a week before the hatching starts, and the fish bulge at them like anything. In that light it is impossible to see the greased gut, so I looped a dark small feather on the cast at the right distance from the nymph, oiled it and used it as a float. Only one trout took the feather instead of the nymph, and I got several fish which I should otherwise have missed.

Since commencing this letter I have worked out some ideas on the best number of strips to use in built-cane. I broke some just now; this is what happens:

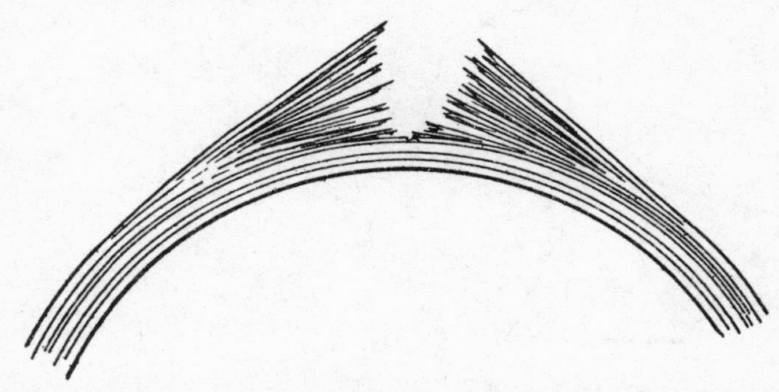

The glue didn't separate at all. The skin on the outside of the curve gave way under a tensional stress. The fracture was progressive; first the outside broke and the outer fibres split down the grain and flew straight. Then the next layer of fibres and so on. I am thus forced to the conclusion that at any rate a flat on the *outside* of the curve is better than a corner.

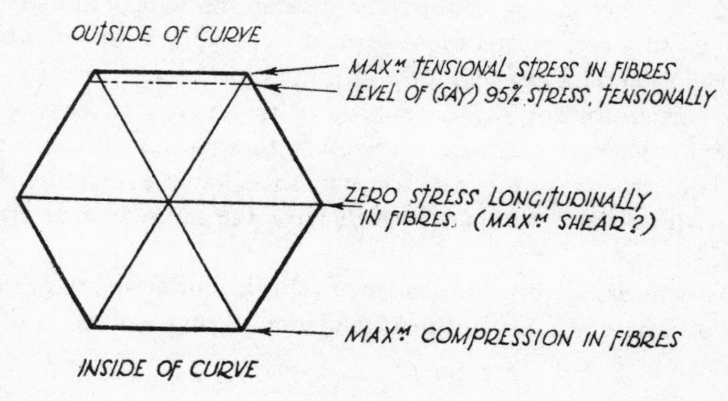

In this construction we have the maximum tensional stresses taken by a band of fibres whose cross-section is

Now take a heptagonal rod, corner upwards

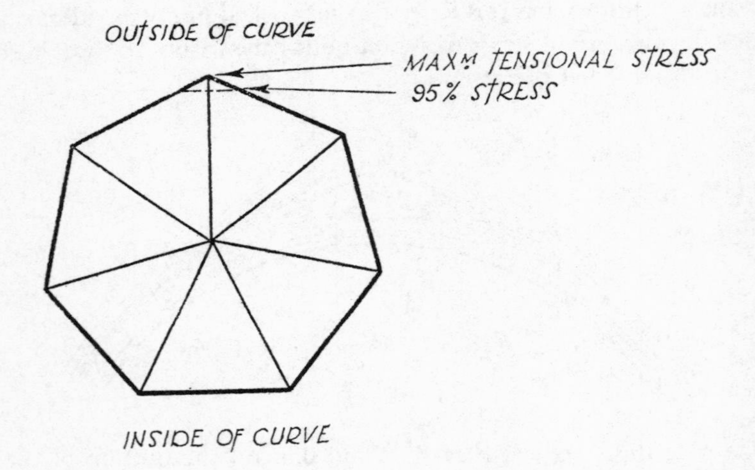

here the maximum stresses are taken by a cross-section like this: The difference is obvious; the tension in pounds per square inch is very much greater in the second case than in the first.

Now, when a rod is used for casting (in which the stresses applied to a rod exceed those applied in playing a fish) it is bent in *both* directions, so that an odd number of sections *must* result in a corner coming on the outside of the curve. It seems conclusive, therefore, that irrespective of other considerations, a rod made of an *even* number of sections is less liable to fracture than one with an *odd* number, if both have the same area of cross-section.

As regards the shearing tendency (?) this is not confined to one plane. There is a displacement tendency throughout the rod, on this basis:

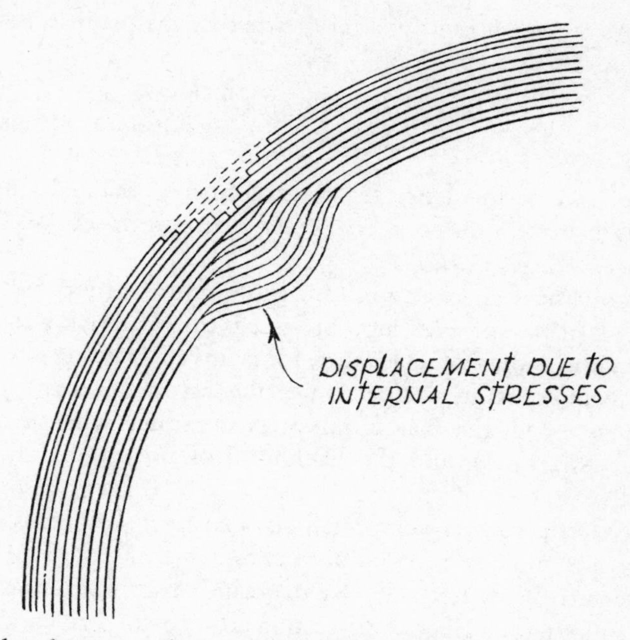

This sketch is to indicate the tendency in each area through the rod from the inside to the outside of the curve. This is a tendency towards relative movement, one area to another or one fibre to another. Actually, as far as I can see, the minimum internal stress is just where *Field and Stream* say it is at maximum. It is also interesting to observe that in the top half of a rod, i.e. the part in tension, the sections are held together; only underneath do they tend to separate through the bending stresses, and even there I am not sure whether separation stresses occur until fracture has commenced on the outside of the curve.

The whole business requires complicated testing machinery to arrive at a definite conclusion, and even then there are factors which may confuse the issue. For example, rings have quite a considerable effect on the stiffness of a rod.

Let me know if you find out anything useful about leeches. I think we shall find this a useful line to pursue. I am trying to get the fishing rights on a disused and flooded gravel pit about six miles from here. If I am successful I intend to stock with mirror carp. At present it is a question of whether the pit is to be used as a refuse tip.

Sincerely,
RICHARD WALKER

Footnote to this letter

Since I wrote this letter to Maurice I have obtained authoritative information on polygonal cross-section from H. W. Phear of Caius College, Cambridge.

No polygonal cross-section rod having four or more sides has preferred planes of bending; provided the material is homogeneous the radius of curvature for a given bending-moment will remain constant, irrespective of the axis of bending.

As I surmised, the maximum stress is greater when a rod is bent across corners, and the likelihood of breakage is thus increased.

In five-strip rods, a very small advantage in stiffness is offset by a greater increase in maximum stress.

Seven-strip rods not only have greater maximum stress but lower stiffness for a given cross-section area, i.e. for a given weight of bamboo.

This is, of course, dependent on the modulus of elasticity remaining constant for all degrees of bending, which is true of metals but which may not be true for woods. Having tried rods of 5-strip construction, I can detect little difference in practice between this and the 6-strip construction.

RICHARD WALKER

VI

March Letters

Dear Mr. Walker,

The rod is now completed, with the exception of varnishing, and it has turned out beautifully. I've not tried it yet, of course, but I like the feel of it very much indeed. I experienced no difficulty with the ferrules, the alignment is perfect, and I'm sure they will never shift. My next job is to finish my landing net, of which I have already woven more than half, and to dress it so as to give it plenty of time to dry before June 16th. Then I have the handle and built cane ring to make and at odd moments I may be able to do a bit more fly-tying.

I like your suggestion for carrying flies. It sounds very simple and effective.

The sink-and-draw technique did not work on my last visit to Revesby, in fact nothing that I tried proved very effective. The conditions were not good and although I caught several small pike—the largest about 2 lb.—I only had three small perch.

This subject of which is the best number of sections in a built cane rod is most interesting. Although the idea was new to me I realized that it is in fact old, and that there must be a good reason for the majority of our built cane rods being hexagonal. In practice I have no complaints whatever with six-strip construction, but the theory is very interesting. Did not Hardy's produce a number of rods of six-sided construction which were twisted so that the sections, instead of lying straight along the line of the rod, followed it spirally? Such construction would appear to eliminate any possibility of preferred planes of action and at the same time cancel out any slight variations in the strength of the sections. I don't know if these rods are still being made, but judging from the small numbers in use I assume that they were not a success, or, which is more likely, that the additional expense resulting from the special type of construction was not justified.

Your argument leading to the conclusion that a flat on the outside of a curve is better than a corner is very logical and convincing. You found that the cane on the outside of the curve fractured under tension but that the glue did not separate at all. That presumably is the answer to *Field and Stream*'s point regarding shearing tendency.

The long-range dapping idea is most ingenious and I will bear it in mind if a suitable occasion arises. For what reason do you doubt the legality of this method? If the 'sausage' is cast on to the opposite bank the tackle *might* possibly be regarded as a cross-line, but I doubt if it could be so regarded if the 'sausage' were lodged in a lily-bed. I can think of no other legal objection—but perhaps you know more about the legal aspect than I.

Thanks for the information on knots. Since writing to you last I have managed to get hold of a copy of the I.C.I. booklet on knots. Your arguments in favour of varnishing knots in nylon are, as usual, unassailable.

What dimensions do you suggest for the cross-section of my built cane landing net ring? I've got my tonking from J. B. Walker, and as I have no facilities—at present—for planing it up myself I intend to have it worked up to size by one of our local joiners. I'm not quite sure what will be the best way to make it up. I had thought of heating and bending the strips roughly to shape before cementing them together; then after cementing, binding them firmly together and, while the cement is still soft, tape it around a 24″ cycle wheel rim, and leave it until thoroughly set. Do you think that would be effective?

I see you have been paid a very nice compliment in this week's *Fishing Gazette*! By the way, when is your article on fly-tying going to appear?

If you need a new net at any time and let me know your requirements I shall be very pleased to make it up for you.

Yours sincerely,

MAURICE INGHAM

Dear Mr. Ingham,

Confessions of a Carp-fisher is at last published and on sale, but do not order a copy—I will send you one when my batch arrives.

I've done the top joint of your fly-rod and shall start on the butt this evening, so you can gather together the necessary rings, corks, etc. Some fly rods have fancy screw grip reel fittings, but I find a plain cork grip is quite practical and far cheaper. I like my handles like this:

but it is a matter of preference. Make the corks fit your own hand. You can cast thumb or forefinger.

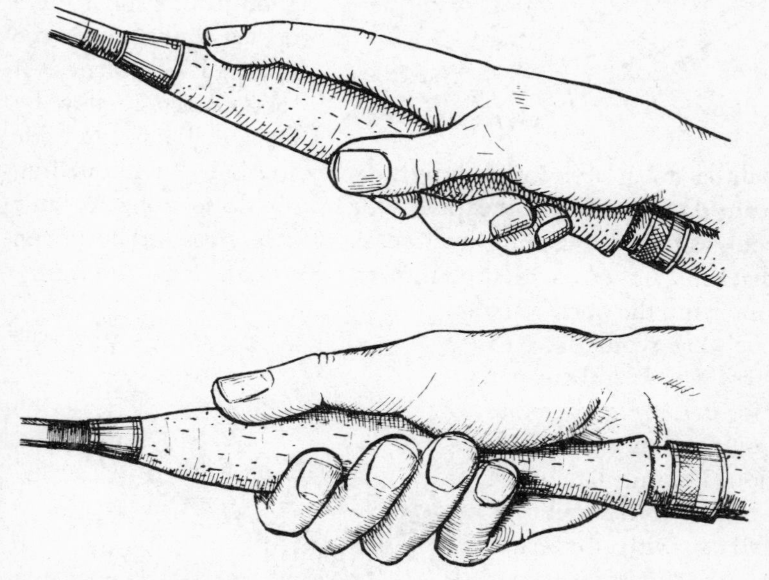

I find that the thumb method is advocated in most of the books, which I expected, as I use the other method! I doubt if it matters very much, but I should say thumb for distance, finger for accuracy, if there is anything to choose.

I forgot to tell you earlier, but must do so now with great emphasis. *Never* try to backcast a sunk line, as it severely strains and may even break a rod. Coax it to the surface if you can. A sharp strike *downwards* with the rod-point usually brings a sunk fly-line to the surface!

Don't worry about getting out a straight line—as long as the fly goes where it should it is an advantage if the line falls a bit wriggly—it avoids drag.

We laid a lovely drag-trap on our trout stream yesterday which will puzzle everyone:

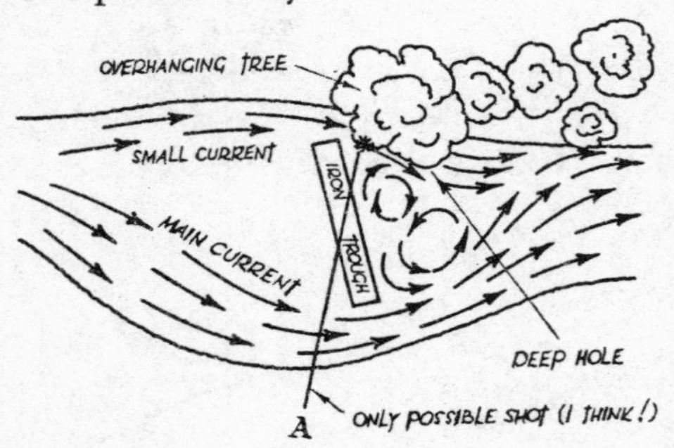

We filled the trough up with earth and gravel and turfed it with long grass so that it doesn't look too unsightly. Now a good trout is sure to take up his abode under the tree and get plenty of food carried to him by the small current. He will be at *. I cannot see how anyone can cast to * without drag from down-stream of the spot. One cannot do so from the same bank as the overhanging tree, because of the trees and bushes on that bank, nor can one dap, as the tree is too dense (it's a hawthorn). And from the open bank one's line would have to cross a powerful current plus at least one lesser one going in another direction. The only likely shot I can see is to crawl to A and cast with as much of the line as possible falling on the trough. I'm looking forward to trying this problem!

I started to write this letter last night; then I cut out three strips for your butt section, so it shouldn't be long before it is finished.

You are evidently finding net-making less tedious than I did, but wait till you try half-inch mesh!

As regards the bamboo ring, if you are having the strips planed up for you, emphasize that you don't want *any* of the outer skin removed. If I were you I would split out the strips myself—roughly—and file down the knots inside and out, before sending for planing. It might be as well to paint the outside and labe 'painted side *not* to be planed'. I think a section $\frac{3}{4}'' \times \frac{3}{8}''$ ought to be about right, but I'm only guessing.

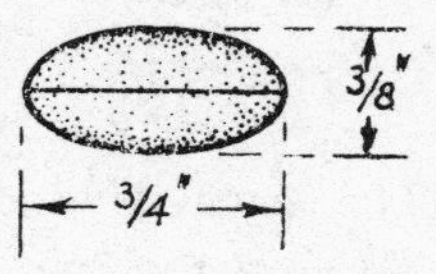

I would take great care to round the edges, as bamboo cane can cut like anything, as my hands often bear witness! Don't forget to 'stagger' the knots, i.e. place the strips so that the knots don't coincide. Of course if you like to use more than two strips you can, and it will make the bending easier, but the outer skin of the inside strips will have to be planed down a bit to get it flat.

I've never seen one of the twisted split-cane rods, but there would be no difficulty in producing one—you can bend and twist built cane anywhere you like while the cement is still soft.

I had a fibreglass rod in for re-whipping last week. It is exactly like greenheart in action, but lighter and virtually unbreakable by comparison. It is not nearly as rigid and steely as built cane of the same cross-section. I still prefer built cane!

The three secrets of good split cane are:

(1) Choice of bamboo.

(2) Preservation of outer skin.

(3) Good fitting and cementing.

When I talk about outer skin, I don't mean that every bit of the enamel must be retained; but one must not remove more than about .005" of the outside.

The cross-line theory was what I had in mind in long-range dapping. I am not sure that a cross-line proper (or improper!) doesn't imply two operators from the legal point of view, though.

I'm glad you reminded me about the fly-tying article—I haven't sent it off yet! Must do so forthwith!

To revert to your net—if you make it round you won't want it quite so big as a triangular one—I should say 24″ diameter ought to be enough. It might be an advantage to taper the bamboo for the ring, making each strip like this:

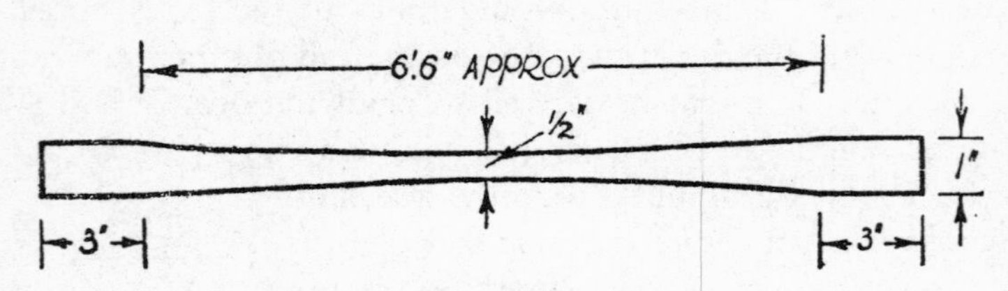

The strips could also taper in thickness, from say 3/16″ at ends to 1/16″ in the middle. This would give much greater strength/weight ratio. Your idea of taping the ring round a bike rim is a good one. Make sure your ring is thoroughly waterproofed. It might be wise to bind it with thin silk tape, not so much for strength but to hold the varnish; a net often gets hard knocks and a bamboo ring ought not to be allowed to get damp inside. Varnish *over* the tape, of course!

Thank you very much for your offer to make me a net-mesh. I will remember you next time I need one; at present I am well supplied.

Let me know as soon as you are able to do some planing, as I can make you some 'formers' on my machine. I have made a few cutters to produce various grooves and can make formers very quickly.

I'm glad you have completed the carp-rod successfully and that it handles well. It now remains to christen it! Good luck! Let each coat of copal get quite dry before applying the next; you've plenty of time before June 16th. Put it on with your fingers, mucky job, but the best way to get it on really thin. I hope you've written your name in indian ink just above the shoulder collar, together with some suitable carp-fisher's motto like 'Nil Desperandum' or 'Semper in Excretum'.

Sincerely,

RICHARD WALKER

Dear Mr. Ingham,

Here is the fly-rod, less handle and rings. I'm rather ashamed of it from the point of view of workmanship—you will notice that the glue-line is a bit wide here and there. That is because I haven't got my machine perfect yet; here and there, there has been a tendency for the bamboo to rise against the cutter. I am fitting spring-loaded rollers to keep it down. I think, however, you will find that the sections will stay together all right, and the action of the rod is correct. After whipping and varnishing the blemishes will be mostly hidden. The butt-end is of course shocking; fortunately it doesn't matter as the bad part is below the grip and will be covered by the corks. If the season had been further off I would have made a fresh set, but I thought you would like to have this one now; it will at least throw a line and catch a fish. Later on I will make you some better sections, and you will be able then to tell me whether you would like any modifications to the action or the length.

Sincerely,
RICHARD WALKER

Dear Mr. Walker,

The rod sections arrived safely yesterday and I'm sure they will make a beautiful little rod. It is most kind of you and I am deeply grateful. The net-mesh is all but finished—another night's work will see it completed—then I can dress it and turn my attention to the fly-rod. I ordered the accessories from J. B. Walker yesterday and in the meantime I can carry on with the intermediate whippings.

The copy of *Confessions* . . . will have a place of honour in my small library. Many thanks. I am looking forward to reading it.

Your new drag-trap sets you a pretty problem and I hope your solution is the correct one. I had a spell this morning worm-fishing in a brook near here. It is very small—one could almost step across it in places—but it holds quite a good stock of small trout. Unfortunately it is so overgrown with alders (damnable trees!) that it is almost impossible to get a bait into the water and I have no qualms whatsoever about worming there. It would be absolutely impossible to cast a fly. The only way to fish it that I know is to push the rod through where there is a small gap in the greenery and to trot the bait along with the current under the overhanging branches. I managed to catch five—largest 14 ozs.—and lost several others in the submerged rubbish, one of which I guessed to be something over a pound. It is a great pity that it should be so overgrown because this little brook twists and turns most attractively and there are some beautiful little corners and eddies.

Please excuse more now—I have all the symptoms of a really good 'go' of 'flu. I've taken a stiff dose of quinine and my head is buzzing like a dynamo, so I think the best thing I can do is to crawl into bed. Don't trouble to reply to this letter—I'll write again in a day or two—D.V.!

Thanks again for the rod.

Yours sincerely,
MAURICE INGHAM

Dear Mr. Walker,

Frequent large doses of quinine and a few days in bed seem to have had the desired effect, and I am more or less fit again.

There are some compensations in having 'flu, though! I have had time to put in a bit of practice at fly-tying, and I am enclosing a specimen for your comments. It is not intended as a copy of any particular insect, but is merely an exercise in tying technique, and I should be pleased to know exactly what you think of it.

Since I last wrote I have also made considerable progress with my other jobs. My net is completed; it has been well soaked in linseed oil and is now hung up to dry.

The little fly rod is also progressing favourably. The rings and intermediate whippings are finished, and there now only remains the handle and varnishing. I am looking forward to using it—I think it will be ideal on our little stream. However do you manage to build cane to such small dimensions? The tip of that little rod is not much thicker than the lead in a pencil, and when one realizes that it is made up of six segments—it is almost incredible.

I have been thinking about that little stream that I mentioned in my last letter. I am sure there are some really good trout in the deep corners, if one could only get at them through the tangle of overhanging alders, hawthorns and brambles, and I have been wondering if a floating plug might not be effective. It could be floated down over a likely looking spot and drawn slowly back against the current. With this in view, I have manufactured a little wooden plug which I intend to try out on my next visit.

Yesterday my friend John got a copy of *Confessions* . . . which he has had on order for some time and we spent most of the morning looking through it. It looks a most fascinating book. I was somewhat surprised to read that 'B.B.' favours the use of wire traces for carp fishing. John and I have had long discussions on this subject and neither of us can see any obvious advantage which 8 lb. breaking strain wire (the size favoured by 'B.B.') might possess over nylon of the same breaking strain. I think 'B.B.' says somewhere that wire is stronger than nylon. Wire with a breaking strain of 8 lb. is no stronger than nylon of the same breaking strain! Certainly 8 lb. wire would be *finer* than 8 lb. nylon, and that may have been implied by 'B.B.'. Therein may lie a possible advantage in certain circumstances.

My wife was most amused when I told her that according to 'B.B.', carp fishers' wives are lean and nagging. She is neither!

It is only of recent years, though, that I have taken fishing at all seriously; it was formerly merely a pleasant way of spending a fine afternoon when I had nothing more important to do. Match fishing does not attract me at all—I do not deny that it requires a great amount of skill, but for me angling is a quiet, restful sport, to be followed in peaceful surroundings. To me the loss of a fish, unless it be a specimen fish, is not a matter of any great moment. The urgency and rivalry of competitive angling would destroy completely the pleasure that I derive from my outings —but *chacun a son goût*. A type of angling which I do deplore —if it can be graced by the name of angling—is the social outing or communal picnic—call it what you will—when coach loads of fishermen, complete with wives, families, cases of beer and even gramophones, descend upon some quiet water and monopolize it. I expect you know only too well what I mean and have no difficulty in recognizing the aftermath of such outings—the litter of paper and rubbish, the broken tree branches, the empty and broken bottles and the inevitable small dead fish floating in the water. I suppose those people do obtain enjoyment from their excursions, but they certainly spoil the sport of the local anglers.

It is reported in *The Angler* that the Ouse and Cam Fishery Board have withdrawn their support for the scheme to introduce Indian laboes into some of our rivers. You are a member of the Board, aren't you? Can you give me any details of the Scheme and the reasons why the O. & C. Fishery Board have dropped out? I quite realize that the introduction of any new fish would have to be done extremely carefully—we don't want any ichthyological 'grey squirrels'—but I do think that it would be to the advantage of angling generally if we had more varieties of sporting fish and fewer roach, rudd, bream, bleak, ruffe, etc. It has been done very successfully in the past, the carp being a notable example!

The autograph and motto on my carp rod have not been overlooked. I had thought of 'Nil carborundum illegitibus' but finally decided on the more grammatically correct, but nevertheless appropriate 'In omnia paratus'.

John and I were discussing the other day the question of fishing for eels during the close season. John is not keen on trout fishing and he thought he might fill in the time before the coarse fishing season opens again by fishing for eels in a manner that would be unattractive to any other fish—possibly by using small dead fish as bait. I can see no moral objection to this, as there is no biological reason why there should be a close season for eels—they never spawn in fresh water. I should be pleased to know your views on this.

Yours sincerely,
MAURICE INGHAM

Dear Mr. Ingham,

This fly is quite all right. You are now a Fly-Tyer. It is only a question of collecting materials now, as far as you are concerned. I see you have used a couple of starling hackles for the wings. Have you been reading some formulae which give 'starling' for wings? Because they mean slips of solid feather from a starling's primary wing feather. Starling hackles make an excellent hackle for a tiny midge imitation.

I am more and more inclined to the belief that *all* imitations of ephemeridae should be tied with hackle point wings and that the majority should have the wings set on flat, spinnerwise. Probably the best all-round fly in existence is Lunn's Particular, which imitates a spent Olive. Body: Rhode Island cock hackle-stalk, undyed. Wings: two medium Blue dun cock hackle-points, put on flat. Hackle: medium Rhode Island Whisks, put on flat (but I use two long grey whisks). Silk: Pearsall's Gossamer, shade 13, crimson. Hook: size 0 (No. 15).

Variations of shade and colour on this theme will imitate all the small ephemerid flies. Light Sussex hen hackle-points make good buoyant wings for all these imitations of spinners. Choose hackles with good, sharply-defined black centres; these centres have an iridescent sheen, if taken from a bird in tight feather. Strip them to fan-shape (*a*). The centre has the shape shown. When the fly is on the water and viewed from below, only the iridescent black part is seen, and gauzy at that. It makes a fine imitation. So a fly which looks to you like this (*b*) looks to the trout thus (*c*).

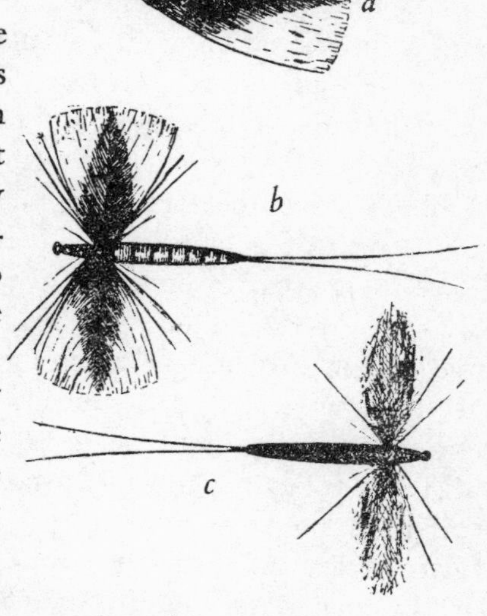

The hook you've used for your fly is rather heavy in the wire; you need fine-wire hooks for dry flies. Try Veniard of Thornton Heath.

I'm glad you are recovered from the 'flu; it has been very prevalent this winter.

Your various projects seem to be progressing well. I hope

the fly-rod will work all right and stand up to use. The whole secret of fine tops is a dead sharp plane, *kept* dead sharp. As for accuracy, if the former is right the section can't very well go astray, large or small. You will find split-cane making quite easy.

I am making a 15′ 6″ spanish reed rod now, for fishing in deep water. I never could make sliding floats work, except heavy ones with lots of lead. I can't see any reason why the small plug shouldn't catch trout; big cannibals will grab anything which appears to be alive. You must use strong tackle and pull hard! I remember a 10 lb. carp which 'B.B.' caught which is referred to now as the skullduggery incident. It was his last day with me in 1947; a carp was moving about in a big weed-patch about twenty yards square, sucking and rolling. It was the only fish to be seen. I fixed up for 'B.B.' an old 10 ft. pike rod, which is dead stiff and would stop a horse, big Nottingham reel and 25 lb. b.s. line, with cod-hook tied on direct. 'B.B.' baited with a crust and by an effort got this out to where the carp was. It was taken within ten minutes. We had decided that the only thing to do was to pull really hard and run backwards, winding. All went according to plan; the carp was pulled out on top of the weed, which was very dense, and slithered along into the net. Time of fight, 20 seconds! No, ten seconds would be more like it; I fancy 'B.B.' is rather ashamed of this performance; I'm not. It was a triumph of mind over matter, of determination over defeatism!

I think some of the wire sold is perfectly awful stuff. I wouldn't use it under any circumstances. It isn't only that I don't like the idea of using wire for carp. If I wanted something stronger than stout gut or nylon I'd use a wire that *was* stronger. 'B.B.' brought some wire in 1947 and I wouldn't let him use it; I fixed him up a trace of banjo 2nd, nitrate stained, which will really hold something. Some wire is as feeble as can be; why anyone uses the stuff is quite beyond my understanding. I have never found it necessary to use wire myself and I've caught quite a large number of decent carp, i.e. over ten pounds. About tackle I would say this. In open water you can use very light tackle, *vide* Buckley. In weedy water you need 12 lb. stuff; where there are very bad snags indeed and fish have to be held hard and not allowed an inch of line, 18 lb. b.s. is necessary. There is hardly ever any point in going above this. If a fish gets you round a lily-root or a sunken tree, half-inch manilla *rope* won't be strong enough! You can get nylon up to 18 lb. b.s. and over, so why use wire? Carp haven't got tackle-biting teeth. When 'B.B.' came here in 1947 we went fishing the first evening and he got into a good fish which promptly broke the .018 nylon cast. 'B.B.' thereupon insisted on wire and landed his next fish, 10 lb. 2 oz., on banjo string. He would have done it on nylon. If he had had wire for the first fish he would have been broken just the same; it got round something immovable just under the bank and having a solid to pull against, broke the tackle. If it hadn't, 'B.B.' would have had to break it from his end anyway.

From which you will deduce that I do not favour wire.

'B.B.' catches carp by being a first-class naturalist. The reason why we make a good carping combination is that 'B.B.' is a more practical angler than I am; he keeps his mind on catching carp and leaves me to see that the tackle is scientifically sound. He is really an extraordinary person—not a brilliant caster, yet somehow when a long accurate cast is essential he produces it perfectly, right against his usual form. I can cast beautifully—except when I have a wonderful opportunity, then I always bungle; I think this is more human!

Confessions was written three years ago and we've learned a lot since then. The Carp Rod had not then been worked out and we were using Wallis Avon rods mostly. Nor had I got my Felton Crosswind. My contribution to *Confessions* contains a classic error; I thought then that big carp wouldn't feed when the rudd shoals were active on the surface. It isn't true. That idea was based on what happened on one water. It applies nowhere else that I've fished, and shows the danger of dogma in angling matters!

On looking back I think the only real contribution I have been able to make to our sum of carp-lore is the technique of margin-fishing, and this is only useful when there is no likelihood of disturbance from other anglers.

The problem of the coach-borne crowds is one which will

have to be tackled, or no one will be able to fish at all. The attitude of some of these people is intolerable. 'We've come x miles to fish here' seems to be their excuse for anything. One wouldn't mind so much if they really came for the fishing, but a very large proportion come for a picnic and bring the whole family; they don't care much whether they actually fish or not.

We had a visit from '——' Angling Club last year. They came to fish on a local lake. I have a favourite corner there where I can usually catch twenty or thirty roach, from small ones up to perhaps ¾ lb. It is a nice little spot, like this

There is a willow tree on the right, for shade; the rushes in front make good cover and the bank a natural seat; it is above one's head so there is no silhouette. I went over in the evening to see that all was in order (I'm a Bailiff) and found three anglers in a row, practically elbow to elbow, in this spot. The rushes in front had been cut right down to the roots and about ten yards of them cleared right out. At the edge of the bank above, which is flat-topped and grassy, a cloth was spread with the remains of tea; beside it was a game of cricket (?) in progress; two mothers and five kids. There was paper everywhere. All the bankward branches of the willow tree had been pulled down; broken but not detached; you know what I mean. In another place, three small boys had collected up some empty bottles, and were launching them one by one and then breaking them with stones.

Two fish were caught that day by that club; a roach of 6″ and a little tench of 9″. In future we are thinking of making it a rule that visiting clubs must not bring non-anglers, relations or no.

I don't want to be too stuffy about visitors; after all it's hard luck if a man who lives in a town can't get a bit of fishing in the country; but I think it is up to him to avoid spoiling other people's pleasure more than he can help.

Yes, I am a member of the Ouse and Cam Fishery Board. I was not at the meeting when it was decided not to back the Laboe scheme. I don't think it is quite correct for the Angling Press to say that we have *withdrawn* support. We never *offered* support that I know of; the Nene and Welland people asked if we would like to come in on the scheme and we said 'No, thank you.' I think probably on the advice of Colonel Foster, Vice-Chairman, who knows the Laboe in its native haunts. I myself am quite neutral on the project. There is always a big bleat in our district for re-stocking. To hear it one would think the Ouse was short of fish. In fact it is stiff with fish and it would be a good thing if the small fish were drastically thinned out so that some of them could grow. I wish I could get someone to bet me I couldn't catch a hundred fish any day on the Ouse. The truth is that a great many anglers are ill-informed and lazy; they start fishing at the wrong time in the wrong place, with the wrong tackle and the wrong bait, wearing the wrong clothes and fishing in the wrong way. Having miserably failed to catch a decent fish: 'Oh, there are few fish in the Ouse, it badly needs re-stocking!' I have a friend, Pete. He and I take great delight in showing up these fellows. Our club often goes to Offord; complaints were that Offord was fishing badly last year. Pete and I went over and caught forty pounds of fish between us, chub up to 3¾ lb., bream to 2½ lb., two roach over ¾ lb. and Pete had a nice perch of 2 lb. 10 ozs. The next time the club went there the best fish they caught was a bream of 1 lb. 4 oz.; I had 5 chub weighing 12 lb. and a bream of 2¼ lb. Next thing was a complaint that the fee we pay annually for the river Oughton was wasted, there were so few trout there. So Pete went and caught nine in one evening over 1 lb., besides several smaller ones. Best fish 2 lb. 14 oz. All on fly.

I suppose I must sound rather boastful and superior, but it isn't that we are so darn clever, it's the other people are such pessimists!

I can't see any objection to catching eels at any time. They are most rapacious things and eat any amount of spawn and fry. The Nene and Welland Board allows eels to be taken at any season and so does the Ouse and Cam Board, except that we prohibit the use of 'a hook or other metal appliance'. A sliver of bamboo does very well to catch eels, tied thus

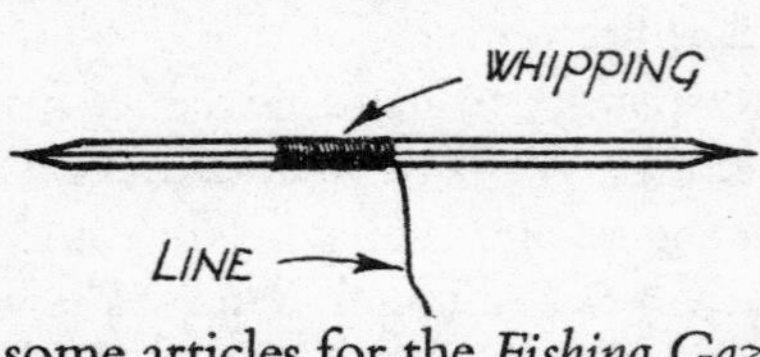

You thread a lob on it, allow the eel to swallow the lob, then pull, when the bamboo catches the eel crosswise in the gullet.

You really ought to write some articles for the *Fishing Gazette*. I shall repeat this at regular intervals until you do it!

Confessions has arrived—here's your copy.

Sincerely,

RICHARD WALKER

Nor is my wife lean or nagging!

Dear Mr. Walker,

Many thanks for *Confessions*—I have enjoyed reading it immensely and it has made me look forward even more to 16th June.

I was elected a member of the Croxby A.C. last Wednesday evening and this afternoon I took the family out for a ride and called to have a look at the Pond en route. There is a very wide fringe of reeds all round the lake and the bottom end by the sluice is badly silted up, but there is quite a large expanse of water and so far as fishing is concerned I don't think that any extensive dredging operations are essential. A number of small jetties have been built out to the edge of the reeds—this was apparently done some years ago—and when the reeds have grown up I imagine that anyone fishing from the jetties will be fairly well screened. The hut which for the past few years has been used as a café has been moved down nearer to the Pond and will serve in future as a club-house, rod room or what-have-you. I met the Secretary of the Club last week and he showed me a photograph of a day's catch by one of the ticket-holders last year—six fish, average 7½ lb., best 10 lb., all common carp. I gathered that there have been no really big carp caught in the past few years—the best was, I think, about 12 lb.—but our meeting was very brief and I hadn't a chance to ask him more than a few of the host of questions that I intend to fire at him the next time we meet. Whenever you feel like having a crack at the Croxby carp I shall be very pleased to take you along.

The starling hackle wings—I take your word that they were starling hackles—on the fly I sent you were chosen by chance, being the most conveniently sized feathers I had when I made the fly. I have read no formulae and intend to follow your advice of copying as closely as possible the natural insect.

Again I must plead ignorance! You refer to cock and hen

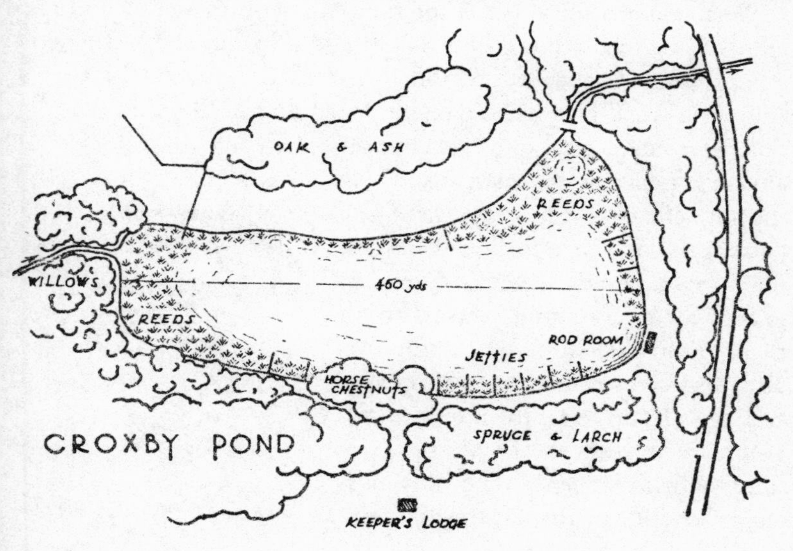

hackles, but how does one tell the difference? In your formula for Lunn's Particular you give—'Wings: two medium blue dun cock hackle points . . .; do you dye the hackles the appropriate colour?

I haven't given my little plug a try-out yet, as I've not been again to the stream where I intended to use it. Since writing last I have had two goes at the trout in our local stream, but the place where I fished was two or three miles above the town. I was worming, with no float or shot, and caught quite a lot of small trout up to about half a pound. Except for a few very short lengths the stream is completely overgrown and most difficult to fish—and flows too swiftly for a plug to be effective. The majority of the trout I caught were small rainbows which must have escaped as fry from a trout farm a mile or so upstream which specializes in rainbows. There must be a very good head of fish in that small stream now and if the food supply is sufficient there should be some good fish to be had in a year or two. I only saw one fly in my two outings, and that at a distance, but suspect it was a March Brown. There should be some good sport with fly on the few lengths that are fishable, as I know there is usually a good hatch of fly on that stream.

What pattern do you use for the plugs you make? The little fellow I made is a copy of a Snapdragon Sprite, complete with diving vane, but with a wooden instead of a plastic body. I have seen small plugs in the tackle shops shaped like this but have never used one. Have you any experience with this pattern? If they are effective it is a much simpler pattern to copy than the Sprite design.

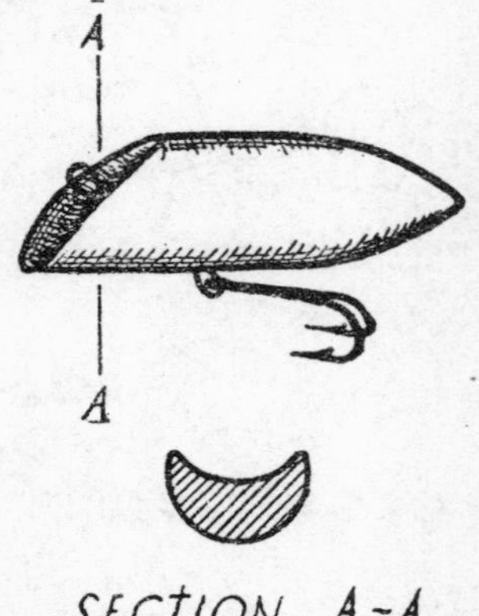

I have had no experience with wire, except for pike spinning traces, but in theory I must say I am not very favourably disposed towards its use for carp-fishing. It appears to me that the comparative stiffness of wire is a very definite disadvantage. The only possible advantage that it might have over nylon—and it is a very doubtful one—is that it might cut through weeds more easily than nylon of the same strength.

Has 'B.B.' ever tried floating crust at Swancoote Pool? He said that he hoped to return one day.

I can imagine your feelings when you saw how that visiting club were disporting themselves! I couldn't agree more with your sentiments concerning the pessimism of the average angler. One morning last summer I had been fishing for tench in the small pond I mentioned in an earlier letter. I had been fishing from sunrise and about 10 a.m. I was thinking of packing up when two anglers arrived. They have both had considerable success in matches and I decided to wait awhile and watch. Their first move was to stamp up and down along the top of the bank, silhouetted against the sky, surveying the water. Then a rod-rest was hammered into the hard clay bank with a convenient brick, with such force that the vibration sent ripples across the water. A large bag of ground bait was then *thrown* in to soak, sending more ripples across the pond. The setting up of the tackle necessitated much further stamping back and forth along the top of the bank, and by the time this operation was completed the ground bait was soaked and ready for use. The bag was opened at the water's edge, two hands were buried in it and a large quantity was scooped out and deposited into the water with an appalling splash. This was repeated several times before the pitch was prepared. Then began a demonstration of casting—a heavily shotted cast being lashed in and out at least half a dozen times before it was satisfactory—in a pond which is so small that I, who am not a good caster, can reach the middle with an 'underarm' cast! All was now ready and the fishermen settled themselves on their baskets. There was comparative quiet for about ten minutes, and then, 'They don't seem to be very hungry this morning!' and another bout of casting. I waited a while longer, during which time two fingerling roach were caught, and then, like you and your friend, I took great delight in slowly and, I admit, rather ostentatiously, returning three nice tench from my keep net to the water!

You ask me why I don't do an article for the *Fishing Gazette*.

Now I'll ask you one—Why don't you write a book? From what I have read of your writing I am certain you could write one which would immediately place you in the literary field along with 'B.B.' and Michael Traherne, or even H. T. Sheringham. (Michael Traherne's book is amazingly popular amongst my friends and relations!) If you will write a book I will illustrate it for you!

As a matter of fact I have been toying with one or two ideas for articles for the *Fishing Gazette*. When they take more definite shape I'll tell you about them.

Yours sincerely,
MAURICE INGHAM

VII

April Letters

Dear Mr. Ingham,

I am glad to hear you are all fixed for Croxby. I think it is about time that a definite distinction was drawn between common and mirror carp for the purpose of angling records. I would say a common carp of 10 lb. is as creditable a catch as a mirror carp of 15 lb., not only on a basis of the ultimate size reached by the two varieties, but also on fighting qualities. My best common carp was 12 lb., from Temple Pool, and I am far prouder of it than of the best mirror of 17 lb.; it fought harder and was much faster in its runs.

Croxby sounds an attractive water, but reeds are awful tough, as I know from having spent last week-end cutting them. You'll have to use reasonably stout tackle and keep a fish's head up at all costs; if they get round the bottom of a reed you will be broken;

if you keep them off the bottom the reed will be pulled over and the tackle *may* slip clear, with considerable luck.

I only guessed they were starling hackles! Whatever they were, they were well set on, which is the main thing. You must specify fine-wire dry-fly hooks. I prefer these even for wet flies, you can always make a wet fly heavier by winding the shank of the hook, under the body, with gold wire or 5-amp fuse wire. You then retain the keener penetration of the fine-wire hook.

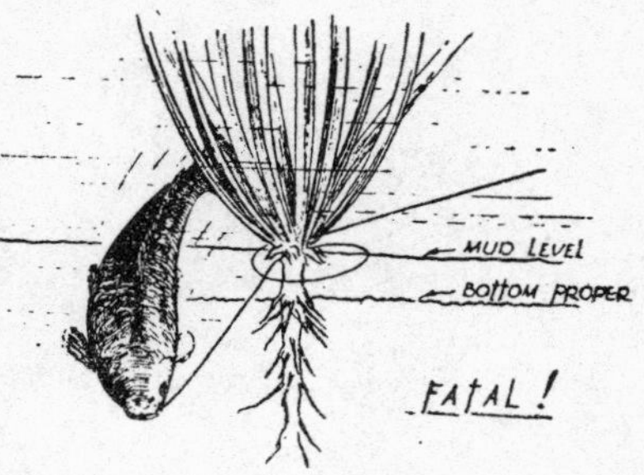

The force required to drive a hook in depends, among other things, on the square of the wire diameter.

If you could get leave to 'tinker' with your small trout stream you could do a lot to improve the fishing, by making pools, which help to improve size a lot. If your stream bed is thus, and you put in a low dam so

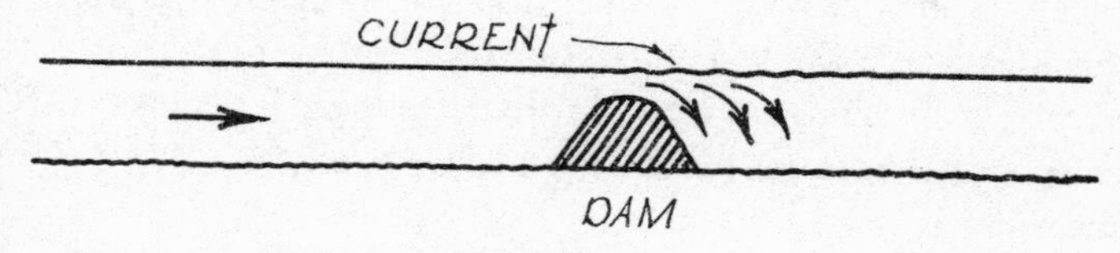

you will eventually get

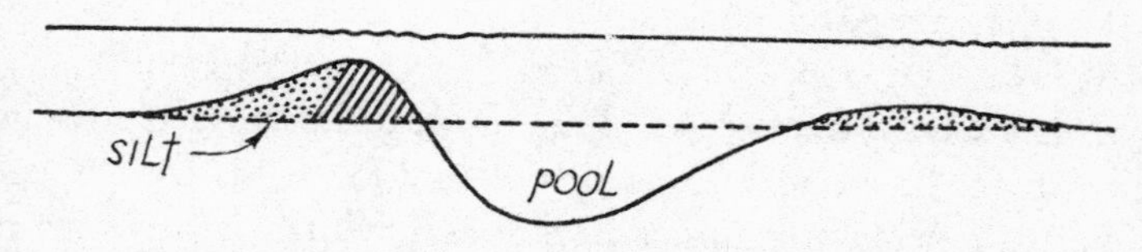

We have put in two dams and two breakwaters in our lower stream and it has greatly improved the fishing.

Oh, yes, I forgot. Here are two hackles:

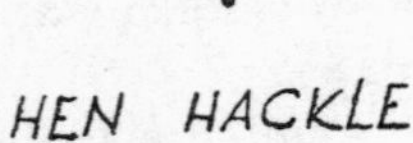

COCK HACKLE

ACTUAL SIZE OF HACKLES ATTACHED TO ORIGINAL LETTER

Hen hackles are, as you see, quite differently shaped from cock hackles, and much softer in feather. Generally speaking, cock hackles are necessary for dry flies, hen hackles for wet, but hen hackles make a good wing on dry flies.

There is a fly that has been known for many years, the Red Quill (so called because the quill part is *not* red).

The dressing is:

Body, stripped peacock quill, undyed.
Wings, medium starling primary.
Hackle, red game cock.
Whisks, red cock hackle fibres.

This has always been a useful dry fly and, in its right size, will catch fish feeding on almost any ephemerid. This fly has been 'developed'; tied with ginger hackle and whisks it becomes the Ginger Quill; blue hackle, etc., Blue Quill; olive, Olive Quill, etc. Now of these, the Red and Ginger will cover most cases. A fish on Olives will take Red Quill and maybe Ginger. A fish on Pale Watery will take Ginger and Red, but not Olive or Blue—as a rule; one cannot be too dogmatic. Of the Red and the Ginger, Red will take nearly if not quite as well as Ginger when the Pale Watery is on, but beats Ginger hollow when Olives are up. Red is therefore established as the best all-rounder of these Quills, so much so that there have been anglers who carried nothing else but various sizes of Red Quill.

Recognizing the virtue of this fly, various people have dressed variations of it; Lunn's Particular is, of course, one of these; the essentials of well-defined body stripes, reddish hackle and greyish wings are all there. Rhode hackle stalk is much cheaper and easier than peacock, and is more buoyant.

Another well-known and good fly is Greenwell's Glory.

The dressing is:

Body, greenish-yellow silk, ribbed gold wire.
Wings, medium starling primary.
Whisks, omitted, or as hackle.
Hackle, ginger furnace or sometimes red furnace.

Recognizing the utility of this fly, I 'crossed' it with Red Quill and called the offspring Cussy's Favourite, which is:

Body, stripped undyed peacock quill *or* Rhode hackle-stalk.
Wings, Light Sussex cock hackle points, upright to imitate sub-imago, flat if for spent imitation.
Hackle, furnace.
Whisks, grey or red! I usually use grey.

You can use blue dun hackle-points for wings if you like. You will see that one can play many tunes on this theme, all of which are effective. My spent Mayfly is of course Cussy's Favourite tied big and with raffia or paper body. It kills wonderfully well.

I expect you're wondering at this, having heeded my warnings against 'fancy' flies? My only answer is that this one works!

Blue Dun cock hackles can be got from Andalusian cocks which are wrong! The Show Andalusian has black hackles, but they breed blues. Most Blue Dun hackles are white ones dyed and are probably just as good, but they must *be* white and not cream, which comes out a greenish colour when dyed. Blue Old

English Game fowls and Blue Leghorn Bantams also give good Blue Dun hackles. Some natural Blue Dun hackles have a kind of brassy freckling in the fibres, and these are supposed to be very attractive. They certainly make a nice-looking fly. Natural 'Blue' Dun is usually more of a mousy colour than blue.

Plugs. I've tried all shapes. The small two-hook ones are quite effective; I've caught several decent chub on them. If your cannibals are anything over 4 lb. you might try a calf tail at dusk, or a rabbit's tail.

Wire will cut weed of the soft kinds; if I wanted to use wire to do that I'd use Banjo D string (1st), which is no thicker than 3x gut and will lift about 20 lb. It is silvered as bought, but turns black if dipped in silver nitrate (10%). It is far and away the best single wire I know; of course, like all single wire, one has to watch it for kinks.

Your description of the assault on your tench-water was one that could be applied to the majority of such ventures. Our club members usually go one step further and drag the chosen spot with grapnel and rope. Curiously enough, I have sometimes caught tench very soon after such an operation, when I've been forced to do it myself where weeds have been solid. But the things I really object to are stamping and conspicuous clothes.

I'm in the middle of writing *two* books! You write one yourself! My trouble is lack of time and the fact that there is always someone calling to talk fishing.

My wife duly produced her twin boys with amazing nonchalance on Good Friday. I went off and caught a brace of trout, 1 lb. and 1¾ lb. to celebrate the event.

I shall look forward to seeing your articles in the *Fishing Gazette*. Have you tried scraper board for illustrations?

If you want to cut reeds at Croxby I recommend these two implements:

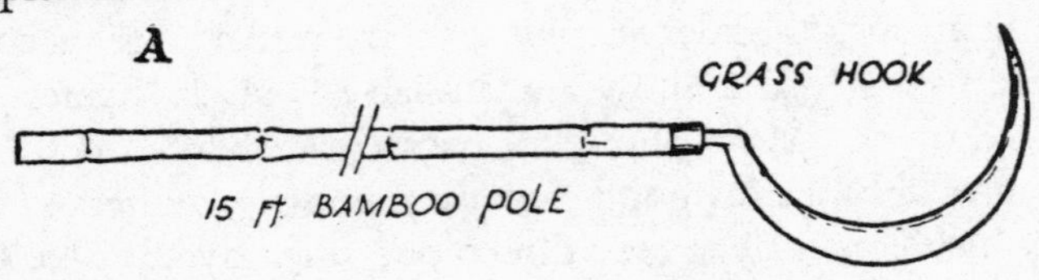

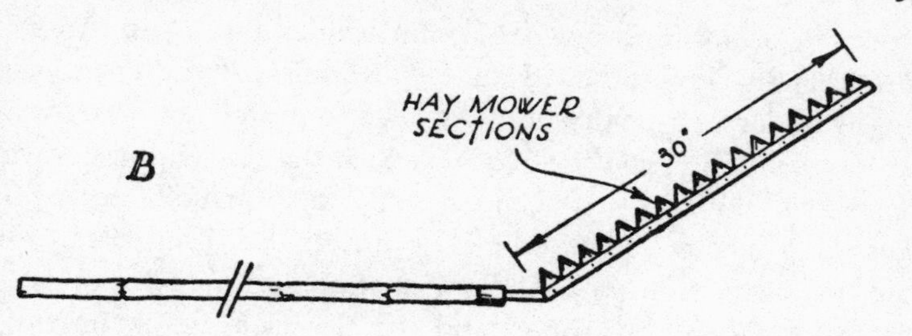

The technique is to get the cutting edge of (*a*) against the reeds and then give a smart jerk on the pole. The grass hook does best on old hard growth, the haymower affair is best for the young stuff; work it backwards and forwards. The edges must be kept nice and sharp.

Best of luck,

RICHARD WALKER

Dear Mr. Walker,

Congratulations on your family increase. You certainly have qualified for family allowance! I expect in two or three years' time you will be busy making small rods and imparting to two budding anglers the rudiments of the art. They will be lucky lads to have such a teacher.

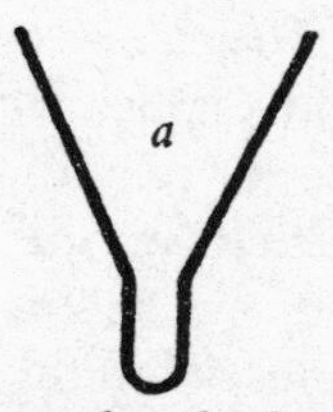

Before I forget—I understand that Otto Overbeck died a few years ago, either during or shortly after the war. He was at one time analyst for Hewitt Bros., a Grimsby firm of brewers. I gathered from *Confessions* that 'B.B.' is interested and you might care to pass the information on to him. I'm afraid I don't know any details, but perhaps some of the members of the Croxby A.C. who are mostly Grimsby men, will be able to tell me more.

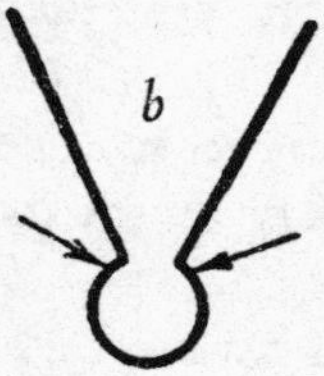

There was another point that occurred to me when I was reading *Confessions*. Would not a rod-rest shaped (*a*) be more satisfactory than the one which you recommend, which is shaped (*b*).

It may be an insignificant detail, but it does appear, in theory at least, that there may be a remote possibility of the line's being caught under one of the points I have indicated with arrows, if there is slack line and the rod is taken off the rest with a sideways motion and not lifted off vertically. As I say, the likelihood of this happening in practice may be *very* remote, but it appears to me that my suggestion would avoid it completely. I've no doubt you have a perfectly sound and logical scientific argument in support of your design and I am quite prepared to be squashed! For instance, you will no doubt say that when a carp takes bait there is no slack line—agreed—but if one's rod is fitted with high stand-off rings is it not *possible* that the point I have arrowed might be forced between the rod and the line if, in the hectic moment of picking up the rod to strike, it is lifted off the rest sideways? No! On second thoughts, and after again examining your dimensioned illustration, I am satisfied that that could not happen as, unless one is using a very thin rod or excessively high stand-off rings, the line when taut could not possibly be below the point where the arms of the rest would meet if produced. Excuse my 'thinking on paper'—I should have thought this out more carefully before I started writing. Nevertheless, I can see no advantage in your design which is not also in mine and mine is *perhaps* more foolproof.

The cane for my net frame is now in the hands of the joiner, with explicit and very detailed instructions. What cement do you use for joining cane? I have some of J. B. Walker's casein glue. Is that suitable, or do you recommend a waterproof glue—Durofix or something similar? Another question! What do you suggest for the handle of the net, not forgetting that the cane ring will be ¾″ deep? It is not going to be easy to make a neat job of attaching the ring to the handle without reducing its strength very considerably. Any suggestion will be gratefully received.

The net mesh, by the way, is very nearly dry after its soaking in linseed oil. As there is still plenty of time I may repeat the process.

Not only are reeds awful tough, but they are also awful sharp!

On two occasions I have had the mortifying experience of seeing a good fish depart with several yards of line attached when fishing over reeds, due to the line being severed by the sharp edges of the reeds. It has not happened again—one learns by experience.

The evolution of Cussy's Favourite from Red Quill and Greenwell's Glory is most interesting. I must really get down seriously to fly-tying when I have got this net out of the way.

There seems to be a wide divergence of opinion on the best size of hooks to use for carp fishing. 8 and 6 seem to be the most popular, but I think you favour something bigger. With your very first letter you kindly sent me some taper-shanked Model Perfects which look to be about size 3 or 4. I have got some of them mounted on .016 nylon and intend using them in my first assaults on Croxby. Do you think that they have any advantage over the eyed Model Perfects, apart from the fact that there is no weakening of the nylon due to knotting? With regard to size, it seems to me that a large fish such as the carp can take a big mouthful and that the bait can conceal a big hook. If a big hook can be used without risk of its being detected and provided the tackle is strong enough to drive it home, I think it must have considerable advantages over a smaller hook.

You are a most amazing person! How you find time for half the things you do that *I* know of I can't imagine, and then you casually announce that you are in the middle of writing two books! Is it permitted at this stage to enquire further about your books?—subjects?—likely date of publication, etc.? I am most interested.

Re leeches, I have not yet had a reply from the Secretary of the Lincolnshire Naturalist Trust, but I have also written to the Curator of the Natural History Section of the British Museum. We should get some useful information from one, at least, of these sources.

I hope Mrs. Walker is making a rapid recovery and that the infants will continue to thrive.

Yours sincerely,

MAURICE INGHAM

Dear Mr. Ingham,

Thank you for your good wishes for the twins' welfare. As they are identical we had thought of bringing them up as poachers; their elder brother can do the fishing.

I think you are right about the rod-rest. The original reason for the shape was that with the big fixed-spool reels and heavy lines there is a lot of 'slap'; but since I always have the big butt ring bankwards of the rest, the advantage (if any) of the larger space in the rest is lost, and I think your idea is the better one. Further development of the rest has also taken place since *Confessions* was written and the y arms bent round to give this shape (*a*). The next one will be (*b*).

The attachment of the cane net ring is something I hadn't foreseen. I think you will have to get a block of good wood and set it on a bamboo shaft like this:

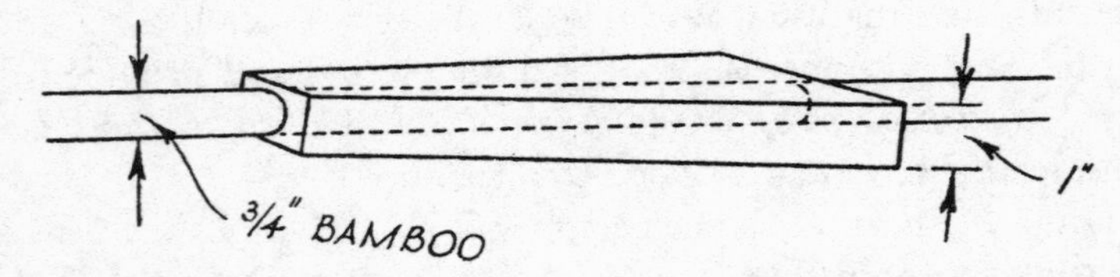

Roughen the bamboo where it goes in the wood so that the glue can bite. Then plane and file the wood so that it merges nicely into the bamboo:

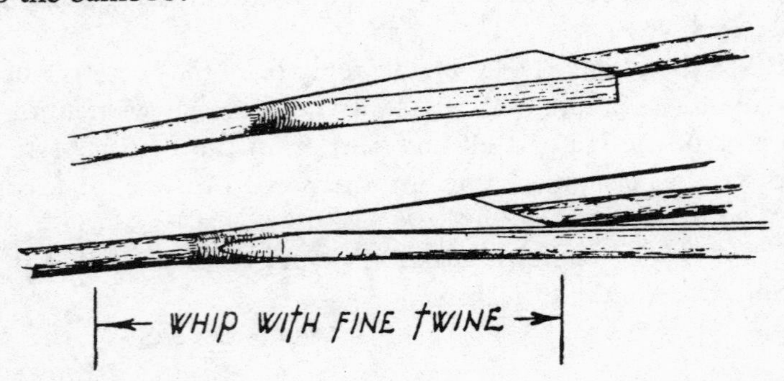

It might be worth while to get a knuckle joint so you can reduce the thing to more reasonable dimensions.

The best adhesive I know is urea-formaldehyde. Where glue-line gaps are under 0.010", use the ordinary cement. If over, use gap-filling cement. The trouble is that these adhesives have a store life of about three months and are only sold in bulk to professional users; however, if you ask nicely you can usually get small quantities of say 2 lb. You put cement on one surface and hardener on the other, bring together and clamp (or lash). Presently the cement becomes bakelite.

It has occurred to me that if you make a wood block of fair size you can use this form of construction:

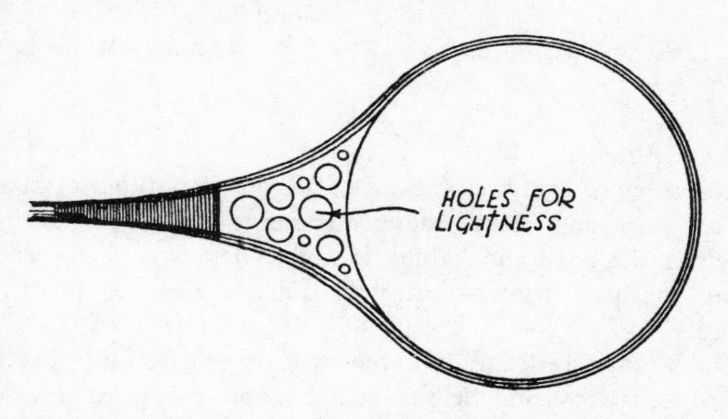

and save the extra strip and extension of handle. If you use urea cement you will have no trouble from water, nor will you need much binding to hold things together. Once the cement is set it is quite impossible to separate the woods.

Casein glue is unreliable, especially under damp conditions.

A second dip in linseed oil will improve your net greatly. I must get busy and dress some line soon with it.

I think that the Model Perfect hooks are the best I've struck for carp so far. Those I sent you were 2's and 4's. I wouldn't recommend 2's on tackle under 8 lb. b.s., or 4's under 6 lb. b.s., for you may not get them home. Of course the rod must be stiff enough too, but your carp rod will stick a size 2 in all right.

I never make much attempt to conceal the hook; perhaps I

ought to. I think eyed hooks are quite as good as taper-shanks, especially if you varnish the knot. I happen to have these taper shank Model Perfects by me so I might as well use them.

I find crust stays on a big hook much better than on a small one, and if you really have to use force on a fish the big hook is less likely to tear out.

One of my books is on rod-building for amateurs.[1] The other is just another fishing book, on similar lines to "Be Quiet". The former ought to be finished this year. The latter won't be, at this rate!

I am sorry to have been so long in answering your letter, but I followed your example and caught 'flu last Wednesday.

Good luck,

RICHARD WALKER

Dear Mr. Walker,

I was sorry to read that you have had 'flu, but in this weather it is not surprising. I had the misfortune to-day to have to go out along the coast and I think it was colder than at any time during the past winter—not very suitable weather for fly-fishing!

I think your idea of training the twins as poachers is brilliant! One to act as decoy and establish an alibi, while the other gets the goods. Have you ever read *I Walked by Night*? It is the 'Autobiography of the King of the Norfolk Poachers, written by himself and edited by Lilias Rider Haggard'. There must have been many occasions when that old chap would have been very pleased to have had a 'double'. I should be pleased to lend it to you if you haven't read it and could find time amongst all your other activities to read it. I'm sure you would enjoy it.

I appreciate now the reason for the Grecian harp shape of the rod rest as originally designed. The large circular space for the passage of the line served the same purpose, presumably, as the large butt ring which one uses with a fixed-spool reel. That explanation had not occurred to me because, like you, I prefer

[1] *Rod-building for Amateurs*. Belfield & Bushell, 1952.

to have my rod well back on the rest—there is much less likelihood, in an unguarded moment, of the rod's being tipped into the water by a running fish. Your revised rod rest design is similar to the one that I made after reading your first article on carp fishing in the *Fishing Gazette* last year. Mine is shaped:

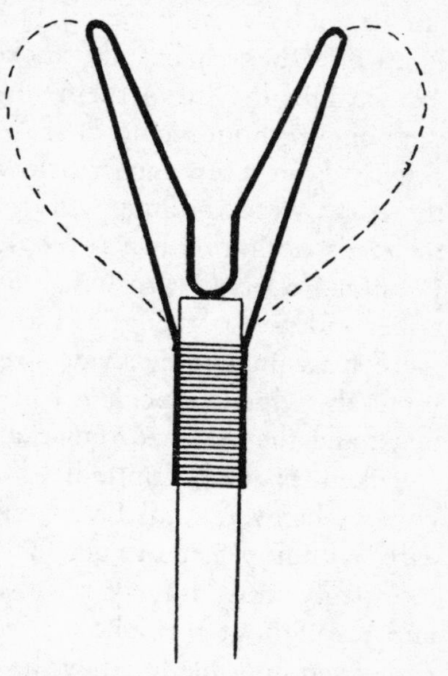

The material I used was a piece of Woolworths' brass valance rail, which is unnecessarily heavy, but the best that was easily available at the time. I think it is a slight advantage to have the arms of the outer Y as nearly vertical as possible, and for this reason I think there is less likelihood of a line fouling on mine than on yours, which I have dotted; though in practice I should imagine there is very little chance of fouling with either.

Thank you for your suggestion for fastening my net to the handle. It seems to provide a very satisfactory solution. Having the cane all planed down according to instructions, and being very impatient to get on with the job, I foolishly did not wait for your advice on adhesive and have stuck the sections with casein glue. If it proves unsatisfactory I shall have to take it apart and start again with urea formaldehyde—the stuff we had great fun experimenting with at Government expense in West Africa!—but if the whole of the cane is bound with silk tape as you suggested and adequately whipped and varnished, it may be all right. Anyway, I intend to give it a trial.

I saw the secretary of the Croxby A.C. for a short time last week and learned amongst other things that the Pond contains carp, tench, roach, perch and some brown trout, so last Sunday I decided to see if I could interest a big trout in a Devon. I arrived about 10.30 a.m. and had every intention of returning home for lunch, but although I only spent about 15 minutes spinning I did not arrive home until about 3.30 p.m. It was a beautiful sunny day and I had not been spinning long when I decided that it would be far more entertaining and instructive watching the carp—and so I spent nearly four hours just sitting and watching, fascinated by a sight that I have never seen before. Croxby Pond must be *very* heavily stocked with carp, because the water seemed literally full of them. It was not possible to look across the pond without seeing dozens of dark shadowy forms moving slowly about a few inches below the surface and the shallows at the edges were absolutely alive with carp. In one small inlet in the reeds, not more than 25 feet square and only a few inches deep, I counted over 60 carp which appeared to be from 18 inches to 2 feet and more in length. I assume that the fish in the shallows were spawning—they made spasmodic twitching movements at intervals, which coincided, I presume, with the extrusion of the eggs; and they seemed remarkably disinterested in my presence. I walked forward admittedly slowly and quietly but without any cover whatever, until I was standing ankle-deep in water with carp within 5 feet of me. It was most fascinating. When I eventually moved away the fish again ignored my movements and throughout the whole time I was watching them I might have been invisible for they showed no signs of fright or even of being aware of my presence at all. I saw no mirror carp unless some of the big fellows out in the middle—and there were some big ones—were mirrors.

In wandering around the Pond I found the remains of two carp. One had been completely eaten, apart from the head and backbone, but the other was more or less intact. The tail had gone and a large piece from one shoulder, but sufficient remained for me to be able to form a pretty good idea of its size. I estimated that its length would be about 24 inches and girth 16 inches. What do you think would be its weight? I took a few scales and enclose a couple. I suppose it was the work of an otter. An otter would easily catch spawning carp.

Croxby is, I believe, a noted 'potato water' and certainly the secretary tells me that potato is *the* bait for carp, but whether this is because it has become the accepted thing to bait with potato at Croxby or whether it is a fact that the carp there definitely prefer that bait is something that I shall have to prove for myself.

I hope you are fully recovered from your bout of 'flu.

Yours sincerely,

MAURICE INGHAM

Dear Mr. Ingham,

I'm very glad to hear there are so many carp at Croxby. 'B.B.' and I had formed the idea that there were not large numbers. It seems that a good deal of breeding goes on. If I were in possession of such a water I should keep an eye open for other waters, especially flooded gravel and clay pits, which can usually be rented for a few pounds a year. Then I should get busy with a net and stock other places.

The wriggles and vibrations are common to all spawning fish and at such times you can almost catch them by hand. The scales you sent came from a good fish which I should say would weigh from 10 lb. to 12 lb.; carp are not easy to judge from measurements, even when you know the girth, as they vary so much in shape. A really high conditioned one is shaped rather like a perch, with humped shoulders: and will weigh quite a bit more for the same girth and length. This fish is about ten years old, as far as I can judge, and if so might easily weigh 12 lb. or even more. The scales are almost exactly the same size as one I have from a common carp which weighed 12 lb., from Temple Pool.

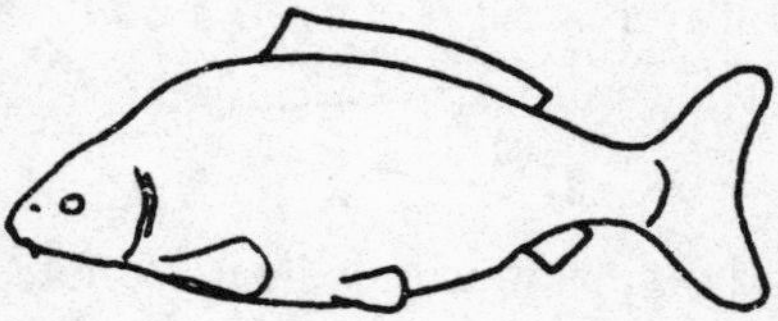

If you have repeated depredations by otters you will have to deal with them severely. At this time of year otters travel a good deal and yours may be one that just dropped in and passed on; but you must guard against a pair settling in to raise a family, or they will decimate the stock of carp. We had trouble with them at

Temple Pool and they killed dozens of lovely fish; I sat up several nights with a .22 but although I saw them several times I never got a shot; eventually the head keeper got the dog in a steel trap and the bitch moved on with the kittens. The method is to use a strong gin trap set under water where they go in and out, a place not difficult to find.

Of course the carp you found may have died from spawning and then been eaten by rats or crows. You can soon tell if otters are about by looking for their seal in the mud, and for 'slides' anywhere where the banks are steep enough.

It may be that potato will prove to be the best bait at Croxby, but I never fancy it much, perhaps because I have never done much with it. Common carp seem more inclined to feed on the bottom than mirrors and are therefore not so susceptible to floating bread. I expect you will find lobworm as effective as anything, and it has the virtue of being a bait that is taken decisively, whereas potato is often nibbled and messed about.

I am making a few floats for carp fishing, as I am beginning to think an unobtrusive float might be advantageous in reducing the amount of sunk line, which not only interferes with striking but which may put more drag on a running fish than a float and one shot. If a full two yards is on the bottom the carp oughtn't to mind. I bought a cycle tyre repair outfit last week, to mend a puncture, and it contained some shaped valve rubbers, like this:

I thought of using a float without rings and two of these rubbers, so as to pass through the weeds easily:

I doubt if there is any need for the float to cock, but it might be made self-cocking, leaving about an inch showing, which would take one more shot to pull right down, so that if the shot on the cast were lifted the float would react.

I think the best place to pinch on the shot is thus:

This avoids nipping and possibly weakening the tackle. The float could be of balsa and bamboo, stained weed-colour.

I went trouting last evening and got four from $\frac{3}{4}$ lb. to $1\frac{1}{2}$ lb., all on the same fly, which is as effective an imitation of an Olive as I know, especially for rough weather. It has a single wing made of the secondary wing feather of a song-thrush, a long golden-olive hackle, grey whisks and a body of blue-dun hackle-stalk, dyed in old gold *after* stripping, which gives rings of brownish yellow and olive-green. The hackle fibres are about $\frac{5}{8}''$ long, the wing about 5/16". About these proportions. No. 1 square-bend hook.

I should have had another fish but got caught in a trap of my own setting: I had moored a fly-board to a spike driven in the brick of the mill-bridge last week, thus:

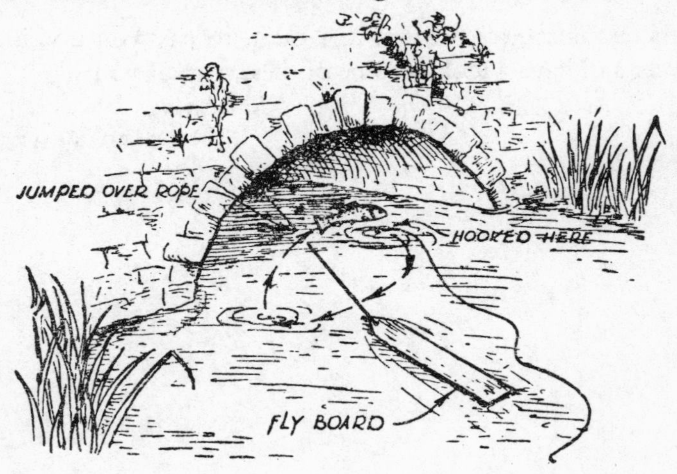

As neat a trick as you could imagine; of course the .006″ point of the cast broke instantly.

It was very windy yesterday, which reminds me that I didn't tell you the trick of pushing a fly into the wind. You do it by casting in the ordinary way but with an exaggerated follow through (which is called the 'downward cut'). The rod-point finishes almost touching the water.

I have always meant to read *I Walked by Night* and would be very glad to take advantage of your kind offer to lend it to me. I've done a great deal of poaching myself in the past; unfortunately I have to appear more respectable nowadays.

I've just realized that you will have to put your net mesh on before attaching the ring, unless you tie each loop on separately—or I suppose you could fix it thus?

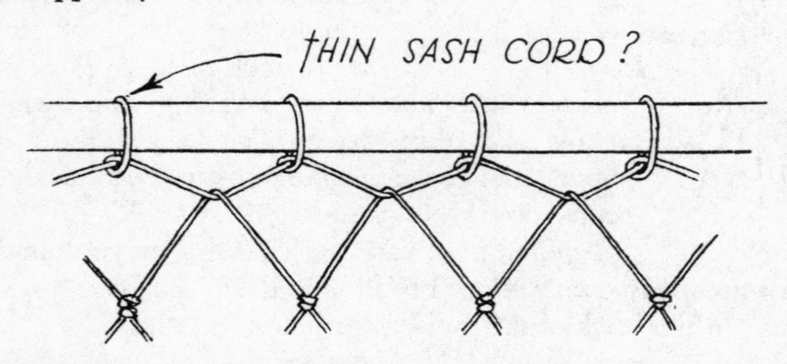

Unless circumstances prevent it, I mean to pay you a visit this summer and have a look at some of these carp of yours.

Sincerely,

RICHARD WALKER

VIII

May Letters

Dear Mr. Walker,

The time has come when my garden cannot be neglected any longer and for the past few days—or evenings, rather—I have been busy getting things shipshape. Now it is more or less up to date so I can get back to my net, which will soon be ready for its first coat of varnish.

I mean to have another visit to Croxby in the near future, when I will have a good scout around for signs of otters. The fish from which I took the scales which I sent you had been killed, I imagine, some three or four days before I found it, and the heavy rain which had fallen during that time would have wiped out any prints in the soft mud. The things that made me think otters were responsible were the way in which the shoulder had been eaten away and the way scales had been scattered around. It seems tragic that carp—in fact the majority of fish—should be so helpless and such easy prey at spawning time, and if I find any evidence of otters in residence I shall certainly advocate drastic measures, much as I admire otters.

Your idea for a non-weed-fouling float is excellent and I shall have to make some for use if a suitable occasion should arise. I understand Croxby contains quite a lot of 'soft' weed but no lilies. The Secretary tells me that the Pond is nowhere more than five feet deep and during the few minutes I spent spinning on my last visit I found it very shallow. The need for a float would only arise, presumably, when fishing well out from the bank. With a short cast the amount of sunken line would not be sufficient to warrant a float, and I must say that in theory at least I prefer a floatless, shotless tackle, though I appreciate the possible disadvantage of having a long length of sunken line.

I had not overlooked the fastening of the mesh on to the ring. I propose to do it as below: double twine woven into top row of mesh.

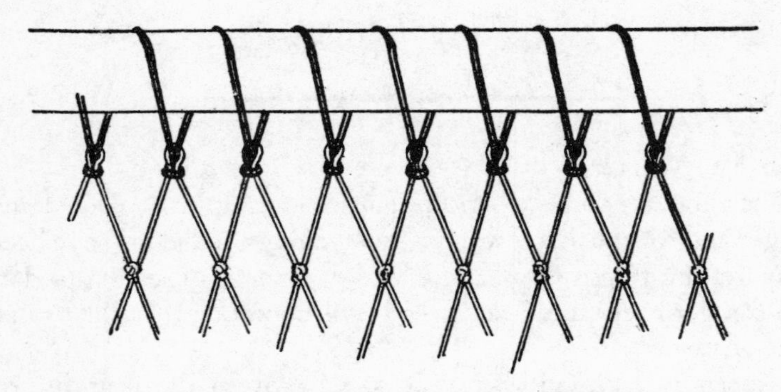

If the weather is favourable this week-end I hope to have my first shot at fly-fishing. Last Monday morning I found an Olive fluttering in the kitchen window and I take it as an omen! I only hope I can put my fly down on the water—the brook is so narrow it is not a very big target! Your single-winged imitation Olive sounds very simply and effective—I must try to manufacture some before the week-end.

I was most interested to read your article on Mayflies in last week's *Fishing Gazette*. If your theory is correct—I call it a 'theory' for want of a more appropriate word: 'assumption' might be better—it opens up vast possibilities. I cannot add anything constructive, but one point does surprise me. Your entire argument is based on the fact that on a given river the Mayfly's time of appearances varies very little from year to year, and from this you deduce that the fly's life cycle must be almost exactly two years, irrespective of climatic conditions during that time. I do not suggest that you are wrong, and I have no more acceptable theory to offer, but I find it difficult to believe that two batches of identical eggs, one subjected to exceptionally warm conditions and the other to exceptionally cold conditions (provided the embryo or nymph remained alive throughout) would both develop into flies on almost exactly the same day. As you know, my knowledge of entomology is strictly limited, but I know of no insect that has a definite fixed life cycle such as you suggest and which is unaffected by climatic conditions. For the sake of your 'theory' I hope your assumptions are correct. Your article should start some interesting correspondence.

I am very pleased indeed to learn that you hope to come up here this summer. Any time would be convenient to me, provided it does not clash with our fortnight in Devon (5th–19th July) or with my Assistant's holiday, the dates of which I will let you know in my next letter. Neither of us is indispensable but the 'powers that be' would frown upon our both being away from the office at the same time. We will have a crack at Woldale and Croxby and I would also like to see you in action with a fly rod. My interest is purely selfish as I have an idea that I might learn a lot. You might be interested in Thimbleby Mill, which I mentioned in an earlier letter. It holds some good trout and is one of the few places around here that contains chub. Mr. Joker, a Dane, who started a hatchery and trout farm there shortly after the war, after being driven out of Denmark by the Germans, has made very clever use of the layout of the place in adapting it to his purpose. The layout now is something like this:

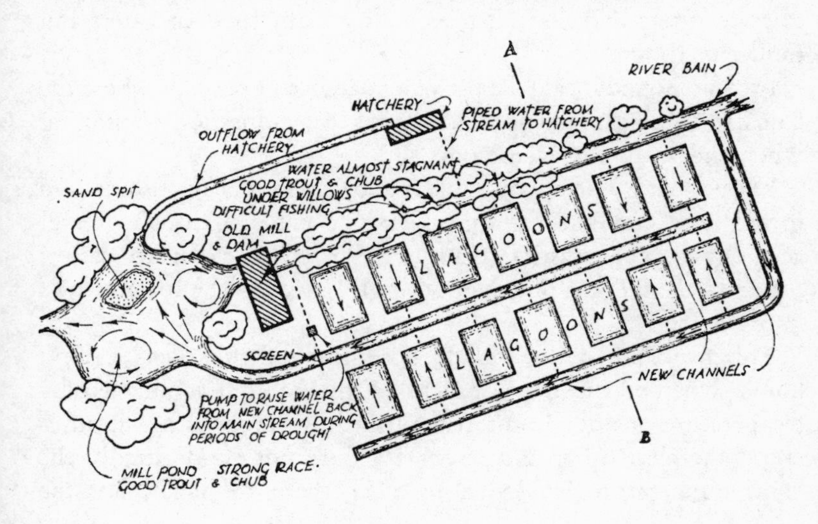

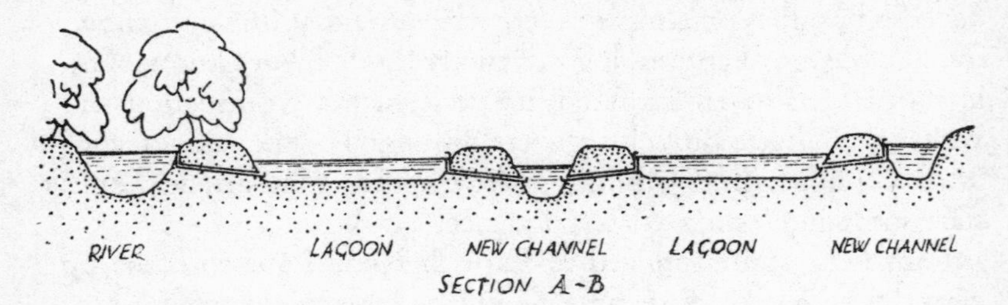

After that pictorial effort I think I will turn in.

Yours sincerely,

MAURICE INGHAM

Dear Mr. Ingham,

Thank you for *I Walked by Night*, which I have read and enjoyed very much; my wife is reading it now. I was surprised to find so much use was made of a gun, as I have always found other methods preferable. I have used a .22 rifle fitted with telescope and silencer, but generally speaking I like the completely silent devices. Poachers who bang about with guns never fail to get themselves caught sooner or later!

I doubt if there is any fish, spawning or not, which an otter cannot catch if he wants to, and on enclosed waters you cannot tolerate otters and have fish as well. I am fond of otters but fonder of fishing.

I would not advocate the use of a float except perhaps where the bait had to be cast out some distance; it is a question of judging when and when not to use one.

I hope that by now you will have had a shot at fly-fishing and found how easy the casting is. It is capable of much greater accuracy than bait-casting. I am by no means an expert fly-caster; I used to *think* I was pretty good until I saw a real expert; now I know better!

This problem of the Mayfly is a most difficult one. I don't know whether the development of the nymph is affected by temperature or not. I doubt very much if the *egg* is much influenced thereby; other and larger eggs are not. Admittedly the right temperature is needed to *allow* them to hatch, but the hatching *time* is constant; one's chicks emerge on the appointed date (or thereabouts) or not at all. Mayfly eggs hatch in about thirty days. The curious thing is that the annual 'hatch' (which isn't *really* a hatch but the transformation of nymph to sub-imago) is so remarkably constant; it never varies by more than a few days, as far as I can ascertain. It certainly doesn't on our water. Last year the first fly was seen on May 6th; this year on May 7th. Now the spring of 1947 was perishing cold—fuel crisis, etc., remember? One would think that the 1947 flies would have been late and hence the 1949 ones, if temperature affected the nymph. 1948 was a mild spring and one might have expected its fly, and subsequently the 1950 fly, to be earlier; yet there it was yesterday, May 7th; and for all I know two or three flies might have been out on Saturday; I wasn't there as it poured with rain all day.

Added to all this is the fact that the nymphs live in burrows in the mud at the bottom of the river, and I doubt if the temperature varies very greatly there, especially on a chalk stream, which is in no wise subject to spates.

There is undoubtedly a great deal to learn about ephemeridae, and any enthusiastic entomologist looking for fresh fields to explore might very well do some investigations in this one.

I'm very interested in your plans of the hatchery. I like the idea of trout and chub under the willows; are you allowed to fish for them? The mill pool sounds interesting too. I like chub-fishing.

It looks as if the best time for me to come would be either the last week in June or the last in July; what do you think? It is very good of you to have me, and I appreciate it very much. I very much doubt if I can teach you anything and I think it likely that I shall learn a good deal from you.

I had a letter from Lt.-Col. Milward last week enclosing a tapered nylon cast, 2½ yards .017″ to .008″ *without any knots*.

Let me know if you would like some more of the large Model Perfect hooks, as I have quite a lot; you can't get them in the shops.

Sincerely,

RICHARD WALKER

Dear Mr. Walker,

I have had a word with the secretary of the Croxby A.C. to-day and he tells me that the dredging operation has been postponed until late summer, so that it is not likely to clash with your visit. I think the last week in July would suit me better, but before we make any definite arrangements I will have a word with my Chief. Shall we say, provisionally, Monday, 24th, to Friday, 28th July—week-ends, of course, are my own to do with as I please, so I have not counted the two week-ends.

I'm pleased you enjoyed *I Walked by Night*. It is out of the usual run of autobiographies, isn't it?

The otter menace at Croxby is receiving attention. The keeper, who lives close by the Pond, has instructions to eliminate all otters in, on or within striking distance of the Pond.

I have yet to try my hand at fly-fishing. I went down to the river last Sunday morning and again last evening and on neither occasion did I see a fly or a single rise. I caught two brown trout last night around the $\frac{3}{4}$ lb. mark and examined minutely the contents of their stomachs, both of which were very full. There were caddis, shrimps, nymphs, a few beetles and worms, two very small creatures which I took to be a variety of leech and considerable numbers of small cream-coloured maggots about 3/16″ long, which I could not identify—but no trace of a fly.

I fished at Thimbleby Mill several times last year and I've no doubt I could get permission to fish again this year—and for you also. I had some dealings with Mr. Joker early last year in a professional capacity and he gave me carte blanche to fish there as and when I wished. The chub are not large by any standards—my best, caught on a Devon while spinning for trout, was about $1\frac{1}{2}$ lb., but to fish for them under those overhanging willows would, I think, be a severe test even for your ingenuity. I took my brother along on one occasion last year and he had an interesting experience. Spinning a 1″ gold Devon just above the Mill dam he caught a rainbow of 2 lb. 3 ozs. Mr. Joker examined it and informed us that it was one of his stock fish that had only been in the open river a matter of about six weeks. Asked how he knew this, he explained that when artificially fed a trout's fins are a pinkish-white in colour, but in their natural state, of course, they are a clear bright pink. The fins of the one my brother caught were pink except for a small whitish tip at the extreme edge. How had that fish escaped from its artificial lagoon into the river? The bank between the river and the lagoons is of considerable width and the water level in the lagoons is, I imagine, at least three feet below the top of the bank. To escape via the water inlet duct is virtually impossible. A heron might have picked it out of the lagoon and dropped it into the river, but there was not a mark on the fish to indicate such a happening. The only possible solution I can think of is the obvious one—that the fish leapt out of the lagoon on to the bank and flopped across and into the river, but it was no mean feat and most unusual as I understand that fish in captivity, particularly the larger ones, show no desire to leap.

I hope during the coming week to get some snaps of Woldale and Croxby and if they are satisfactory I will send you some to give you some idea of what you are coming to!

If you can spare me a few more Model Perfect hooks I shall be most grateful. My experience of playing large fish is very limited and I have no doubt that I shall lose a good many, so I would like to have a small reserve in readiness.

I hope Mrs. Walker and the twins are thriving.

Yours sincerely,
MAURICE INGHAM

Dear Mr. Ingham,

July it shall be, then, barring accidents. Would it be possible for *you* to spend one of the week-ends involved *here*, and have a crack at Temple Pool? We could travel one way or the other together. I have no car, so that Temple Pool has to be attained per bicycle, seven miles. I have two bikes, so you wouldn't have to ride on a step! Let me know what you think about this.

When you can't see fly or rising fish you have to try other less pure methods, as for example a wet March Brown or Wickham in all the likely spots; grease the line and glycerine cast and fly. Watch the reel line, and strike if it stops or twitches, or if you see a boil or the flash of a turning fish. It is more difficult than dry fly, in spite of what some of the books may say. Partridge and Orange is another excellent wet fly.

Wickham; gold tinsel body with red hackle as ribbing, starling wings, red main hackle. Wings are set back, thus:

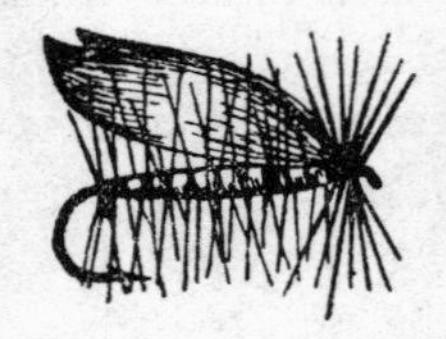

as are most wet flies. I won't attempt to give dressings for March Brown, as no two dressers seem to agree, but the hackle is partridge, brownish wings, buff and green mixed wool or hare's ear fur body, ribbed with yellow silk. Orange Partridge is very easy to tie, orange silk body, partridge hackle. You can put a rib of gold wire on if you like.

Nymphs are good at all times. I carry only three, which are as follows:

Olive nymph. Body, heron herl dyed in yellow dye to give light greeny-olive, ribbed with fine gold wire; hackle, whisks, olive hen hackle. Thorax, slip of solid feather, or raffia, dyed medium sepia; silk, shade 16 (olive). The tie is like this:

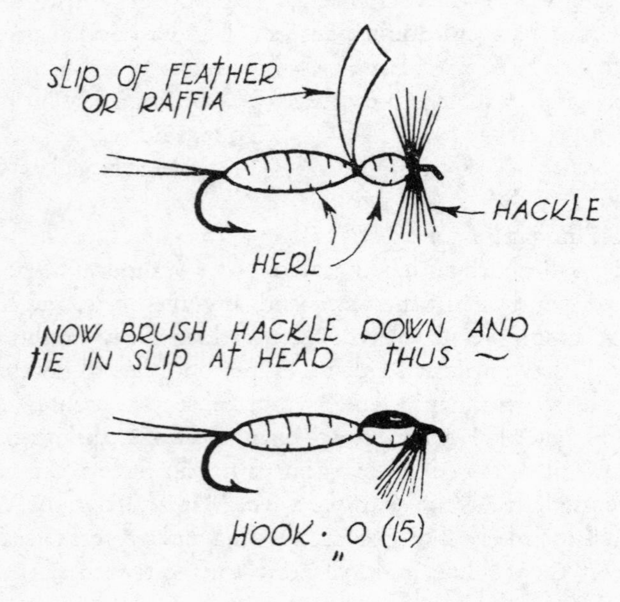

Pale Watery nymph. As above, but herl dyed dirty pale yellow-brown. Hackle and whisks, cream. Thorax, natural raffia. Hook, 00 (16). Silk, shade 6 (yellow).

Mayfly nymph. Good a week before the Mayfly and during Mayfly season. As above for shape. Body, swan secondary feather fibre, dyed pale khaki. Tails, pheasant. Thorax, raffia dyed dark chestnut. Hackle, grouse. Hook, size 9 (of ordinary scale, corresponding to 14 for Olive). Silk, 16.

Keep tails short, about 1/3rd the length of those of a dry fly. Hackles must also be shortish, especially the Mayfly.

Don't be bound by dressings you read; if you haven't the materials use the nearest you have; fish aren't usually very fussy. One of my friends advocates a different colour for Mayfly nymph. Instead of the pale khaki herl he uses cream wool, ribbed with black silk, thus:

2 WIDE BANDS OF 4 OR 5 TURNS EACH

When you fish nymphs you can grease part of your cast to control depth at which you fish, as you usually fish them over quarry which you can see; this makes it 'pure'!

I've had lots of fun this week with Mayfly nymph at dusk. You can see great boils and swirls into which you throw your nymph, striking if the boil is repeated, on chance. You fail to connect four out of five times (probably the boil was another natural being taken, but you have to strike, in case it's your artificial). I cannot claim great slaughter, as I got only three up to 1 lb. 5 ozs., but there was a big one between 3 and 4 lb. which got away! It got mixed up with a moorhen's nest and made the moorhen very cross. All this in near darkness.

Your account of the rainbow fin coloration is most interesting. We have some rainbows in our water, but I don't like them, except to look at. They are not nearly such good fighters as the browns, they'll take anything offered if not alarmed, and they're spawning *now*, which is a nuisance, as we can't disturb the gravel. No doubt for Mr. Joker's purpose they are superior, as they grow much faster than browns, I believe. It is amazing what feats they can perform when they mean to go somewhere; at Temple Pool they manage to get down from the upper lake in spite of grids and other obstructions.

I'll send on the Model Perfect hooks presently—I'm writing this from the office. Be sure and whip them on soundly, especially with nylon. I tie a knot in the nylon to prevent slipping.

I wouldn't mind betting that there *are* some bigger chub under those willows, cunning old ones which know how to keep out of sight. I am looking forward very much to seeing this set-up; I like problems of that kind. This doesn't mean that I can always solve them! There are plenty of spots on our little trout stream which I know hold good trout, but which I have found quite unfishable so far. Some of them are virtually copses, but one looks quite easy until you try. Visitors are always tempted. Here is the set-up:

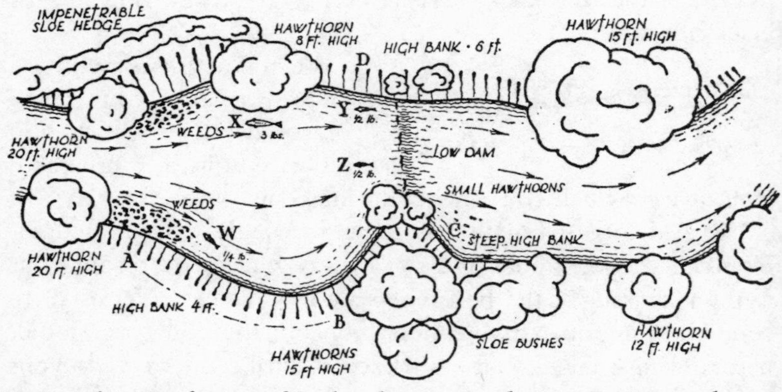

Puzzle: Catch Oswald, the three-pounder at X. He is always rising merrily if there's any surface fly at all; he takes everything that comes down. We've tried sending down handfuls of wood-lice from higher up and Oswald hardly missed one. Visitors who don't know this little trap usually try from B. Oswald knows it directly they start, because in order to avoid getting hung up on the back cast they have to emerge to some extent from behind the bush. From A to B they are perfectly silhouetted against the sky. To a really first-class caster, who could throw enough slack to avoid drag and still put his fly over Oswald from behind the bush at A, it might be possible, except for trout W, who has a close view of the proceedings and if disturbed bolts under

Oswald's bush, as indeed do all the trout in this pool. The same applies to approach from below the dam: as soon as the reel line touches the water, trouts at Y and Z go and inform Oswald that a nasty man is fishing for him, whereupon all retire under the bush (which is *in* the water). If there were only one of these half-pounders one could snatch it over the fall and then get on to Oswald, but if you hook one the other is always aware of it. Besides which, the footing at C is perilous; you have to hang on with one hand and cast with the other, which makes it awkward to shoot line, especially as the *back* cast has to be kept accurate and short to avoid getting hung up.

Our next attempt will be from a point between A and B, but seven yards from the bank, an observation post having been established somewhere near C. I forgot to say that D is no good because of Y and Z, and it also involves a back-handed cast for a right-handed angler. If Oswald survives another two seasons it will be easier, as he will by then probably have eaten W, Y and Z; in fact if I were W I'd be a bit apprehensive even now!

Sincerely,

RICHARD WALKER

Dear Mr. Walker,

The holiday is all arranged. I take the 4th–20th July for the family fortnight in Devon, return to the office for the 21st and 22nd, and then have the whole of the next week free for fishing. I would like very much to spend one of the week-ends with you at Temple Pool—if I might suggest the last week-end in July. I shall be very pleased to come back with you for the week-end, either by car or train, and I am not deterred by the prospect of a seven-mile cycle ride in the early hours, though I must admit that I would prefer to go by car. Doesn't 'B.B.' say somewhere in *Confessions* that fishermen are naturally lazy?

Will you come on the Friday evening or the Saturday? My work on Saturday morning will not detain me after mid-day and you could no doubt amuse yourself by inspecting our town or by wandering along the river, which runs through a very beautiful valley just above the town.

My net is now completed with the exception of a handle. I have been unable to get a $\frac{3}{4}''$ diameter bamboo locally and I see from his catalogue that J. B. Walker will only supply them in half dozen lots. I don't anticipate that I shall ever need any more $\frac{3}{4}''$ canes, and to buy half a dozen for the sake of one seems unnecessarily extravagant. I wonder if you have one that you could let me have, or if you can suggest a suitable alternative.

I managed to combine business and pleasure yesterday afternoon, to the extent of visiting Croxby and Woldale and taking some photographs. I expect they will be ready by the week-end, and if they are any good I will send you some when I write again.

I entirely agree with you on the fighting qualities of the rainbow trout—he cannot compare with the brown. The little stream where I do most of my trouting contains large numbers of small rainbows. I think I told you that Mr. Joker has an establishment a short distance upstream, which was used for the first time early last summer when he introduced about 80,000 rainbow fry—ten weeks old. Many of them must have escaped downstream and I have caught several around the ½ lb. mark. I don't know to what size the ones in captivity have grown, but with artificial feeding I know they grow at a terrific rate.

Have you put your combined ops. against Oswald into opertion yet? It is a most interesting set-up. I hope you will find Thimbleby as interesting.

When I was at Woldale yesterday I saw several carp, one of which was a whopper. He was basking on the surface and I got quite a good look at him. As you know it is very difficult to judge size in water, but I would have no hesitation in estimating his length at something over three feet, and he was very broad in the beam. From what I have seen this spring I would say that Woldale does not contain anything like the numbers of carp that Croxby does, but it would not surprise me if the bigger fish were at Woldale. This is quite understandable, as I suspect that the Woldale carp are all mirrors, while those at Croxby are, I understand, all common carp.

I hope to have lunch with the secretary of the Croxby A.C. during the next week and as our conversation will be confined mainly to angling topics, I hope to learn a lot more about Croxby and the peculiarities of the carp there.

Kind regards,

Yours sincerely,
MAURICE INGHAM

Dear Mr. Ingham,

If 'B.B.' thinks fishermen are naturally lazy he is mistaken! It's true that there are some kinds of fishing which give opportunity for *physical* inactivity; carp, tench and barbel fishing come into this category. *Mental* laziness is fatal in all kinds of fishing. But some kinds of fishing permit no laziness of any kind. I don't know why I have said all this, because you know it as well as I do!

If it is all right with you I will come on the Friday evening.

I've looked through my stock of canes and there is not one over $\frac{5}{8}''$; but J. B. Walker will let you have a single $\frac{3}{4}''$ all right. Don't forget to ask for $\frac{3}{4}''$ at *small end.*

The Mayfly is on thick now. I went out yesterday afternoon and got seven fish, all between 1 lb. and $1\frac{1}{2}$ lb. One of them had someone else's fly in its mouth, plus a 2-yard tapered nylon cast, minus loop. Bad knotting on somebody's part, by the look of it. The really big trout are not on the fly yet.

My friend Pete has invented a rather surrealistic Mayfly which we have found very successful as an imitation of the sub-imago. It's called the Bitsa, as Pete claims the original was made of 'bitsa' material left over from tying orthodox patterns. It has four hackles and no wings:

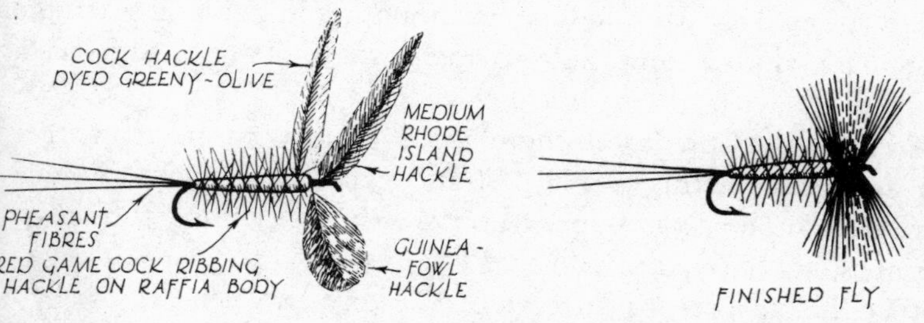

Pete claims that a fly ought to be an impressionist rather than an imitative copy. The idea of the combined effect of the guineafowl hackle and the greeny-olive is to give the impression of the veined greenish wings; the Rhode hackle gives the idea of the brown legs. The ribbing hackle is simply to aid flotation, which it certainly succeeds in doing; the fly is practically unsinkable. I got all of yesterday's seven on one of them. It may be that this is an idea that could be profitably followed for smaller flies. I am going to see what can be done on these lines when the Mayfly is over.

If the carp you saw at Woldale was three feet long it ought to weigh between 25 and 30 pounds, or even more if in really fat condition. If you saw *several* carp it bodes well for the chances of catching one, and if they are mirror carp, they ought to be bigger than they look. If they are mirrors they will be more inclined to surface feeding and may succumb to floating bread. The thing to do is to take a loaf every time you go there, break it up into pieces about matchbox size or a little bigger, and throw them in at a suitable spot. Carp very quickly become 'educated' to bread and where they *will* take it, it has great advantages; you know exactly what is happening; there is no waterlogged line to hamper the strike; you know what fish is biting (if any!) and you are not concerned with the kind of bottom or depth of water.

It might be worth while for the Croxby Club to get a hundred or so small mirrors, to increase size in years to come. They will breed with the common carp, as they do at Temple Pool, and you get all sorts of interesting variations, of which my favourite is the one with scales all over, but only about half the normal *number*, each scale being three times the normal size. This makes a beautiful golden-coloured fish. I had one of these, 6½ lb., last year, and was in two minds about mounting it, but let it go in the end. It's almost impossible to retain the metallic colours in a stuffed fish.

I have still not sent you those hooks; I must try and remember to get them off this evening. I am trying to get some French nylon to mount some up. About 10 lb. b.s. I think should be right, suitably dyed of course.

We'll have a record carp out of Woldale between us!

Sincerely,

RICHARD WALKER

Dear Mr. Walker,

I have caught my first trout on dry and wet fly! I went out for a couple of hours last Monday evening and although the river was somewhat highly coloured and swollen after the week-end rain a few fish were rising and I managed to tempt one with an Olive. As the water was so 'thick' I decided that I might do better with a wet fly in the eddies and got three more on Partridge and Orange. They were all small rainbows but I was quite satisfied with my first attempt. When the water has fined down I will try again and perhaps I shall do better. Incidentally I have not seen any signs of Mayfly yet.

I think I shall be able to manage the trip by car. I have been hoarding my 'basic' petrol as much as possible, but our trip to Devon will take about 30 gallons—however by careful budgeting I think we shall make it.

Of *course* 'B.B.' is mistaken when he says that fishermen are naturally lazy! Most of the fishermen I know are extremely active and energetic people, but they are, generally speaking, of placid disposition. I think it is that placid, contemplative disposition which makes a really good angler—perhaps 'philosophical' would be an appropriate adjective too. On second thoughts I am not sure whether it is correct to say that placid people become good fishermen, or that people who spend a lot of time fishing become placid—perhaps a bit of both. Certainly angling is the most restful occupation I know and the time passes more quickly when I am fishing than in any other way.

I may have some more chub fishing for you when you come here, if you are interested and if we have time. There is a river that holds some good chub, I am told, and a few trout. It is private water but I think I can get permission to fish a two-mile stretch—if so, I hope to have a look at it and perhaps try for some of the trout this week-end. I'll tell you more about it later.

The enclosed photographs of Woldale and Croxby may interest you and give you some idea of what these waters are like, and the sketch plans will give you a more complete picture.

Taking Woldale first, both photographs are of the House Pond. One is taken from the north-east corner looking north-west, with large horse-chestnut trees overhanging the water. The other is taken from the southern bank near the boathouse, looking across the Pond. You will see from the photographs that there is already a considerable amount of weed out in the middle—far more than I saw at any time last summer. Fortunately it is all soft weed; there are no lilies, except in the S.E. corner (pp. 192–93).

One of the Croxby photographs is a distant view from the road looking eastwards along the valley in which the Pond lies. You can just see the hut at the far end of the Pond. It was a café before the Club took over the place and was perched up on the hillside near the Lodge, with 'TEAS' in huge white letters emblazoned across it. Now it has been redecorated and moved down to the waterside, where it will make a very useful shelter—rod-room—clubroom, or what-have-you. The other photograph is taken from the north bank looking southwards across the Pond. You can see the Keeper's Lodge on top of the hill and some of the jetties sticking out from the southern bank. You can also just see a white dot over by the far bank, which is the solitary swan that inhabits the lake. I am not greatly enamoured of those jetties; there would appear to be danger of a fish running between the piles of the jetty and the result would be a break and a lost fish at least, possibly a broken top joint. There are one or two places on the north bank where it will be possible to fish from the bank itself and it is there that I intend to try first of all. The northern side is considerably shallower than the southern and for that reason, no doubt, will provide better fishing, except in rough weather.

The north-eastern corner of the Pond is badly silted up and overgrown with reeds, with the result that there is only the merest trickle of water under the sluice gate. Most of the outflow seems to be seeping through the bank at the eastern end. The main object of the proposed dredging operations, as I understand it, is to clear the reeds and silt from the north-east corner to get the sluice functioning properly again. If we can get a flow of water through that corner again it may prevent further silting.

It was in a small open patch of water amongst those reeds where I saw so many spawning fish last May. There were several carp moving in the water when we walked round before taking the photographs. One biggish carp stood on his head at the root of some reeds and waved a tail like a whitewash brush in the air. Then he took fright and bolted through the reeds to run headlong, with a resounding 'thwack', into the base of an old reedmace, causing it to sway violently. The reeds are fairly thick at that point and it is very easy to follow the movements of the fish by the swaying of the reeds.

The Friday evening will suit me beautifully. If you will let me know in due course what train you will be arriving on I will meet you with the car to give you a lift with your gear.

Did I tell you that I had not been able to get any information from the Lincolnshire Naturalist Trust on leeches and had written to the British Museum? The result there was equally unsatisfactory—they have never heard of the name 'vamps'.[1]

So it looks as if we shall have to experiment ourselves.

Have you ever heard of a worm spinner? I have been very impressed by the attractive way a worm spins when drawn slowly against the current and the majority of my trout this year have been caught that way. I think I shall fix up a proper spinner for worm—with very small celluloid fins and with a Pennell or Stewart type flight. I've an idea it might be very effective against perch.

Yours sincerely,
MAURICE INGHAM

Dear Mr. Ingham,

I am glad to hear you are now a fly-fisher. I thought you would soon pick up the trick of casting and I am sure you will agree that it is really one of the easiest ways of fishing once you get started. I expect your Mayfly will be a good deal later than ours, which is exceptionally early. Ours has been rather spasmodic this year; on some afternoons the hatch has been very sparse. The really big chaps haven't got on the fly yet, the best I've had so far being 2 lb. 10 ozs.—Oswald! I got him casting blind, without seeing the water at all. I put out enough line to just *not* reach the

[1] I wonder!—R.W.

bush, let it fall and struck at the 'plop'. I put him back, so the problem is still there!

You will find that the ability to throw a fly will come in very useful for other fish besides trout; you can catch rudd, chub and dace on a fly, as of course you know, but I usually use a bunch of maggots instead of a fly for rudd; it is a deadly way of fishing for them when they're feeding on the surface, as they usually are.

These are excellent photographs of Woldale and Croxby. Woldale is much smaller than I had visualized, which is a decided advantage. It is often difficult to locate the fish in large waters. It looks as if one could cover practically every part of Woldale with the 'Felton Crosswind'. It is a very 'carpy'-looking place, especially in the view with the fence running down into the water—handy place for a fish to bolt under!

I am pleased to observe that Croxby 'reeds' are rushes! My botany is extremely sketchy, but I *believe* these are called giant reed-mace, and by the uninitiated (even less initiated than I!) 'bulrushes'. They are like this (*a*):

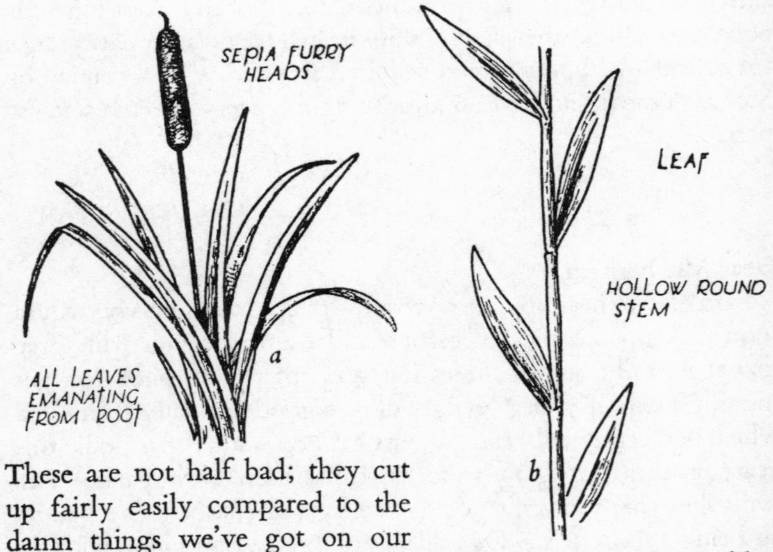

These are not half bad; they cut up fairly easily compared to the damn things we've got on our trout water, which are the Norfolk type reeds, almost like miniature bamboos (*b*). Your sort of reed or rush is very easily cut indeed by the grass-hook-on-a-pole affair, which after some weeks of trial I do not hesitate to say is the best thing I ever tried for general *single-handed* weed-cutting. You can, of course, cut your stuff with a link-scythe, working one end from a boat, but I find the link-scythe tends to be unselective, besides being much more likely to cut fish. If you had grass hooks on poles you could cut back straggling rushes and leave a solid wall of the thicker stuff to provide cover (for anglers).

Like you I do *not* like the platforms at all. Anyone on one of them is going to be pretty conspicuous! And every vibration of the structure is going to be transmitted to the fish. And as you say, if a fish bunks underneath one, well . . .! I think you are wise to fish from the bank. If there is a boat there you could clear yourself one or two pitches. I must say, however, that from what you have told me and from looking at the photographs, Woldale looks much more like producing a good fish than Croxby, besides being a more restful-looking place to sit by!

I observe that there are swans at Croxby. The only good swans
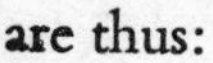
are thus:

They are the only wild creature I really detest. 'B.B.' hates them and carries a catapult specially to deal with them. There is a pair on the upper lake at Temple Pool, and sometimes they come down to the lower lake and make themselves a nuisance.

I have never heard of a worm spinner designed as such, but I've seen worms spun on natural bait tackles. I think an error lies here. These tackles spin the worm much too fast. What is wanted is a slow undulating spin to resemble the progress of a little eel.

It would be worth experimenting with a vane on the lines of a plug, so as to get the head end of the worm to follow a track through the water thus: ~~~~

It ought to be a horizontal and not a vertical undulation. It may be necessary to have a little bit of lead to give a keel effect.

A small eel or lamprey is a deadly bait for many fish, chub and barbel particularly. If you can devise something to imitate an eel's movements it ought to be very effective indeed. I must experiment myself.

I am enclosing a dozen each of 2 and 4 Model Perfects. I'm making up some myself, No. 2's on .017″ nylon and 4's on .016″. I shall probably do a few 4's on .014″ also, in case it looks safe to use lighter tackle at Woldale.

I had a bit of luck the other day; a man came to order a match rod and brought his old one to see if I could allow anything on it, which I did—£2. When the paint (!) and solidified groundbait had been cleaned off, I began to open my eyes. Now, after a complete strip-down, re-blueing of ferrules and cleaning and polishing of reel-fittings, sandpapering cork and re-whipping and varnishing, I have a Hardy 'Gold Medal', 10′ 6″ 3-piece steel centre fly-rod, present price £19.10.0 or thereabouts. It will be fine for chub and for any biggish water, or if I go sea-trouting. It would even do for salmon at a pinch. And of course it's worth at least £12 secondhand if I ever wanted to sell it.

It will soon be carping-time now. I must begin getting ready.

Sincerely,

RICHARD WALKER

Dear Mr. Walker,

My outing to the River last Monday was a dismal failure so far as trout were concerned—I got one rainbow about six inches long—but I have satisfied myself that it does contain some nice chub. I tried all ways to catch trout—fly, worm, quill minnow, devon, plug, etc.—and caught chub every time, in remarkably good condition considering they are out of season. My best two were 1 lb. 12 ozs. and 1 lb. 10 ozs. but I am quite sure there are much bigger ones. It is a most attractive stream and looks ideal for trout but the effluent from a sewage disposal works runs into it at one point and I suspect that the pollution is sufficient to eliminate trout but not bad enough to affect the chub. Incidentally the one trout which I did catch was from above the sewage outfall.

My best trout since I wrote last was $\frac{3}{4}$ lb. and I have had several over the $\frac{1}{2}$ lb. mark. That is very small by your standards but for the little stream where I fish it is a good average. I *may* have some better trout fishing to offer you when you come—if we have time for such small fry. I am making a few discreet enquiries and hoping something will come of them.

I have heard from J. B. Walker to-day that a cane is on its way, so I hope to have my net ready by the 16th.

Congratulations on catching Oswald. I thought it wouldn't be long before you found the answer to that problem!

I may have a day at Slapton again this year when we go down to Devon and I will try out your suggestion on the rudd there. It should be good sport. It is a great pity that I cannot get down to Slapton in the winter. I would very much like to have a crack at some of the pike there when they are in really good shape. I caught a few on my two visits last summer, but as you know the weather was very hot and they were poor sport. The best fight I had was with one of about 12 lb. that took a perch that I was reeling in on my light rod. We had a grand tussle for about an hour and I had played him almost to a standstill, but when he saw my net he disgorged the perch and sank out of sight.

There is a boat—of sorts—at Croxby and some time during the next week or so I will try to get over and clear one or two pitches as you suggest. There are one or two spots that are naturally open, but it is as well to have a choice of pitches.

After trying out a worm spinner with a very small homemade celluloid spinning vane last Monday, I have come to the conclusion that your suggestion is very sound. Spinning up against the current the worm was rotated so rapidly that it lost that attractive wriggle that I had observed previously. I think your plug head suggestion is a good one—I must experiment when I have time. Have you any suggestions as to design?

Thank you very much for the hooks. I must get some mounted and varnished. They really are beautiful hooks.

You had a lucky break in acquiring a Hardy 'Gold Medal' rod for £2, didn't you? The man must have been a bit 'dim' if he couldn't appreciate the real worth of his rod by its action and 'feel'—and to *paint* it . . . ! You will now be able to boast that you have been given a Hardy 'Gold Medal' rod in part exchange for one of your own make! An unsolicited testimonial to the excellence of your rods.

Yours sincerely,
MAURICE INGHAM

Dear Mr. Ingham,

Don't you worry about finding trout fishing for me: I would rather fish for carp any day! It might be fun to have a go at those chub, but we mustn't let the carp feel neglected!

I'm glad you've managed to get your ¾" cane. J. B. Walker is a most helpful chap and can always be relied on to do his best. He found me some beautiful poles for splitting some time ago and I am just beginning to find how good they are. I've practically abandoned my machine, as I find that the extra time involved in hand-building is more than compensated for by the superiority of the finished job. The difference is this:

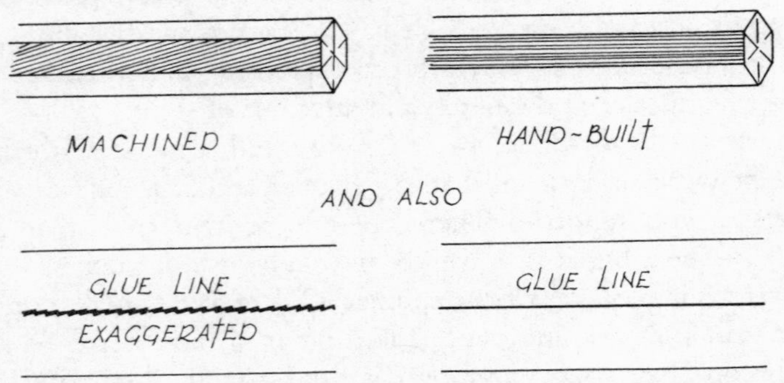

On fine tops 3/32" or 5/64" corner-to-corner, the width of the glue line and straightness of the fibres make a very considerable difference.

Actually I am beginning to wonder if we are on the right lines at all in making rods polygonal. I rather fancy it would be better to make them of this section: 'f' being the face used for casting and 'x-x' the line of neutral stress. The rod would be built of bamboo strip, the tension side flat and the compression side on edge. When bent back, i.e. at the point where the forward cast is commenced, the edgewise fibres would all be in compression and their recovery ought to put a considerable kick into the cast. I believe archers are well up in this form of construction. I'm going to make a couple of rods this way when I get time.

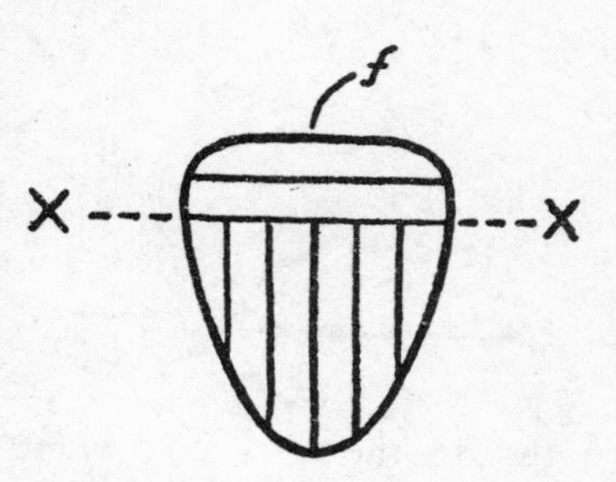

I am convinced that a well-made flat-strip rod is quite equal to the conventional kind. I made one for a friend about 18 months ago, an 8 ft. 2-joint, extra-powerful dry fly rod, and have just had it returned to have the top agate replaced. It has been in constant use, both in throwing a heavy (H.B.H.) line for trout and during the winter with a wet fly or worm for chub. It caught fish of both kinds up to 3½ lb. and a pike of 8 lb. on a worm. It shows no sign of weakening whatever and I am very pleased with it. Of course the proportion of hard outer fibre is much higher in this kind of rod, and you surely can feel it! You get the same feeling in using it that you get in driving a really powerful car—elation tempered with caution! This is an octagonal rod. It is, of course, the easiest kind of split cane there is to make. I am glad you are coming here for a few days as I can show you some of the rod-building tricks. When you get the space you will have lots of fun building rods. It really is a fascinating thing.

I've never been to Slapton. Of course you would want a more powerful fly rod, to get more distance, on a biggish water. I find the best technique for rudd is to use as long a line as I can comfortably cast, with the line greased and the cast glycerined to sink, size 8 hook and six maggots. You usually lose a maggot or two in casting! You can see the greased line shoot along the surface when you get a bite, and the fish hang on longer than when they have a float to drag.

I haven't had a chance to try a worm-wriggler yet, but I should think a celluloid head vane like this:

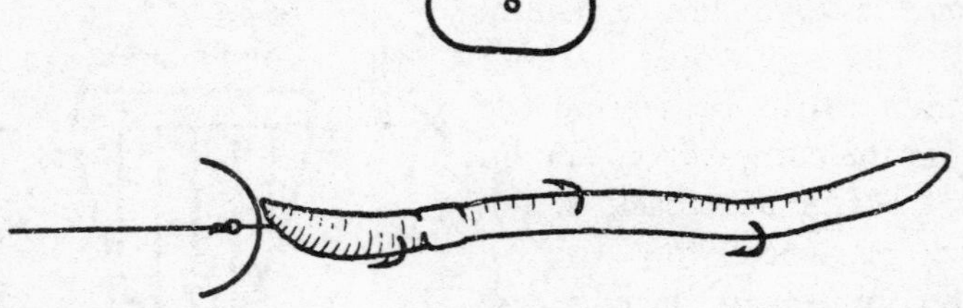

might do the trick. It wants experiment . . . trial and error. There's no reason why this should be limited to worms. Why must natural bait spinners spin? Why shouldn't they 'plug'?

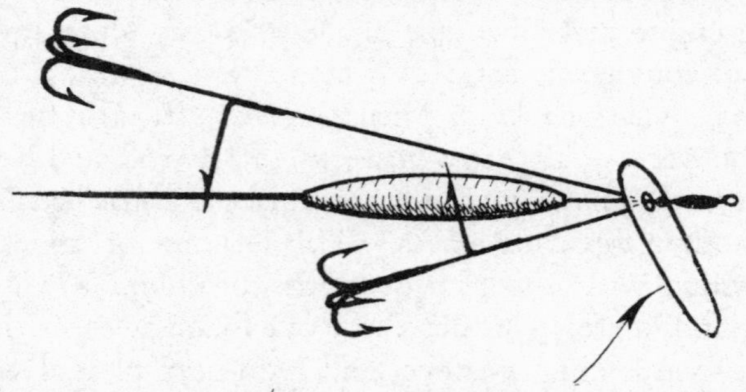

CELLULOID VANE INSTEAD OF SPINNING FANS?? WHY NOT?

The hooks *are* very nice. They were specially done for big carp. Major Courtney Williams of Allcocks got them done for me. We had a lot of correspondence about it. The hooks are all picked and tested and have extra long sharp points, the idea being to avoid any danger of 'padding' in the bend and consequent inadequate penetration. They are designed to go home with a *pull* and not need so much of an *impact* as ordinary hooks of that size.

The chap that had the 'Hardy' rod is not a fly fisher, and the rod is much too limber for coarse fishing. I'm making him a nice hollow-built split cane job which will be much more satisfactory. Not long now to carp-time.

Sincerely,

RICHARD WALKER

IX

June Letters

Dear Mr. Walker,

How do you like this tropical weather? The fish at Woldale certainly seem to be enjoying it. Last Sunday my wife decided we would go for a picnic, and as all the seaside places were likely to be crowded we thought we would have a nice peaceful afternoon at Woldale . . . my suggestion, as I wanted to see if there were any carp in evidence.

I took a walk round the Decoy Pond and saw some movement in a very thick bed of weed which stretches halfway across the pond from the western bank. I had my binoculars with me but couldn't identify the fish which were making the disturbance, but after negotiating a bed of nettles and reeds and some very marshy ground, I managed to climb a tree which was overhanging the water and had a perfect view of the fish moving almost directly beneath me. They were tench, but such tench as I have never seen before in my life. They were absolute monsters. They were rolling on the surface amongst the weed, dorsal fins and tails frequently sticking out of the water, and I'll swear that the dorsal fin of one was nearly as big as my hand, and if it was not a record tench I should be very surprised. I mean to have a crack at those big fellows before long, but it will not be easy. The west bank is unfishable and the east bank, which is fairly clear of weed, is very heavily fished. I think the only chance of getting one is by a long cast from the east bank to the edge of the weed bed in the middle of the pond. You may be able to make some other suggestions when you see the set-up.

On Monday afternoon my work took me again in the vicinity of Woldale and I made a slight detour to see if there was any sign of carp—and there was. I got a really close-up view of three mirror carp basking on the surface within a few feet of the bank. Two were, I imagine, about 12–15 lb., but one would be nearer 20 lb. He was a beauty and most considerately turned slowly round so that I had a good view of him from all angles. He had a real 'hog's-back' and was distinctly balloon-like in 'front elevation'. He had two whitish marks on the back of his head or on his shoulders, which reminded me of the tale about the King of the Carp in *Confessions*. I took a loaf of bread with me, but hadn't time to wait and see if any of the carp showed any interest in it. Masses of small roach were very interested in the bread, attacking it in vast numbers immediately it touched the water, and I suspect they would be a nuisance if one were fishing a floating crust. The weed bed in the House Pond has extended considerably since I saw it last and is now much bigger than at any time last year—but the Pond is still fishable.

I hope to go over to Croxby next Saturday or Sunday to cut out one or two pitches so that we can fish from the bank.

Your theory of flat-strip rod construction is most interesting—it would appear to put the strength where it is needed instead of spreading it evenly on all sides of the hexagon as in the present orthodox method of construction. I should think it would be ideal for a spinning rod, which, incidentally, will be my first job when I get my hut, I hope, before the autumn.

I have never been able to understand why one is always told that natural bait spinners must spin. It is even emphasized that the spin must be 'true' and not a wobble. Surely a wriggler appears far more natural in the water than a spinner. The sight of a small fish rotating rapidly as it passes through the water must be an awe-inspiring one to any self-respecting pike, etc. Perhaps it is the fact that a fish—obviously a fish by its appearance and 'smell'—is behaving in a completely unusual manner that makes it so attractive, but I would have thought that a 'plugged' natural bait would more nearly resemble an injured fish, which, presumably, is the reason why a pike takes any of the usual lures. Anyway, I think it would be worth following up.

I get the final component for my net to-morrow—the tapered

connecting piece which you suggested—and I hope to get it completely assembled and varnished before the week-end. I fear it will not be fully varnished by the 16th, but I hope to have at least two coats on it by then and subsequent coats will have to be applied between outings.

It won't be long now!

Yours sincerely,
MAURICE INGHAM

PS. I am enclosing a Mayfly, which I think must be a female imago of Vulgata or Lineata. Am I right? One tail seems to be missing.

Dear Maurice,

What a pleasure it is to find one's information used! Your diagnosis of the Mayfly is perfectly correct. It is a female spinner of Vulgata or Lineata. I can only tell the difference in the sub-imago, Lineata is greener than Vulgata. It is hard to describe the colours; Vulgata is called 'brown' and the other two 'green', but the 'brown' is pretty greenish in most cases. If you have one of each it's easy enough. I expect yours is Vulgata, as Lineata is pretty rare. Yes, there is one tail missing. They come adrift at the least provocation. If you're going to fish Mays, use a stronger point on your cast than usual. I use 0.010″ now! Trout usually take a Mayfly with a sudden loud PLOMP! which makes one jump and strike much too hard!

I am baiting at Temple Pool every evening and *hope* to have a great pogrom of carp on 17th. We dragged a nice pitch on Saturday and thoroughly scoured the bottom. I have a fine gadget for the purpose, like this:

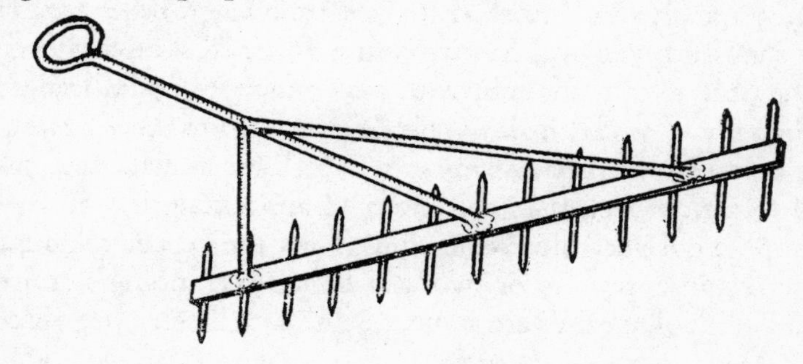

made of welded steel and 17″ wide. Whichever way it falls, it's the same effect. I designed it for match fishing, where one often draws a pitch choked with weeds and practically unfishable without dragging.

The tench at Woldale sound exciting. I expect they were spawning when you saw them rolling about. I think the best way to catch tench is to drag a pitch in a bed of weeds in the evening and fish it early the next morning. If there are bulrushes near, so much the better. I never mind weed if I can only get to the bank to drag a pitch. Is this possible at Woldale? It sounds as if one would have to drag late and arrive early the next morning or the pitch might be appropriated! The dragging is as good as groundbaiting.

The fact that Woldale is extensively fished is no detriment if one is prepared to go in for nocturnal adventures, or to rise very early! The 'deep and weedy claypit' where I caught dozens of big carp was fished by up to thirty rods nearly every evening in summer, yet hardly ever was a carp even hooked. I used to get them after dark, or in the early morning, especially on week-days when there were no daytime anglers before about 6.30 p.m. If the carp at Woldale bask near the bank you can bet they will be catchable at night, by the technique that Traherne sets out in *Be Quiet* .... You can circumvent the roach by drawing up the crust on the hook and throwing small pieces of crust to the roach until a carp comes 'clooping' around. Then you lower the hook-bait and look out for squalls! Another advantage of the waters being well-fished is that the carp are sure to know bread is edible. I doubt if much floating-bread fishing has been done there; you will not usually find more than one freshwater fisherman in every thousand who will fish without a float and shot, and even then he only does it for eels, with two ounces of coffin-lead. I shall be very surprised if the Woldale carp won't take a floating crust, especially as they are mirrors, which are much more in-clined to surface-feed than commons. I am getting the mirrors at Temple Pool very bread-conscious; I got the keeper to chuck some crusts in every day or two, and he has been doing so since April. I am looking forward to next Saturday! There were three

20-pounders cruising round yesterday and one took a crust very unsuspiciously; but there are so many small fish from 2½ to 6 lb. or so that the big fish are odds against when it comes to getting a bait. I mean to start off with an enormous ball of paste for bait, about the size of a tangerine, on a No. 2 Model Perfect.

I have tapers for a variety of spinning rods and will be glad to give you dimensions. Your carp rod has the dimensions of a medium salmon spinning rod, spread over 10′ instead of 8′, if that's any help. When you get your hut fixed you will be surprised how easy it is to make rods.

Are vamps leeches? Didn't the 'vamps' wriggle back into the river at high speed? I think leeches would be a good bait, but I'm not convinced that vamps *are* leeches. They sound too quick to me. (I was looking over some old *Fishing Gazettes* the other day.)

Latest American lure (believe it or not) is the 'Virgin Mermaid', made of pale pink plastic and in appearance exactly as its name implies, decidedly Jane Russellish. The accuracy of the first part of its name is ensured by the presence of a large treble hook. You fish it like a plug and it comes in blonde, brunette or redhead. Marvellous country, America. They also will sell you synthetic salmon eggs and 'otters' (paravanes).

Sincerely,

RICHARD WALKER

Dear Richard,

Yes, I think it is time we dispensed with formality.

Well, I've christened my carp rod! I met the secretary of Croxby A.C. last Friday and learned to my surprise that for some inexplicable reason the season at Croxby commences on 1st June. Anyway, I hied me thither on Saturday evening—fished from 5–11 p.m., had a sleep in the hut from 11 p.m. to 4 a.m. and then fished again until 9 a.m. My bag was 8 carp and two tench—3 carp and 1 tench on Saturday evening and the remainder on Sunday morning. They were only small—5 lb. 8 oz.; 4 lb. 10 oz.; 3 lb. 6 oz.; 3 lb. 4 oz.; 2 lb. 10 oz.; 2 lb. 8 oz.; 1 lb. 12 oz.; 1 lb. 4 oz., and the tench about a pound each—but it was a promising beginning.

I went again last evening and fished from 5.30 p.m. to 10 p.m. This time the average was a little better, five fish—6 lb. 9 oz.; 5 lb. 2 oz.; 4 lb. 10 oz.; 3 lb. 6 oz. and 3 lb. 4 oz. (I used bigger balls of paste—about golf ball size.)

On each occasion I was fishing with two rods; my old light rod with 6 lb. 'Terylene' line on a centre-pin reel, .013″ nylon and No. 8 hook and my new rod with 'Felton Crosswind' reel, old 11 lb. braided nylon line, .016″ nylon on to which I have mounted one of your No. 2 M.P. hooks. Fishing on Saturday and Sunday I tried lobworms, potato and honey paste and found that the carp showed a marked preference for the paste—at least on that occasion. Last night I commenced with potato and from 5.30 to 8.30 p.m. I didn't have a single run. My five carp were taken on paste between 8.30 and 10 p.m. and I also missed one run during that time.

I don't know if it is a case of beginner's luck or if your teachings are already proving their worth, but on both my visits I have been far more successful than any of the other members fishing at the same time. On each occasion I have fished from the bank, but in different places. On Saturday and Sunday, of the dozen or so other members fishing, not one was fishing from the bank.

They were all perched on baskets or deck chairs on the jetties, clad in garments of varied and striking hue, and made little attempt at concealment. Last night one old boy was fishing from the bank, but instead of sitting quietly behind the reeds—now grown up to form a most effective screen—he stood for the greater part of the time at the water's edge in full view of the fish *holding* his rod. He caught three small tench and a carp of about 2 lb.—I got my five carp from a pitch about 30 yards away. As I say, it may be beginner's luck—certainly I do not claim any great skill on my part—but I am inclined to think that my modicum of success has been due to my being quiet and keeping, as far as possible, out of sight.

I am delighted with the way the rod behaves. It casts beautifully and although I have not yet really had to put it to the test, it gives a feeling of great confidence and immense power. My old rod, of course, is quite inadequate to deal with anything but small fish.

The Pond must contain vast numbers of carp and I think the problem there will be the same one that you are faced with at Temple Pool—of giving the big ones a chance of taking the bait before it is seized by the small ones. Big ones there certainly are—a 14-pounder was landed last year, and 'B.B.' records the capture by Otto Overbeck of a 17-pounder in, I think, 1902. If there were fish of that size in 1902 it is reasonable to assume that there are some of at least equal size to-day, though I suspect that the water is over-stocked and the size of the fish suffers thereby. The biggest haul by one member last season was 487 carp!! A member was telling me that he contacted one of the big fellows on the first day of the season and suffered a broken middle joint in consequence!! (I may have a suspicious mind, but I am prepared to bet that he tried to net his fish too quickly.) As soon as the fish saw the net it made a terrific dash for a bed of reeds, the angler had to clamp down and hold on, with the result I have described. He then tried to hold the line in his hand and got a cut finger and finally he put his foot on the line, with the inevitable result.

It may be that floating crust would be more effective against the big ones—I have yet to try it. I am throwing crusts in on all my visits in the hope of making them crust-conscious.

This week-end I am going to have a crack at the big fellows at Woldale. I shall not have the advantage that you will have at Temple Pool of months of pre-baiting with bread, but I may be lucky. While I am there I want to try to persuade the keeper to let me clear a pitch in the Decoy Pool, so that I can have a go at some of those monster tench.

I certainly am prepared to go in for 'nocturnal adventures' as you call them, and for early rising. To me it is one of the greatest attractions of summer fishing. I think the most satisfactory arrangement, particularly when fishing at Croxby, is to do what I did last week-end—fish Saturday evening, sleep in the hut or in the car in the small hours and fish again in the early hours of Sunday morning.

The difficulty in applying the margin-fishing technique to

circumvent the roach shoals at Woldale is that the reed fringe, by which the carp are most prone to bask and where they can always be heard 'clooping' at night, is too wide for my rod to span it. I must try to find a spot on Saturday where this difficulty doesn't obtain.

Best of luck for the week-end.

Yours sincerely,
MAURICE INGHAM

Dear Maurice,

You *did* make a good start, and in excellent weather too. I am pleased for several reasons, perhaps most of all because you have shown that our ideas are not far wrong on yet another water. Of *course* it isn't beginner's luck. If you'd only caught *one* carp, however big, it might have been luck, but not when you get *eight*. I am also pleased that you have seen just how careless many carp-fishers are. I believe that for anyone who takes trouble and thought, as you do, carp are reasonably easy to catch, but they are very sensitive indeed, and it takes very little to scare them. Just a little thing like a clod being accidentally kicked into the water is enough to make them very suspicious. I should think the vibration of anyone moving or even coughing on one of those platform contraptions would be enough to scare the carp a hundred yards away.

You might have a better chance of getting a big one with a big bait of paste, about golf-ball size or near it, with some ground-bait round it, slung as far out as you can pitch it. I don't think you will find floating crust so good at Croxby as the common carp are not as a rule such keen surface-feeders as the mirrors. I don't mean that they won't take a floating bait, just that as far as my experience goes it is not nearly so effective with the common carp as it is with the mirrors. I have never caught a big common carp on floating bait.

It pleased me too that you like the action and feel of your new rod. Of course it was designed for fish of 10 lb. and upwards and is inclined to be a bit rough on smaller fish. I have a lighter version with some extra tip-action which I used for lighter-tackle work. When you get your workshop you will be able to experiment and perhaps produce some even better designs; this is by no means final.

If the Croxby carp like paste, they will be highly susceptible to groundbaiting with mashed bread. You may find the bigger ones feed by night; is the lake deep anywhere? I think the question of night fishing depends mostly on depth, the deeper the lake the later it will fish. I know you told me it is shallow at the side, but has it deep holes in the middle? I imagine you used the floatless technique; did you get good decisive runs? Were you fishing far out?

Our venture to Temple Pool was not very successful; the weather turned much colder last Thursday and the carp were not much in evidence when we made the first attack on Friday evening. I saw 'Pickle-Barrel' (the monster) out in the middle, about 40 yards away, so I slung him a bit of squeezed breadcrumb —to sink—off the Felton, 6 lb. 'Terylene'. After about five minutes he disappeared and off went the line. An enormous cloud of bubbles came up when I connected and I was hopeful, but after a fifteen-minute fight in and out of weed-beds, the fish emerged as a neat common carp of seven pounds two ounces. Two others chased him all over the place during this battle. That was all my score on Friday, but Pete, who was with me, had a leather carp of the same weight on floating crust, margin-fished. It put up a fine struggle on the 4½ lb. line he was using and really his playing of it was as nice and skilful a bit of fishing as ever I saw, considering the weeds and snags. We took the two home in a wet sack and put them in a pond near my house, about 40 yards across.

On Saturday morning I went with another friend, Bob, who is also a carp addict, and got a 5¾ lb. common carp on lob. He went round a branch and towed it about, an unexciting dragging fight. Bob got a pretty mirror of 5½ lb., also on lob. Later on I got a splendid brown trout of 2 lb. 14 ozs. on the lob, in topping condition, small neat head and a hump-back like a perch; it put up a splendid fight, but of course had little chance on 0.012″ nylon and 6 lb. 'Terylene'. And to finish the day I tied some fine roach-tackle, 6x and 16 hook, to the top ring of the carp rod, tight line, and promptly connected with a roach of one pound one ounce, which several times had the rod top in the water and which I expected to break me any minute, but it didn't and was safely landed at last.

One of these days I am going to have a great 'slaughter' of roach over there, and perhaps catch a three-pounder. It is a roach-fisher's paradise; you get a bite at every throw with paste or maggot, provided you keep a good cloud going. We have had two-pounders more than once on lob while carp-fishing. They are good fighters on delicate tackle. Sometimes we have had a minor roach-pogrom, and it has once or twice resulted in a carp being hooked; then there is a new cast and hook to attach!

My 'Felton Crosswind' got rather scruffy-looking where the paint had chipped off the conical part between flyer and drum, so I cleaned the paint right off the part with cellulose thinners, 'Vim' and 'Brasso'; it has polished up nicely and looks better in polished aluminium than it did painted, to my mind. If you find yours gets chipped likewise you'll know what to do. My 'Altex' has been completely paintless for years!

Your idea for Croxby sounds excellent. A *hut* to sleep in is positively luxurious! Will it be possible to have a night at Woldale too? It sounds somehow the kind of water where one might connect with whackers in the dark and have considerable excitement.

I expect you will have some more news of last week-end, which I am looking forward to hearing.

Best of luck,

RICHARD WALKER

Dear Richard,

I'm sorry to have broken the routine of our correspondence, but the past week seems to have slipped by without giving me a chance to write. I never seem to have time for all the jobs that are waiting to be done!

Well, to begin at the beginning: last Saturday week a friend,

John, and I went to Woldale to try our luck with the big carp. Conditions were not ideal—there was quite a cool wind blowing down the lake—and our results were not very good. We started fishing about 9 p.m. when the other anglers had packed up and neither of us had had a run when we knocked off about midnight. Four hours' sleep in the car and we were fishing again. Soon after we started again I had a very feeble run which proved to be a bream of about 2 lb. which had somehow engulfed a walnut-sized lump of paste. A sad anti-climax! About 5 a.m. John connected with a really big carp which ripped out fifty yards of line in a flash. He was just beginning to turn the fish when his line came slack and examination showed that his .016″ nylon had parted at the loop. The line knot was still intact, but there was no monofil attached. John had pinched a half-moon lead on to the loop of his cast to ensure that it laid flat on the bottom, and I suspect that it had damaged the nylon. A lesson learned the hard way! In future I think he will attach his lead to the tail of the loop knot. He was fishing with an 11 lb. 'Terylene' line; do you think it could have cut the nylon? Since I have taken up carp-fishing I always make a practice of doubling my reel line before tying on the cast. It may be my imagination, but I feel that by making the knot more bulky the strands of nylon are not nipped so tightly together and there is a cushioning effect. I tie my knot like this—if I can draw it—it has never let me down—yet!

A few minutes after the catastrophe, a very big fish leapt twice out in the middle of the pond. No doubt it was John's fish trying to rid itself of a size 1 Model Perfect hook and 2 yards of monofil. We had no more runs that morning.

Last Tuesday evening I decided I would have another crack at Croxby. It was a lovely evening. I dumped my tackle in the car and had gone about half a mile on my way when there was a loud crack and I discovered that the top two leaves of one of my front springs had snapped in half. There was no fishing that night!

On Friday evening I went over to Woldale with the intention of clearing a patch of weed in the Decoy Pond prior to an attack on the tench on Saturday morning. I had a chat with the Keeper, and he told me that the boat was leaking badly and out of commission, so I had to do my bit of cleaning from the bank. After a while I gave it up as a bad job, as the margin of the pond where I wanted to fish is so soft and quaking that the slightest movement sent ripples out over the water. I decided that it would be futile to fish under such conditions. Nevertheless I did turn out at about 4 a.m. on Saturday and fished from the firm bank which is so much frequented by anglers. Again there was a cool wind and there was not a sign of a tench on the move. Fishing with two rods—one paste and one worm—I caught two large eels on worm and then two more 'fishermen' arrived. They were apparently strangers to the place—they tramped up and down inspecting the pitches and then came and stood on the top of the bank, behind where I was in hiding amongst some reeds and commenced a lengthy barrage of questions about the fishing at Woldale. I was very patient and gave them all the information they required, and then packed up in disgust and was home in time for an early breakfast.

Last Saturday evening I took John to Croxby. He has been longing to go ever since he learned that I had joined the Club, and having promised him a visit I could not cry off in spite of the most wretched weather. We arrived at Croxby in a downpour and as all the bank pitches are fully exposed we decided to fish from two jetties which are overhung by a large horse-chestnut tree. The rain continued steadily and we never had a run until about 10 p.m. when John connected with a carp. He had not landed a carp before and was agog with excitement. In the battle he forgot, I suppose, where he was, took a step sideways and fell up to his waist in mud and water, from which position he continued to play his fish. It proved to be a common carp of 2½ lb., but to John it was ample recompense for his ducking. Then we returned home for dry clothes, scoured the town for petrol at 11.30 p.m. and were eventually successful, slept at home until 3 a.m. and then off to Croxby again. Once again it was raining when we arrived, but it soon stopped and as soon as the sun got up over the trees it very quickly became blazing hot. I got one fish of 4 lb. 10 ozs. and then began a most disconcerting series of incidents. I had six more runs without landing a single fish. On three of the runs I failed to connect with the fish at all, twice the fish was hooked but shed the hook very quickly, and once the fish ran straight out for about 40–50 yards and then swung round at the extremity of the line and headed straight into the reeds, where he very quickly transferred my hook from his mouth into some immovable object. My hooks were sharp, and I was striking at the height of the run—the only possible explanations I can think of are (1) my paste was too stiff (2) the fish were not taking the bait properly into their mouths—it was very hot and sunny, remember—or (3) they were small fish which were incapable of taking the bait fully into their mouths. John had a similar experience—he missed five runs.

A man fishing at the next pitch to me did not appear to be having the same difficulty. He caught several fish on potato. Do you think it is possible that when the fish are *really* feeding they will take potato or paste equally well—but that when they are not quite so hungry they can only be tempted to feed properly on potato?

So all things considered I have not had a very successful time since I wrote last.

Now to answer your queries about Croxby. I don't think it is very deep. The Secretary told me that at its deepest it is about 5–6 feet. There may be deeper holes, but I doubt it. I have fished without a float on each occasion so far and in almost every case the runs have been very decisive. I have found in my very limited experience so far that in the late evening and early morning I do best fishing close to the bank, but during the daytime I fish as far out as I can cast.

Have you contacted 'Pickle-Barrel' yet? I'll bet you were

anticipating a fight when he disappeared over your bait on your first visit to Temple Pool last Friday week.

I hope to have another evening at Croxby this week and at the week-end John and I are going to have another crack at Woldale. I am determined to get one of those big fellows this season—but I will save one or two for you!

I am looking forward now to hearing what you have to report.

Best wishes,

MAURICE INGHAM

PS. As you will have gathered, one *is* allowed to fish all night at Woldale. The weed, which a few weeks ago had shown signs of covering the greater part of the pond, has now died down and there is very little surface weed. Croxby has practically no surface weed.

Dear Maurice,

Too bad about the lost carp at Woldale, but at least it shows that they can be tempted there. I suppose that one was on paste? I expect you are right in surmising that the lead was responsible for the break. Your idea of a double-line knot sounds all right. Pete often uses a bit of that hard-fibred marshgrass and puts it in like this:

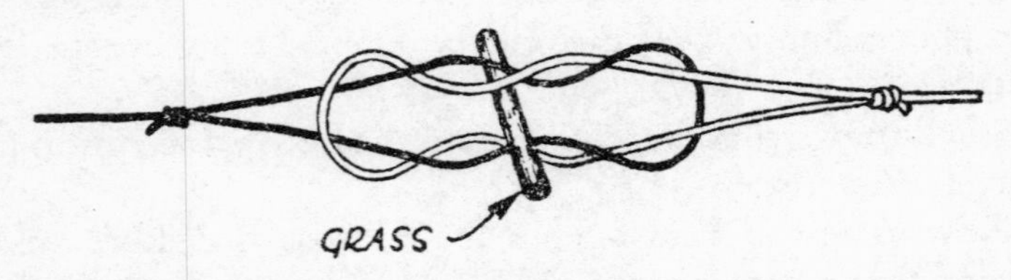

pull tight and cut ends of grass short. My usual method is this:

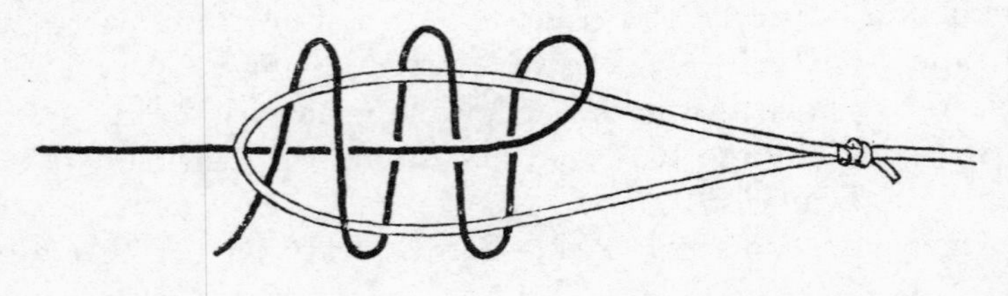

I should think a piece of rubber band would be best:

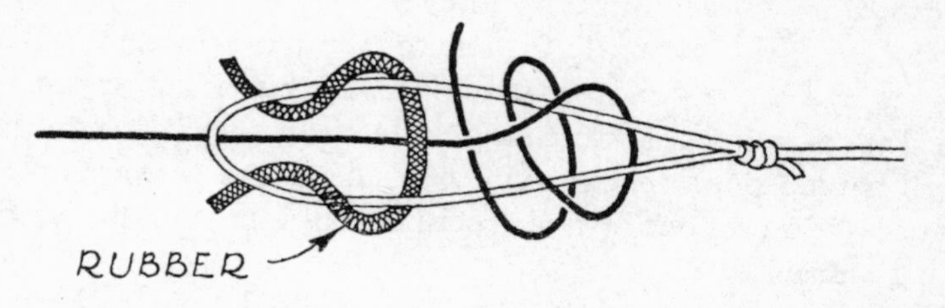

The rubber would be pulled up tight first before tightening the reel-line.

Both French and Belgian monofil appear to be superior to British. I wouldn't like to express an opinion as to whether 'Terylene' might cut the nylon; I think that it sounds possible. It may be that the best way would be to attach each cast to a tiny metal ring by a half-blood knot, and then attach the reel-line to the ring by the same means; that half-blood is a very strong and reliable knot. A small swivel would probably be just as effective as a ring; it wouldn't weigh as much as a shot. I think I will fit my casts up like that and see how it works out.

What you say about potato at Croxby is interesting, and it looks as if the carp there are well educated to it. I have often had a series of misses, exactly as you describe, on both worm and paste and have never come to a definite conclusion as to the reason. It can hardly be too-hard dough, because it happens in the same way on worm. And it isn't always small fish, because I rolled a fifteen-pounder over in one such a spell of misses last September. I think your second suggestion, that the fish were not taking the bait properly, is probably the right answer. I usually find that the runs which end in these misses are very fast and sudden ones, as if the carp were suspicious and, having plucked up enough courage to take the bait, had then become scared and bolted, ejecting the bait en route. Pete says the proper thing to do under these conditions is to use a float and strike at the slightest touch. Your friend John and my friend Pete appear to have some water-spaniel inclinations! Peter never hesitates to go in, if necessary up to the neck! Tell John that, having involuntarily learned the art, he will be a great asset to you in future. You can take up wildfowling and use him as a retriever.

No, no 'Pickle-Barrel'! I went to Temple Pool last Friday evening and had my eye wiped by Pete; he caught a 4½-pounder and I a 2-pound mirror, a dear little chap, which is now in Pete's garden pond, being trained to take bread from people's fingers, as do the four or five crucians from ½ lb. to 2 lb. which he has already.

On Sunday morning I went to Temple Pool alone and got a nice fish, 13½ lb., on a big piece of honey paste, with a bit of crust on the hook as well. I put that one back. I also hooked another fish which I didn't see, but which felt pretty powerful; it got into a fallen tree and I had to break after waiting about an hour to see if it would unravel itself. These were on 6 lb. 'Terylene' and there were some anxious moments before the 13-pounder was landed.

I asked about the depth at Croxby because I think it has a lot to do with night-fishing. When it gets cooler in the evening the surface is cooled. This cooler water sinks and is replaced by water from below. If a lake is shallow it is soon chilled right to the bottom and the fish go off feed; at Temple Pool they stop feeding before dark except in unusually warm evenings. Where the water is deeper, fish feed later, and in waters which have an ample reservoir of deep water they feed all night and are not very inclined to feed at any other time. This is theory of course, and liable to be upset!

Have you noticed much bubbling or mud-stirring at either Croxby or Woldale? In some waters it is very easy to find the carp by the soda-water bubbles which come up in clouds, or by the smoke-screens of disturbed mud which they put up.

I forgot to say I was using a float when I caught the 13-pounder on Sunday, a two-shot heron quill.

It's nice to hear that the weed is diminishing in your part of the world; our trout stream is about choked. We don't like to cut weed until a month after the Mayfly is over, as it may destroy their eggs. There has been a good hatch of Vulgata at Arlesey Lake; Danica finished on the trout stream about June 10th and

Vulgata commenced at Arlesey about the same time. I hope to transfer fly from Arlesey to the trout water and thus extend the season. Vulgata is a far darker fly than Danica and even the male imago has a decidedly buff body; Danica is ivory-white. I am going to try Mayfly nymphs as a bait at Arlesey. Perhaps one day I may hook that monstrous carp that lives there!

I have got wind of another carp water near a village called S——, which is about 18 miles away. It is not fished. My informant says there are carp there as big as sucking pigs! Actually he didn't say carp, but 'bloody great dark blue fish'. It belongs to a farmer who doesn't care who fishes there, so I'm told; I hope to investigate at the week-end.

I smashed my favourite fly-rod last week—22 years old. Now I must fix up a new top for it.

Not long now before our combined operations commence.

Good luck,

Richard Walker

X

July Letters

Dear Richard,

Yes, the carp at Woldale *can* be tempted, as I have proved today (Sunday).

John and I set out yesterday evening about 7 p.m. but had to wait until nearly 10 p.m. for the tiddler-snatchers to depart. It was a perfect evening and I had high hopes, but although we fished until midnight we didn't have a run. After a sleep in the car we commenced fishing again at 4 a.m. As I think I have told you, I have been in the habit of using two rods when carp-fishing —my carp-rod proper and another which is really quite unsuitable (actually it is one that I made by way of experiment last summer from one of the ex-W.D. tubular steel aerials that were so much advertised at that time). On the steel rod I was using my 6 lb. 'Terylene' line on a centre-pin reel, and a size 8 eyed Model Perfect hook on what I *thought* was .012″ nylon. I have since discovered that it was .010″ and not .012″. Careless, I agree, but very lucky that my rod *was* weak.

Both rods were baited with large lumps of honey paste and I felt confident that something would happen before long—(it was an ideal morning)—and it did! At 4.45 a.m. I had a terrific run on my light rod. By the time I picked up my rod and struck, the fish was halfway across the pond, and I only just managed to turn him before he gained the sanctuary of the overhanging horse-chestnut trees on the far side. I won't burden you with a detailed narrative about the long battle that ensued—it will suffice to say that it was most unspectacular, a test of patience and endurance rather than skill. He made no more fast runs, but put up a *most* dogged and determined fight and showed the most amazing strength. Fortunately, owing to my weak rod I was not able to exert the full strain that would have been possible with the .012″ cast which I *thought* I was using, and so the .010″ cast which I was actually using was not taxed as severely as it might have been. For *four hours* I could see no sign of weakening in the fish, then gradually the strength of his runs diminished and I was able to keep him more or less on the surface, but it was not until 11.25 a.m.—after playing him for 6 hours, 40 minutes—that we were able to land him. The landing *was* spectacular. John wielded his home-made net, a triangular one 24″ × 24″ × 30″, but in the heat of the moment he tried to lift the fish instead of dragging it and the net parted from the handle at the fork. Fortunately the net was deep, and I was able to grab it before the fish escaped. Throughout the battle the fish appeared to be getting bigger and bigger (and the net smaller and smaller) but it proved to be a mirror of 17 lb. exactly, in beautiful condition.

As the fight progressed I began to have grave doubts about the durability of the cast where it was rubbing against the fish's mouth, but I need not have bothered. The fish was hooked in the corner of the mouth with the shank of the hook protruding—*all* the cast was outside the fish's mouth.

That fish is going to be mounted in some form or other. At the moment he is reclining in my butcher's refrigerator.

I suppose that should be a lesson to me to use more appropriate tackle in future. I might—but I would not have missed that fight for anything. It didn't *seem* to last for more than an hour. I can now vouch for the fact that at least one half of that pond is virtually free of weed of any consequence!

How Albert Buckley managed to land his record fish on such fine tackle in such short time, I cannot imagine. I am positive that for the greater part of six hours I was applying a pressure that would have been the absolute limit possible on Buckley's 3½ lb. line and 4 x cast.

I am looking forward to seeing you in contact with one of the really big ones. There are many much bigger than mine and I'm sure some are record-breakers.

Please excuse me from replying to your letter this time. There are many jobs waiting to be done before we depart on our holiday on Wednesday morning and I am weary after the exertions of the past 24 hours.

We shall be in Devon from the 5th to the 19th. Please don't call a halt to our correspondence while I am on holiday. I shall be pleased to know if you have improved on your 13½-pounder and if the 'bloody great dark blue fish' at S—— were worth investigating—also what time you will be arriving on the 21st.

Sincerely,

MAURICE INGHAM

Dear Maurice,

What an excellent show! You've started your carp catching career in a big way. A seventeen-pounder is a whacker in any water. It will look fine stuffed, but don't let them do the usual dreadful embellishments in the case! If I were you I would just have the fish stuffed, and do the case myself. I saw a tench (only a three-pounder) done professionally yesterday, and it was terrible. The fish had a bright orange belly, a drawing-pin eye, and the symmetry of the verdigris-coloured bunches of rush in the case was ghastly.

I can see that you played the fish in a very careful way. 6 hours 40 minutes! If you had hooked it on the carp rod you'd have had it out in an hour. Harry Grief of Dagenham has just pulled out a 25 lb. 12 oz. fish in half an hour on 6 lb. line. I have seldom had even a 15-pounder out in that time! It is obvious that you are a cool-headed sort of bloke and there is no greater asset in playing big carp. Many congratulations! You have now the right to wear a large and flamboyant feather in your hat!

I am getting very excited indeed at the prospect of fishing Woldale. I hope the fame of your capture doesn't result in too much overcrowding there!

I failed dismally at Temple Pool on Saturday morning. I had no lobs and was forced to use paste or bread, which I don't like when carp are bubbling, as I think they are apt to mess about more with paste. Anyhow, I had three bites, missed one clean, hooked a scale off the next fish and was well and truly broken by the third, which was a real whacker, going on for 20 lb. He went under the same tree as last week's fish. Pete never had a bite. The previous evening was also a bad show. Pete hooked two big ones. The first, about 15 pounds, broke the line with a loud noise; it had apparently got caught twice round the pick-up. The second came unstuck. It had taken a crust within half a minute of its being cast out and I think the hardness of the crust prevented the hook from penetrating. I got two five-pounders on crust weighed with paste to just sink. There is a lot of flannel weed on the bottom and I want a bait that would not sink too deeply into it. It has rained since and I now have plenty of lobs.

On Sunday Pete and I went tench-fishing at Southill Park. I got three nice ones, 3 lb. 6 ozs., 3 lb. 11½ oz. and 4 lb. on 0.008″ nylon cast and lobworm. Pete drew a blank except for numerous perch up to 1 lb. Another angler had a tench of 3 lb. 10 ozs. and Bob a 2 lb. 9½ oz. perch which I am stuffing; it isn't a specimen but it's good practice and it will make a decoration (?).

The tench-fishing was quite amusing. I used my 15 ft. roach rod and watched for bubbles to come up, then dropped the lob in the middle of the 'froth'. It worked every time. These tench each took over ten minutes to land and were in excellent condition. They fought very hard indeed. We went over at 7 a.m. and at 9 a.m. the Club arrived in the coach. There was a suggestion that Pete and I should move to make room for match pegs, but we pointed out that the swim had been dragged and baited. (Yes, we dragged thoroughly as soon as we arrived and I had a tench on within five minutes of the drag's being put away.) So they put a peg in 10 yards away, each side of us. The man who drew the pitch on our left had a wooden rod rest.

As the ground was hard and dry, he found it necessary to hammer this in with a bit of branch about four inches thick. He had a shirt of Persil whiteness, as did our right-hand neighbour, who was using a 2 oz. coffin lead. Not a sizeable fish was caught in the whole match, except the 3 lb. 10 oz. tench, which was caught by a friend of mine who drew a pitch fifty yards from the main mob, on the far side of a bed of reed. He weighed in 10 lb. 14 oz. and won easily. The perch was caught on a small 'Vibro'. These 'Vibros' are pretty good; in addition to the perch about ten pike were caught, but they are not in season until October here. Bob doesn't fish in matches, and caught his perch well away from the crowd. We put the tench—my three and the 3 lb. 10 oz. fish—in the small field pond about half a mile from my house, where I told you we had previously put some carp. This pond is of fishable size, about 40 yards × 30 yards and 10 ft. deep in the deepest part. It is fed by a pipe from the trout stream. We hope to get some more carp to put in and to fish it next year. It will be nice for an occasional evening, unless it becomes too well known. I'm still looking out for a disused gravel pit to rent, and then we shall net all these fish out and transfer them.

Several carp have been seen in the club water at Arlesey Lake, probably some of those we put in last year.

I'll send up my box the day before I come, or perhaps before that, and it can wait at the station until I arrive. The pond at S—— is being investigated on Saturday next; I'll let you know what we discover.

Sincerely,
RICHARD WALKER

Dear Richard,

Please excuse this ghastly notepaper, which is all my wife could get in this remote corner of rural England.

After making a number of enquiries I came *very* reluctantly to the conclusion that I cannot afford to have my seventeen-pounder set up. I had not realized that it is such a costly business—and it grieves me that I have killed that fish unnecessarily. If I had had more time before my holiday I would have had a shot at setting it up myself, or of making a cast of it. As it is, I have had to content myself with a good photograph, which I am having enlarged to full size and which I may one day attempt to colour.

John took some photographs on the spot, which I have just had developed and printed. I am enclosing two pictures, one of me with the fish, and the other a delightful sylvan scene with me in the later stages of playing the fish. As you can see by the angle of the sun, it was then fairly late in the morning and the fish had been battling for several hours. He was beginning to get very tired and I was taking advantage of it to have a rest myself. After the first few minutes of the struggle my difficulty was not one of slowing the fish down, but of getting him to move around sufficiently to tire himself. Time after time he would make a short run, which I would check, and then he would bore down to the bottom and remain there motionless, and I would be powerless to shift him. A few well-placed stones thrown by John would set him moving again for a short time, and then the whole business would be repeated. I am not proud of the fact that it took me so long to land that fish, and I've no doubt that I could have landed it sooner if I had cared to play it a bit nearer to the safety limit of my tackle, but when I saw him for the first time I decided that I *was* going to land him and I would not risk a break for the sake of playing him a little longer.

I don't think you need fear overcrowding at Woldale. A number of local anglers have displayed a certain amount of interest and envy over my fish, but I think the chances of any one of them turning up at Woldale at a time that matters is very remote. One of the oldest members of the local angling club said when he saw the fish, 'Well, I'm damned! I've been fishing for xxx years and that is the fish I've always dreamed of, but never caught. I'm going home now to burn my rods.' I am prepared to bet a considerable amount that he has never fished all night in his life, and I imagine it is most unlikely that he has ever started fishing before breakfast.

Your tench fishing sounds very interesting. I have caught tench at Woldale Decoy Pond using exactly the same method that you used—dropping a worm into the midst of the bubbles.

I have not caught any there so far this season, but I mean to have a go. There really are some monsters.

I haven't done any serious fishing since I arrived here. I have offered a silver Devon to the bass in the estuary on two occasions without result—I may have a crack at them from a boat next week.

I'm looking forward to hearing about S—— and what you discovered on your visit to-day. These 'unfished' ponds are always immensely attractive, but rarely live up to their reputations. I hope yours is an exception.

Sincerely,

MAURICE INGHAM

Dear Maurice,

I suppose it's too late to hope, but if that carp is still refrigerated, get it sent here. I can stuff it! My goodness, why ever didn't you telegraph me or something; I *like* stuffing fish and can't get enough; I don't like to kill carp just to practice stuffing on. If the carp isn't actually buried or burned or fed to the pigs, get it sent to me pronto. If it's too late, you'll have to catch another and I'll stuff that. I did the perch of 2 lb. 9½ ozs. last week, and it looks *exactly like a stuffed perch*, according to my wife.

I find that I can get a much more pleasing result by using coloured spirit ink, rather than opaque paint as the professional stuffers do, and just brightening up the natural colours between successive coats of cellulose varnish. I've been examining some samples of professional stuffing lately and I don't think much of them. I want to do a big chub as soon as I can catch one, to see if I can devise a way of preserving the silver on the scales.

If you get another good carp while I am in Lincolnshire we can bring it back here and I'll stuff it 'while you wait'! If *I* get one, I'd like to bring it back alive and put it in our small pond. We got two small fish last Sunday, 3 lb. and 4 lb., so the population of the pond, which is called Oughton Pond, is now:

Carp, 7, 7, 5, 4½, 4, 5¾, 5½, 4, 3.

Tench, 4, 3¾, 3–10 oz., 3–6 oz., 8 oz.

I am hoping to go to Southill next week-end, and catch some more tench for the Oughton Pond. I am also negotiating for the fishing in another small stream-fed pond, about a mile from where I live. It is a made stew-pond and big enough to fish. I rather like ponds of 'farm' size, say 30 yards wide, and have had some fine sport in such places.

I couldn't go to S—— after all, as it was necessary to tackle my bees. Pete went, accompanied by our club secretary. The water undoubtedly contains carp but they didn't see any, so we don't know about the size. There was a Carp-Fisher actually on the job there, complete with 'Water Rail' rod and 'Felton Cross-wind'! After some conversation, this chap asked our secretary if he knew the name and address of the secretary of our angling club. He also recommended Pete to get hold of the back numbers of the *Fishing Gazette* containing articles by 'Water Rail' on carp-fishing. I understand some hilarity ensued. While they were there this carp-fisher got himself attached to a carp which went up a tree and broke him. He also caught a whacking great eel. Pete says the water is very badly choked with trees, both dead and alive, growing (or standing) on the bottom, but that he thinks there must be plenty of carp, judging by the mud-stirring.

I have lots of lobs. Shall I send some up to you next week, or can you get them easily?

I like the photograph of you playing the carp very much, the composition is fine and the whole atmosphere of the picture is pure carp-fishing. I am writing a book *Still-water Angling* and I would like very much to use this picture in it, if you would agree. I should also like a whole-plate enlargement of it to decorate my workshop, so if you can get a couple of good size prints I shall be very grateful indeed.

Wasn't it a *fat* carp! Lovely condition and a back like a fat little pig. I hope I manage to get one like it! I think you were very wise to take your time about playing it. In any case the end justified the means. When these big fish settle down to a really dogged fight, as they so often do, one just has to be patient. Of course the more you can keep them on the move the sooner they are beaten, but you can't expect to lift seventeen-pounders off the bottom with light tackle.

I understand perfectly what you mean about the comments

on your fish. It always irritates me when people who are lazy, clumsy and stupid tell me how lucky I am to have caught a good fish. One of our club members told me I was 'a lucky old bug-bear' (or some such expression) to get those three tench I told you about. He arrived at 10 a.m. He hooked a tench, which I think was over 3 lb., but 'couldn't hold it'. He wears a beautiful white shirt. Not content with standing up on the bank, he wades in as far as his gumboots will permit. I've never known him catch a fish over 8 oz. According to him, Pete and I are *born* lucky; some people are, he says; others, like himself, are just unlucky, but in spite of being dogged by ill-fortune, they remain keen as ever and come up smiling, their heads 'bloody but unbowed'. Poor fellows! Once I was rash enough to explain concisely to one such, exactly *why* he never got a decent fish. He has hardly spoken to me since!

If you're doing some sea-fishing, be careful with your tackle, and wash everything thoroughly, dry, and oil, or you will find the sea-water has had an appalling effect on it.

I have just heard that 'B.B.' is on holiday near Kingsbridge, too. What a coincidence—why don't you call and see him?

See you soon. Good luck.

RICHARD WALKER

Dear Richard,

Your letter has just arrived and I am dashing off this note for posting in Kingsbridge this morning.

Many thanks for the offer to stuff my fish. I am extremely grateful. I left the fish with my father, who was hoping to keep it in his butcher's 'frig' to show to my brother when he returns from his holiday. I am sending him a telegram this morning asking him to send it, if still intact, to you by the quickest possible route, and to advise you of its time of arrival. It will no doubt have been badly mauled by the various people to whom I'm quite sure father will have exhibited it. If you think it is too badly damaged don't bother about it.

Yours,

MAURICE INGHAM

Dear Richard,

I have sad news. The carp has been disposed of—buried, I think—so I'm afraid I cannot take advantage of your kind offer to stuff it for me. Too bad, but there it is! I'll let you know in double-quick time when I catch my twenty-pounder though.

I was very pleased to hear that 'B.B.' is staying down here and I paid him a visit yesterday. What an interesting chap he is! We spent the whole afternoon talking—mostly fishing talk—it was a wretched wet afternoon and the time passed most pleasantly. He was particularly interested in Woldale and Croxby and in my seventeen-pound carp. I am hoping that he will pay us a visit next season and have a crack at some of the Woldale monsters himself. He was very distressed to learn that my seventeen-pounder has been buried—he is quite convinced that I shall never catch another carp as big, but I really cannot see any good reason why I should not get a twenty-pounder sometime.[1] I'm quite certain there are twenty-pounders at Woldale and if the seventeen-pounders are catchable I don't see why the twenty-pounders should not be catchable also. Anyway, I mean to keep trying.

My capture of the seventeen-pounder found its way into the local papers by devious routes and the report, as usual, contained several mistakes, the most amusing of which was a description of the fish as being 'a little over 27 feet in length'! Some fish!!

I have been out twice bass-fishing, and have caught a few fish. They put up quite a good fight on reasonably light tackle, but there is not much skill required. We merely 'stooged' around in the boat, trailing a sand-eel behind us, the fish hooked themselves and it was just a matter of giving sufficient line and allowing the fish time to tire themselves. With limitless water to play the fish in and no obstructions to foul the line, he would be a very poor angler indeed who could not land every bass he hooked.

John has written to say that he will be very pleased to let you use the photograph of me playing that carp, as an illustration in your book. He is a very capable amateur photographer and seems

[1] We have *both* caught twenty-pounders since this was written.

to have an instinctive appreciation of grouping and light and shade.

I expect this will be the last letter I shall write to you before our combined ops., so until I meet you off the train,

Best wishes,

MAURICE.

Dear Maurice,

I'm glad you got in touch with 'B.B.'. He's a most interesting chap to talk to, and knows a lot about carp. I expect he was interested in Woldale and Croxby—he and I have had them marked for a visit for a long time—in fact, 'B.B.' would have been at Croxby in 1947 if I hadn't lured him down here (to catch his best fish so far).

Too bad about the fish, but I don't see why you shouldn't catch one even bigger. If you do I'll gladly have a shot at stuffing it; I don't see any difficulty, although I've never tried stuffing a carp. I'd a lot sooner tackle a big fish than a little one. The only kinds of fish which I'm not confident about are silvery ones. I did another perch on Sunday evening, just for practice, a fish of 2 lb. 2 oz. and the actual skinning and stuffing took 1 hour, 40 minutes. If I take another two hours (a generous allowance) to paint and varnish, it still comes out at under four hours' work. I doubt if it would take more than double that time to do a twenty-pound fish. If I ever do stuff a fish for you, you'll have to cope with the case and herbaceous border yourself!

The perch was caught on Sunday morning at Southill Park on a medium lob. We started at 3 a.m. and it was raining cats and dogs. The rain stopped at about 5 a.m. and then the wind started—a real gale which lasted all the time we were there, i.e. until lunch-time. I got this perch and a couple of tench, 3½ lb. each, which we transferred to Oughton Pond. That makes six tench in there over 3 lb. 6 ozs., four females and two males. Pete hooked a whacking tench, the biggest I ever saw on a line. I would hesitate to guess its weight. He played it well—he only had a light 8 ft. split cane threadline rod, which I made him—and had about a yard to pull it over the net, when the split-shot holding the pierced bullet came off, allowing the bullet to drop down the line straight into the tench's mouth, knocking out the hook instantly! There are some splendid tench in that lake; they average over 3 lb., but I never saw one as big as this before. I like tench. We must try our luck on those at Woldale. I'll bring some lobs.

I'm glad you got some bass, but like you I find sea-fishing rather dull from the point of view of skill and intelligence. It may be that there's more in it than there appears to be. I like quiet ponds myself, though I mean to go to Christchurch and catch a barbel and a chub some day.

Please thank John for letting me use the photograph. It's the best fishing picture I've ever seen, though I think it would take a carp-fisher to appreciate it properly.

Are *your* local papers like that, too? I've featured in our local paper on numerous occasions for one reason or another (all legitimate, so far) and I've *never* known them print an accurate report. My sixteen-pounder was reported as follows: 'Described as a specimen fish, Mr. Richard Walker landed a carp . . .', etc. The boys had plenty of fun out of that, asking me whether I preferred worms or paste and if I'd prefer to be set up by Homer or Cooper.

One of these days I'll have a shot at making a model of your carp, full size. I think it might be possible to make a presentable job of it, working from the photograph and a small mirror carp which could be stuffed first of all. I must collect some scales.

See you soon,

RICHARD WALKER

Dear B.B.,

Your letter about Lackey's Leap was waiting when I arrived home. I've been to spend a few days with Maurice. I'll tell you all about it!

We spent the first morning examining one another's tackle! Maurice's net was a magnificent affair and beautifully made. It looked gigantic leaning against the wall; I was greatly impressed with it. In the afternoon we set out for Woldale Lake. It is a beautiful spot, well sheltered with trees and with a strong *smell* of carp. There is a definite indescribable smell which is always associated with waters where there are carp; whether it is the smell of the carp themselves, or of natural gases released by their stirring-up of the bottom I don't know, but there is no doubt about the affinity between the carp and the smell!

This first visit was a reconnaissance. It was a perfect evening, calm and warm. We didn't see any carp, but there was one tremendous swirl as we walked round, obviously made by a big fish disturbed by our footsteps. I liked the look of the water very much.

The following evening we went to Croxby. Croxby is one of those waters which is disturbed by the slightest breeze. It lies in a valley which funnels the wind, and on this occasion there was a decided chop on the water which I didn't like at all. We hadn't been fishing long before it commenced raining, and this continued throughout the evening, night and following morning.

Croxby is in the hands of a syndicate, and a hut is provided where tackle, keep-nets, etc., can be stowed. Pegs on the wall house rods, full-length, and there were dozens of rods all rigged up, resting horizontally against the walls. The popularity of the 'Ambidex' fixed-spool reel was obvious. All these rods were rigged with very light tackle, which surprised me until I remembered that the average carp at Croxby is not of great size.

During the evening Maurice caught a carp, a tench and an eel. The carp was about three pounds, very long and slim. On the ten-pound tackle it hadn't much chance and was soon ashore. The tench was a little one, about half-a-pound, and the eel was even littler, a little wretch of the most efficient line-knotting size. I had one bite and caught a tench about the same size as Maurice's.

At dusk it became cold, wet and miserable and we retired to the hut for food and sleep. I awoke long before light and went out in the drizzle to fish. First I caught tench—four of them, the biggest about a pound. I was baiting with walnut-sized lumps of paste, which these little tench appeared to find no difficulty in absorbing. They were thin, pale-coloured tench and gave me the impression that at the present time Croxby is greatly overstocked.

Just as it began to get light I hooked a carp. It went off like lightning—the line fairly hissed through the water—and before I could turn it, had shot under one of the jetties which have been constructed to allow anglers to get beyond the reeds. I checked it far too heavily, with the result that the cast broke. I don't think it was a very big fish, and estimate its weight at six or seven pounds.

I was soon fishing again, with a fresh cast, and it was not long before I had another run and was into a second carp, a fish of about three and a half pounds. It, too, went very fast indeed; the long thin build of these Croxby carp evidently helps their speed. But it was soon beaten, and then I realized that the landing-net was in the hut. My shouts roused Maurice, who came and netted the fish. Then he commenced fishing and very soon had another fish similar to mine. But the rain was falling more and more heavily; it showed no sign of ceasing, and we packed up and went home.

During the morning we slept, and set out for Woldale after lunch. Great bubblings were to be seen when we arrived, but worms and paste offered to the bubblers met with no response. I put one or two loose crusts along the margin where I was fishing, and just before sunset one of these was stealthily removed. It was soon replaced by another, this time on a hook. This, too, after an interval of about ten minutes, was also removed without the fish being hooked. The next occurrence was a run on my other rod, which was baited with lobworm. This proved to be a fine eel of about two pounds, which was duly landed and decapitated. Then the light began to fail. Presently the crust was sucked down again and the answering strike connected with something solid, which rushed out about twenty yards of line. After a battle lasting about five minutes, Maurice, who had come round with the net, got the fish out. It proved to be a very ugly common carp, with both its gill-covers heavily scarred, weighing about five pounds. This was consigned to the keep-net.

Maurice had a run just before midnight, which he missed. It was quickly followed by another, which produced a bream of about two pounds.

After the disturbance of landing my carp I had moved to the opposite corner of the lake, close to the chestnut tree. I had heard sucking noises there, so I put out another floating crust just over the edge of the bank. At 2 a.m. the rod-top bent down slowly and I struck. Something went away quickly and made the reel scream, but the run was soon checked. The scream of the reel brought Maurice with net and lamp. The fish put up a good fight, but we soon saw that it was another small common carp, about the same size as the first. It was duly landed, and we were pleased to see that this was a much nicer-looking fish than the other—bright gold and in splendid condition. When we went to put it in the net we found that the other fish had somehow contrived to escape!

It had now become colder and we decided that sleep was indicated. At dawn we recommenced fishing, but with no result. Later on, when the sun was on the water, I crept round the lake and found a tremendous fish, close to the bank, in a sort of bay in the reeds. He really was a whacker, every ounce of twenty pounds and perhaps more. I offered him a lobworm. He sucked it in at once. Then I tried to be too clever. He was turning as he took the worm, and I decided to wait until he had turned right round, facing the open water, before striking, so that when he felt the hook he would go out instead of into the reeds. Alas! he spat the worm out before he had fully turned, then departed stealthily into the reeds. Mistake No. 1!

Just before lunch we went home. We discussed the situation and decided that as there were much bigger carp at Woldale than at Croxby, the former was the better water for future attacks.

In the afternoon we explored Maurice's trout-stream with worms. It is a delightful little brook, full of trout, and swift-running. One or two bits are just fishable with fly, and with a tiny six or seven-foot rod a lot of fun could be had. It was obvious that the rod Maurice had made from the split cane I sent him was far too long at eight feet. I used my little six-foot spinning rod, No. 1 Altex, and a lively lob, and got three trout of six ounces, three ounces and two ounces, the last two being rainbows. I saw one or two fish of about a pound, but they were too cunning for me. This stream struck me as having great possibilities; some damming here and there would double the volume of water and make some fine pools.

We went to Woldale again after tea; it was dark when we arrived. I had three runs during the night, each of which produced a bream. It was rather chilly, with intermittent drizzling rain, and I was not surprised to find floating crust ignored, even by the small roach which had attacked it vigorously the night before. Nothing happened in the early morning, but later on I found a carp feeding on the bottom near the west bank. I could see only his tail, but that looked big enough to belong to a fifteen-pounder. He didn't seem interested in lobworms and presently moved off into deeper water.

Then I found another standing on his head close to the bank, with an even bigger tail. This one wasn't interested in lobs either, but stayed rooting about while I got my other rod, which had a large lump of paste on the hook, left over from the night-fishing. The carp took this in his stride and glided off with it, the line running steadily out behind him. I struck; there was a great swirl, and the lump of paste shot past my ear. When I examined it, it was stiff as putty, with a hard crust where it had lain drying on the bank for four or five hours; of course this had prevented the point of the hook from penetrating. Mistake No. 2!

After this I no longer felt competent to fish for carp, and baited with a dead fish—a little roach—and caught an eel. Maurice, who had done likewise, was the sufferer. The eel got round his line, and before we could get it out had made a tangle of line which was almost unbelievable. It consisted of a ball, about the size of a tennis ball, liberally plastered with slime, and it took Maurice two hours to unravel it.

Two other anglers arrived while this was in progress, and they appeared greatly impressed with the size of the eel—which weighed $2\frac{3}{4}$ lb. The conversation soon turned to carp, and mention was made of a Mr. Harry Sheckell, who was said to have a 25-pound carp in a glass case in his house. We were told of the water in which it was captured—called Tubbs' Pit—and of the monster carp which inhabited it—how these chaps had fished there one evening, and a great carp had come up for a floating crust—it had gone 'Bloody gobble, gobble, gobble' at the crust, and lines had been withdrawn hastily in case the fish might decide to take one of the baited hooks.

The appearance of this monster carp was said to foretell a death in the family who owned the water, and there had been two examples of this within recent years; the keepers now had instructions to shoot the fish at sight, but had, so far, been unsuccessful!

Maurice obtained the location of this water; we then wished our informants good luck and went home for lunch.

On the following morning we went to the trout farm, about which Maurice had told me in his letters. It is based on an old mill, from every window of which there peered at us the faces of cats! I like cats, and was pleased to see so many, all with amiable expressions. We were shown round the trout farm and the sight of a shoal of hundreds of great rainbow trout, from three to five pounds or so, was most impressive. Then we attacked the chub. I tried the mill-pond and caught a couple of half-pounders on black slug; then I went below and fished the right bank of the pool with lobworm on float tackle. First came another half-pound chub, then a series of missed bites, then an eel of about a pound. There was a great deal of bubbling from the bottom in the mill-pool, which was obviously being caused by fish and which I should have attributed to bream had I not been assured that there were no bream in the water. I tried lobworms in the midst of the bubblings without result, so I doubt if eels could have been responsible.

After an unsuccessful spell with the worm I made up some breadpaste and tried swimming this round the eddy at the side of the main run of water, throwing in a little soaked squashed bread at intervals. These tactics were rewarded by two better chub, fish of about 1 lb. and 1½ lb. respectively, which put up quite a fight on the light tackle—0.008″ nylon and No. 10 hook, which I was using with the Avon rod.

Maurice, fishing in the same pool on the other side, was swimming-down with float-tackle in the main run of water and checking his tackle as the float reached the point where the depth began to decrease. By this means he caught several small chub and one bigger one of about 1½ to 1¾ lb.

Although very small game compared to carp, these chub were interesting and sporting fish and I enjoyed fishing for them very much. So, too, did Maurice, with the result that we both stayed much longer than we had intended, and were about three hours late for lunch!

We went again to Woldale in the evening. I put out two rods, one baited with paste and the other with a floating crust just over the bank. During the hours of darkness I caught three more bream up to about 2 lb. on the paste; it was rather chilly again and the carp were not much in evidence. In the morning some loud 'clooping' was heard from the rush-beds and I went round to investigate. The sun had risen and on my way round the lake I spotted a shoal of fish basking in a patch of sunlight under the big chestnut tree. For a few seconds I couldn't understand what they were; then I realized that they were chub. It came as a surprise to find chub in such a lake; there were some big ones, too, up to four pounds or so. I offered the assembly a lobworm which was taken instantly and I soon had the fish out; about 1½ lb. I carried it round to show Maurice, who had no idea that the water contained chub.

A return to the rush-bed from whence the 'clooping' had emanated disclosed that a big carp was feeding among them; smackings and wavings of the rushes indicated his progress. I baited with a big piece of paste and dropped it into a clear space towards which the carp appeared to be making. He arrived there about twenty minutes later and looked at the paste, then fled suddenly in terror out into the middle of the lake.

Shortly after this I caught an eel of about 2½ lb., and we then packed up. After lunch, a sleep, and tea, we set off for my home.

My impression of Woldale is that it undoubtedly contains some very big carp indeed, and that they are not too difficult to catch. They are very stealthy and unobtrusive in their movements, except when one leaps occasionally; but a combination of good weather and greater competence on my part ought to have produced two or three good fish. I have every intention of trying there again.

I am not going to tell you what happened to us at Temple Pool, because I have no doubt you will be hearing from Maurice!

The West Midlands Pool sounds most attractive and I should like to go with you very much. If the carp reported caught there *really* weighed 27½ lb. it is a record-breaker. 'Lackey's Leap' sounds a funny name—what's the origin?

Sincerely,

DICK

Dear 'B.B.',

When we met in Devonshire a couple of weeks ago I mentioned that I was going to spend a few days with Dick, and you asked me to let you know how I fared with the Temple Pool carp.

Well, I have just returned from a most enjoyable week-end and although I have little to report in the way of fish actually caught, you may be interested to learn what we did to *try* to catch fish.

We left here on Thursday evening after our combined assault on the Woldale carp—about which I think Dick has written you—and our arrival about 11.30 p.m. caused considerable upheaval in the Walker household. Dick had written to Mrs. Walker on Wednesday afternoon, but for some mysterious reason the letter announcing our arrival had not been delivered and no arrangements had been made for our accommodation. Ruth waved her magic wand, however, and we were very soon fed and bedded down.

On Friday morning we made a tour of the local angling waters. First of all we had a look at the River Oughton, a delightful little stream with a good head of trout. Before we set out Dick had strict instructions to bring back some trout for supper and these we caught very quickly in unique fashion by fishing over the parapet of a bridge and flicking a hook baited with a lobworm upstream under the bridge! That culvert must be a favourite haunt of the Oughton trout because we caught four lovely fish of about ¾ lb. each in a very short time.

Having caught our supper we continued our tour of inspection, visiting next Maylin's Pool. This is a very dark, deep-looking pool, with considerable beds of weeds and lots of willows in the water. Dick tells me that this water contains some good carp, but the fishing is somewhat crowded and being alongside a busy highway and adjoining an airfield this pool did not appeal to me as an ideal spot for serious carp fishing. It seemed to lack the quiet atmosphere which I associate with carp.

Arlesey Lake, which we visited next, is, I understand, a flooded gravel pit. It is a large expanse of water which on account of its great depth, appears an unusually vivid greenish blue colour. The sides slope down very steeply and there are no marginal shallows. Even the reeds, where they exist at all, are confined to a very narrow fringe, and altogether the place presents a cold and forbidding appearance. Dick tells me that he has twice seen a gigantic carp there, which he says must weigh over 40 lb. and there are some very big perch, but it would be a difficult place to fish. It is all so deep and all the pitches look so much alike that I would not know where to start. On our final visit to Woldale Dick caught an eel of about 3 lb., which he took home for his cats, but as they were well provided with food for the moment he decided to try an experiment with it. It would appear that one or two of the members of the local angling club, which owns the fishing rights of the Lake, are somewhat addicted to exaggeration, and having disposed of the eel in a prominent position near the Lake, Dick said it would be interesting to see how long it would be before someone claimed its 'capture', and how much it had 'grown' in the meantime. I shall look forward to hearing more of that eel!

The next two waters that we visited were also flooded pits and like Arlesey Lake were deep and unattractive. The smaller of the two had an area of some two or three acres and was set as if in the crater of a volcano, surrounded by almost vertical cliffs about 50 feet high. The other was a very large expanse of water and I understand that the workings flooded very quickly before any of the machinery could be removed. Dredgers and derricks can be seen sticking out of the water, and Dick tells me that cables and trucks and similar obstructions on the bed of the old workings makes bottom fishing a hazardous undertaking. The water in both these pits has a very decided milky appearance.

Our final call was at Brickhill Pond, where Dick has caught so many of his big carp. You have caught carp there too, I believe, so I will not weary you with a description of the place, except to say that I was surprised to find such a secluded and obviously carpy spot in the midst of a modern housing estate. What a great pity that one is no longer permitted to fish there.

After lunch we retired to Dick's workshop, where we spent a most enjoyable afternoon examining his tackle and trophies and discussing matters piscatorial. I really must have a shot at mounting some fish. The two perch and that magnificent 4½ pound trout which are now adorning the walls of Dick's workshop are the equal of any stuffed fish I have ever seen. I got to know—too late unfortunately—that Dick would have stuffed my 17-pound carp. If I get in a bit of practice I may become sufficiently proficient to stuff my 20-pounder when it comes along. I still think I shall get him one day, in spite of what you say to the contrary![1]

After tea we paid our first visit to Temple Pool. Isn't it a beautiful spot! Dick claims that few people know of its existence and after seeing it I am not surprised. We turned off the main road along a lane which after half a mile or so became no more than a farm track running between high hawthorn hedges and under overhanging trees. Parking the car beside a haystack, we unloaded the tackle and passed through a handgate along a leafy overgrown path. The thumping of the hydraulic ram betrayed the presence of the Pool, but even warned as I was by the sound I did not realize that we had arrived at the waterside until I almost put my foot in it. The sun was slanting through the trees which enclose the Pool on all sides, and several carp could be seen basking or cruising slowly just below the surface, but although we had approached the water with the utmost caution

[1] A prophecy that was fulfilled, July, 1952.

and remained concealed by the trees, these fish seemed to be aware of our presence and sank slowly out of sight, or glided into the sanctuary of the beds of weeds. The Pool is just as you described it, shaped something like an elongated triangle, about 250 yards long, with a small stream flowing in at the apex and an overflow at the narrow base. The water is not deep, being about five feet at the most, but contains plenty of cover in the form of weed beds and overhanging trees and bushes, and I have never seen a more secluded and peaceful spot or a more ideal carp water. After a very careful reconnaissance, during which we saw many carp up to about 15 pounds in weight, we began to fish. I chose a gap in the weeds where the sun was on the water and tried floating breadcrust, on which I have yet to catch a carp. Dick, being a perfect host, took the less attractive shaded side, where he began to fish with lobworms.

From my concealed observation post behind an overhanging willow I watched several big carp come into the gap in the weeds near my bait. One big fellow cruised slowly round the crust, eyeing it very critically from all angles and then slowly turned away into the weed bed. A few minutes later I saw his face appear through the wall of weeds, as he pushed his way slowly through and glided deliberately towards my bait. My heart thumped and my hand hovered over my rod butt, and I thought that here after only half an hour's fishing was carp number one, but for some inexplicable reason, after nosing at the bait for a few moments, he turned and floated back into the weed bed. During the next hour or so several more carp glided slowly across the patch of open water near my bait, but none showed any interest in it.

By now the sun was off the water and I changed the breadcrust for a big lobworm and moved to another spot at the shallow end of the Pool. I had not been fishing long in this new position when I heard Dick over on the opposite bank commence to whistle softly 'Cock o' the North', which I knew from our experience at Woldale, was a sure indication that he was fast into a fish. A glance through the overhanging branches of the tree under which I was sitting confirmed this—his rod was bent over in a most exciting arc and the quivering line slanted down into a patch of weeds out in the middle of the Pool. By the time I had made my way round to Dick's side with the landing net he had got his fish clear of the weeds and it was circling in the open water immediately in front of him, obviously very tired. After one or two more runs, which were easily checked, the fish rolled over on to its side and it was drawn over the waiting net. It was a mirror carp of 7¾ lb., a beautifully proportioned fish, which after being weighed was deposited in Dick's capacious keepnet. He had been fishing with lobworms throughout, but after laying-on for some time without success he had resorted to 'stalking' the fish, a method which was so very nearly crowned with success at Woldale. He crept stealthily along the bank until he saw some bubbling or swirls of muddy water which indicated a feeding carp, and then dropped his lobworm into the midst of the disturbance. The carp that he landed took his bait almost immediately, and so did another fish earlier, with which Dick had failed to connect. It is a very pretty method of fishing, which calls for infinite patience, extreme caution and great skill and accuracy in casting.

During the next hour's fishing I had several feeble runs, which I suspect were caused by roach tugging at the tail of the lobworm, but I did not hook a fish and when we packed up our tackle Dick had nothing further to report.

The carp was removed from the keepnet, wrapped in a wet sack and transported post haste to a small pond near Dick's home where, after a few false starts, it swam away quite happily. This little pond now contains quite a good stock of carp and tench which Dick and his friends have introduced from time to time, and it will be a very pleasant little spot to fish in a year or so when the fish have settled down.

Saturday morning found us again at the Temple Pool in time to see the sun rise and send shafts of light through the trees on to the steaming surface of the water. It was a perfect morning and we had high hopes, but the fish showed little interest in our baits. Again I had several feeble runs—perhaps prolonged twitchings of the line would be a better description—which set my heart racing, but which came to nought. Roach again, I fear. The sun was well over the trees and I was beginning to think our chances of encountering any carp before evening were fast diminishing when Dick had a run from a pitch near where a large hawthorn bush had fallen into the water. This fish put up a grand fight and Dick appeared to have it well under control when it made a last dash for freedom and dived straight into the submerged branches of the hawthorn bush before any side strain could be exerted to change its course. What an amazing faculty carp possess for disengaging hooks from their mouths and transferring them to immobile inanimate objects!

About half an hour later Dick hooked another carp in the same spot and it escaped in exactly the same way as the first, by diving into the fallen hawthorn bush. It was not our lucky day.

We fished a while longer without success and as there appeared to be little chance of catching carp before evening we packed up our tackle and took a stroll through the woods to the upper lake. As you may know, this lake, which was formerly stocked with trout, had become badly silted up and choked with weed and last year it was drained and cleaned out. The few remaining trout were removed to an enclosed stretch of the stream which connects the two lakes, and for some time we occupied ourselves by flicking pieces of paste to these fish. The water was crystal clear, and it was amusing to see how these fish, usually so shy, darted at the scraps of dough for all the world like a crowd of hens scrambling for a tit-bit. The upper lake has now been refilled and presents a strikingly beautiful picture. The bed of the lake is completely covered with a dense growth of weed of the most vivid green, the brightness of which is accentuated by the sparkling clear water above it. A wooded island, a pair of swans, a stately old mansion with lawns running down to the lake and a grand backcloth of trees complete the scene.

After lunch we paid a visit to the tackle shop in town, where Dick appears to have 'the run of the place'. We browsed through the stock, examined all the new items and departed to the poulterers where, again, Dick seems to have carte blanche. Unattended and unannounced we wandered through the shop to the store room in the back regions, where rows of carcases of dressed poultry were hanging. Dick ran an expert eye along the racks, plucked a hackle from a neck here and there and finally dismissed the lot as being of no value for fly-tying. Now that I have started tying my own flies I must try to get on similar good terms with my local poulterer, who would, I think, be able to keep me supplied with practically all the feathers I am ever likely to need.

Our venture to Temple Pool on Saturday evening was a complete failure. The weather had taken a distinct turn for the worse, the sky was full of heavy clouds and a cool wind had sprung up. To make matters worse, the lobworms, the last of Dick's laboriously gathered stock, had been accidentally put into a tin which had formerly contained alum and saltpetre—an adjunct of Dick's fish stuffing activities—and when we wanted to bait up we found that all the worms were dead. All the carp had vanished and one might have imagined that the lake contained no fish whatsoever, but, with the thought strong in our minds of Albert Buckley's capture of his record 26-pounder in a howling gale, we fished with bread paste until it was too dark to see—without success.

After supper we had a worm-hunt on Dick's lawn. It is great fun, isn't it? He had poured several buckets of water on to the lawn before supper and we very quickly collected a supply of fine lobs for our final assault on the Temple Pool carp the following morning.

Sunday morning was bright and clear, but there was still a cool wind, and conditions were not ideal for carp fishing. We fished really hard, determined to make a success of our final combined operation, but it was to no avail. Apart from the now familiar twitchings of the line, nothing occurred to indicate that a carp was taking an interest in my bait, and when there seemed to be no longer any chance of catching a carp, at Dick's suggestion I put up some light tackle to try for some roach. This fishing proved too easy, though—with a single maggot and a good cloud of groundbait I was able to catch fish at every cast—and it soon palled. What strange perverse creatures we anglers are! If the fish are difficult to catch we try our damnedest and endure considerable hardship to catch them, but if they are easily caught we are no longer interested in them. It is not the kill but the hunt, the battle of instinct versus reason, which provides the sport and makes angling such an absorbing and fascinating pursuit.

As the sun rose higher and the water warmed up after the cold night the carp began to emerge from their secret retreats and we spotted 'Pickle Barrel'. You will remember how Dick hooked this fish last summer, how he lost it only after a terrific battle during which the cast adjacent to the hook was worn completely through by prolonged rubbing against the fish's leathery lips, how he twice had it in his landing net, which was not strong enough to support the great weight, and how, even then he might have landed the fish if he had been prepared to use his gaff; the fish is still there uninjured and growing bigger year by year and Dick is hoping for the day when he may again join battle with this monster.

So our fishing trip ended. It was not memorable for the amount of fish caught, but I have never enjoyed a fishing holiday more and I am looking forward twelve months to the time when Dick and I will once again crouch behind the overhanging branches and try to tempt the monsters of the Temple Pool.

Sincerely,

M. H. INGHAM

Dear Dick,

This will not be the usual missive, but I thought I had better inform you of my safe return. I had a very good journey and arrived home about 6.15 p.m.—3½ hours.

The enclosed photograph of my 17-pound carp will add a little more to the piscatorial atmosphere of your workshop. It is not too bad but might have been better—as you will see, the fish has lost much of its depth as a result of the position in which it was photographed.

I am also returning your rod-bag which you left in the car. I seem to have established a record by not leaving anything behind—at least I have not yet missed anything.

To-day I have heard of two more carp waters, one of which I

have inspected. I had a look at it this afternoon. I was only there for about five minutes and saw six carp basking—one about 15 lb., one about 10 lb., and the others between 5 and 8 lb. There was one man fishing, in not inconspicuous attire and I made no particular effort to conceal myself, but the carp continued to bask. I have known about the pond for some years—the fishing rights are held by the local angling club—but I have never seen it before. I have never heard of anyone catching anything but roach and small tench out of it—certainly no carp. To-morrow I am going to join the angling club and see if I can catch one. It should not be difficult. The pond is small—I won't attempt to guess the size, but I could easily cover all the water with my 'Felton Crosswind'. It is heavily fished and I imagine the carp are well accustomed to the taste of bread—they should be good 'cloopers'! It is ideal for margin fishing, or would be if the banks had not been almost entirely cleared of every vestige of cover, but that difficulty can be overcome. There is very little weed and only one visible snag in the water. A children's recreation ground adjoins the pond, the boundary of the playing field being within four yards of the pond, so if it is possible for carp ever to become accustomed to noise and movement these should be. It is not a particularly beautiful spot, but is enclosed on three sides by trees and will serve me in much the same way as Brickhill Pond served you—for odd evenings and mornings before work.

The other place I heard of was a lake in Brocklesby Park—ten miles or so west of Grimsby. My informant is not a fisherman, but he *says* that he has seen fish there that were 3′ 6″ long and from his description of them I am pretty sure they were carp. I must investigate.

I must also investigate Tubbs' Pit. I am anxious to make the acquaintance of that fish that goes 'bloody gobble-gobble-gobble'! I think I will write to Mr. Tubbs when I have finished this letter.

Weather permitting, John and I are going to have another go at Woldale at the week-end. I'm sorry you were not able to contact one of the big boys there—you must certainly come up again next summer, but earlier in the season, and try again—

that is if you do not become so blasé after your experiences at 'Lackey's Leap' that you consider the Woldale carp small fry!!

Any news yet of a big eel being caught at Arlesey?

Good luck,

MAURICE

Dear Maurice,

I'm glad you had a good journey home. I'll bet you slept well after it. Don't worry about the late arrival here—I overheard Ruth telling our neighbour what a nice chap you are, so apparently we are forgiven!

I think with the information I have I can make quite a presentable model of your carp. It would help if you could get an enlargement of the shot John took, as that gives the proportions of the fish better than the other picture.

The small pond near your home ought to be productive. Brickhill Pond was very heavily fished indeed, but hardly anyone except Pete and I ever caught a carp. We found it almost useless to fish for them in the orthodox way for several reasons:

1. We hardly ever had a bite from a carp;
2. Nearly always a big rudd, bream or tench got the bait first;
3. When we did hook one deep down it had too good a start and usually snagged us or got in the lilies.

It wasn't until I invented margin-fishing that we began getting them regularly—and *landing* them! Brickhill carp never minded showing themselves, however many people were about; but they were sensible enough not to *feed* in the public eye. Sometimes one would cloop a crust right out in the middle, but if a hook was in the crust breakage was practically certain, owing to the lilies and weed. I should think you would find margin-fishing as successful in the pond near your house as we did at Brickhill. In the choice of a place to fish I think there are two factors that count a lot—where the morning sun first strikes the water, and where the wind is blowing towards the bank. There ought also, I think, to be at least 2 ft. of water under the floating bread if possible. I don't want to be dogmatic about this, because I may be all wrong, but I don't recollect ever having caught a carp on floating crust over *very* shallow margins; it is perhaps significant that the two I got at Woldale were both at the deeper end. I'm looking forward to hearing that you have caught your first surface clooper. You will find it a much more exciting affair than bottom fishing.

At Brickhill we used to have a jar of honey and water—quite treacly—and dip the crust in it before putting it in the water. I doubt if it made any difference, but you might care to try it some time. If you're going to fish late you might try mooring crusts all round the pond with bits of cotton and listening for the cloops—this will give you an idea of the best margin to fish. It might be worth trying this at Woldale too, though with those stealthy ones you might not hear very much, and would probably have to inspect periodically to see which crusts had been taken. We found at Brickhill that one spot was far superior to any of the others for margin work, and caught most of the fish there.

Don't forget to try clay-ball and maggot for bubblers—perhaps a mud-ball, using Woldale mud, would be better still—just a few maggot heads showing. Those bubblers are eating *something* all right. It might also be worth trying a ball of bloodworms (mosquito larvae) and mud mixed up, and fished like paste. I think that if either of these baits *did* induce a bite, it would be indicated by twitches and a short pull or two, rather than an impressive run, and it might be hard to tell whether roach, carp or bream were attacking the bait; though if the bait had been put square in the track of a bubbler and there did occur a twitch, one would probably be well advised to strike right away. It *might* be as well to use a float. I intend to try this scheme at Temple Pool at the first opportunity. What about small leeches in a mud-ball?

I was very impressed indeed with Woldale and I have hopes of getting Pete to run up for a week-end with me before this season ends—perhaps in the early part of September. We could leave here about 6 p.m. on Friday evening and leave Woldale on Sunday. If I can fix a trip I'll let you know. Woldale is a fine carp water, and the best I've ever fished. I most certainly will come again next summer; thank you very much. It would take some extraordinary carp to make those I saw at Woldale look like small fry! I wouldn't mind betting that there are several record carp there. The one that took my worm was the biggest I've ever seen, except for the Arlesey monster; bigger than 'Pickle-Barrel', I think. 'B.B.' puts 'Pickle-Barrel' at from 25 to 30 lb., I say from 20 to 25 lb. The Woldale one might well have been 25+, if in the condition your 17-pounder was.

If the Woldale carp will take potato, you might try an extensive groundbaiting with that. I doubt if the carp would get very much of any other kind of bait, what with roach, bream and moorhens, although a regular gratuity of floating crust at the ram end might eventually get the carp with the right idea in their minds; those small ones found it quickly enough! Anyhow, you have terrific opportunities at Woldale, and if you don't get a twenty-pounder eventually I shall be very surprised.

I have written to 'B.B.' and hope to try Lackey's Leap this month, and I'll send you all the details. I hope it's a reasonably small water; I don't like large ones. Anything much bigger than twice the size of Woldale is 'unmanageable', especially on a trip of short duration. I'm sorry you didn't get a Temple Pool carp, but at least you saw plenty!

I wrote to Harry Sheckell yesterday. I expect you will go and have a chat with him some time.

Sincerely,

DICK

XI

August Letters

Dear Dick,

You remember when we were talking to that angler at Croxby he said he was going to have a crack at the Woldale Carp? Well, it appears from the enclosed photograph, in this evening's paper, of a 15-pounder which he has caught, that he was not unsuccessful. Isn't his fish long and slender compared with the one I got? A pity you didn't connect with that one while you were here! I must have another trip over to Croxby in the near future —he is always there!—and find out where he was fishing, his bait, tackle, etc. I have no doubt, though, that he was using potato—he is a great believer in potato and caught a fourteen-pounder from Woldale on that bait a year or two ago.

The enlargement of John's photograph of my carp is being done and I will call in at the studio in the morning before I post this letter, so that if the enlargement is ready I can send it. I am enclosing a photograph cut from a magazine, of a 20-odd-pounder common carp caught at Dagenham last year. Have you ever seen such a 'broad' carp? It is even chubbier than mine and you said that that was exceptional.

Yes, I think I have got exceptional opportunities at Woldale and I am fairly confident that sooner or later I shall beat 17 pounds, in spite of what 'B.B.' says. I intend really to concentrate on Woldale until the end of the season and will try all the ideas you suggest and perhaps one or two of my own. John and I are having a night out there to-morrow night, weather permitting, and I propose to use floating crust in the rushes in the evening and paste on the opposite side in the morning, also a bit of 'stalking' with worms. Next week I hope to commence a course of ground-baiting with potato, preparatory to fishing with potato at the week-end. Have you used water snails as bait for carp? If so, how do you use them? I know where I can get some really big ones and I think they might be worth trying. Are freshwater mussels any good?

I sincerely hope you and Pete are able to arrange a visit before the end of the season. You will, of course, stay with us, or if you intend to fish all night you must come here for a sleep during the daytime and for a decent meal.

Didn't you say that your visitors always leave things behind? The shoe seems to be on the other foot this time—I discovered your gum-boots in the boot of the car the other day! Shall I post them to you, or shall I hang on to them until you come in September?

Last Tuesday evening I had three hours at a pond near here which I think I mentioned to you, which holds some very good tench. A man had just finished clearing a patch of weed when I arrived and I had great hopes. It was a perfect evening and there was soon lots of bubbling, but I didn't contact any tench on either lobs or paste. I had a typical tench bite when I was fishing with paste and when I struck I thought I was into the grandfather of all tench—but not for long. It was an eel of about 2½ lb! I got two more eels and several perch. John has had exactly the same experience with bubbling tench that we have had with bubbling carp. He tried every possible bait without being able to tempt them. The more I think about it the more I am convinced that those bubblers are feeding on some particular natural food which abounds at the present time, and that whilst they are foraging for it they will not look at anything else. I suspect that they are grubbing pretty deeply in the mud and may not see a bait readily, but they must get their noses up sometimes and in any case one would think that they would 'scent' a bait. The question is what is the natural food for which they are nosing in the mud, and what can we offer that would interest them at such a time? I think your suggestion of the clay-ball may be as likely to succeed as anything I have been able to think of, but your analogy of the trout feeding on one particular fly and refusing to look at any thing else may be a better one than we realize.

If the Keeper at Woldale gets the boat up on to the top lake I shall get some samples of mud from the bottom at the deep end, where we saw most bubbling, and see if it reveals anything, but that may not be until next year and in the meantime I shall have to resort to trial and error methods. If you have any more ideas I shall be pleased to try them out. Didn't you say that carp frequently take baits more readily if there is a spell of suitable weather in September or October? If so, could it be that the natural food which we suspect is occupying their attention so much at the present time is then no longer so plentiful or totally absent?

Makes you think, don't it?

Sincerely,

MAURICE

Dear Maurice,

I guessed I'd left the gum-boots in the car. What foxed me was that I have another (leaky!) pair, and seeing them I thought I had unloaded my sound ones.

It's difficult to judge that carp from the photograph, but I should think it was an old fish going back in condition. It would be interesting to hear how it was caught and what sort of a fight it put up.

I am enclosing a couple of letters from Harry Sheckell, who appears to know a thing or two about carp fishing, though I don't fancy using wire.

I think you are right about the bubblers—they are feeding on something that is profuse in the mud at this time of year.

Either (a) It is one particular organism whose season is approximately mid-July to mid-August

or (b) Mud is in general much more richly tenanted by a variety of organisms at that time.

There are a number of varieties of mosquito-like insects whose life-cycles are all pretty similar. This includes the biting mosquito. I believe that with one exception (whose aquatic existence takes place in water caught in tree-forks and like situations) all develop in ponds and streams, different species being able to cope with varying degrees of stagnation. The main thing is that most species are tolerant of habitat, and don't nearly *all* hatch from the egg into a fragile jointed larva called a bloodworm—which lives mostly in the upper surface of *mud*? You can collect any amount from old rainwater butts—at *this* time of the year. There are two subsequent stages, both of which are active swimmers. One looks rather like a capital I, which can swim by becoming an S; the final stage is like a wriggly comma.

It is *just* possible to fish bloodworms on a fine-wire No. 20 hook! They're deadly for roach and bream in the Ouse. I think it likely that carp feed on these bloodworms. Perhaps a ball of mud liberally mixed with the worms might tempt a fish?

Silkweed may be what the fish are eating, or it *may* be caddises, in which case a ball of mud round a lot of caddises on a treble might do. I think it ought to be *mud* rather than clay, and only just hard enough to remain on the hooks. Failing any of these things, a lot of very small red cockspur worms (from your compost heap) may do.

I caught a peculiar fish on Saturday morning in the small pit at Arlesey. It looked very much like a common carp, but the fin-ray count and scale-count made it more like a crucian. It had no barbules. But the fin and body shape was not at all crucian-like. It weighed 3 lb. and I caught it on a cockspur worm, 16 hook and .005″ nylon, one-shot crowquill float and light spanish reed rod. It fought hard and took twenty minutes to land. I'm going to stuff it to-night. I meant to take it to Oughton Pond, but it passed away. (A 4½ lb. tench was put in on Friday.) The carp bite was typically crucian. 'At a little after half-past eight this tip trembled'[1]—but didn't disappear! It trembled at five-minute intervals until about nine, when I struck experimentally and connected. I failed to connect with several similar subsequent shivers.

Two friends returned from a holiday in Rutland yesterday with a 6 lb. bream for me to stuff. They lost count of the numbers

[1] Quotation from H. T. Sheringham's account of his capture of a 16 lb. carp.

over 5 lb. they caught. One of them had 27 lb. in one timed hour; five fish. They concentrated on bream all the time. Both are now satiated with bream and don't want to catch any more for a season or two. They discovered that the use of the boat was fatal to success—the bream wouldn't tolerate it nearer than fifty yards or so—and it was not until they began fishing from the bank, making very long casts with heavy float-tackle, that they began catching fish.

The Dagenham carp are notoriously chubby—the lake is full of feed. I'll send the photographs back next time I write.

I've tried water snails for carp and tench without much success. I've only caught an odd small fish on small water snails (Planorbis corneus mostly). I used to get tench up to 2½ lb. or so at Brickhill on smallish *land* snails. You wait till they come out and quickly stick the hook in. It's quite a game in itself. I should think you could stick a hook right through Limnea stagnalis; the shell is very thin.

Further comments on bubblers. It is not always that bubblers are indifferent to ordinary baits. Bubblers among the tench at Southill Park, up to the middle of July, will take a lob twice out of three offers. Carp at Temple Pool in September take a lob when bubbling, quite frequently. But at this time of year they inspect it, refuse it and often bolt rapidly as if scared by something—the gut, perhaps? But the gut is not a seasonal phenomenon: carp take baits on the same gut at the beginning and end of the season (i.e. June and September).

Francis Francis said that there were times when fine watercord, dyed to match the bottom, was superior to gut for bottom-fishing for carp or tench. I myself have never been able to find proof of any advantage of gut over tying an eyed hook direct to the running-line when fishing on the bottom. Gut and nylon *look* as if they ought to be less visible than line, but I'm inclined to doubt whether this is actually so when both are on the bottom—and the line is much more likely to lie *right* on the bottom; the nylon may be springy enough to lie in curls. That's the reason I experimented with that 12 lb gut substitute, which goes very limp in the water. I think it is good stuff, except when whipped to a taper-shank hook; tied to an eyed hook it gives no trouble. It deteriorates rapidly, however, and I shouldn't like to use it for a second time after it had been wetted and dried again.

Why were the carp at Woldale Lake bubbling in the *deepest* part and the Temple Pool ones in the *shallowest*?

It looks as if potato is favoured by the carp in your district. Probably it *is* as good as paste, and my preference for paste is sheer prejudice! One tries first the baits with which one has had past success and it is only when these fail that one turns to others. And of course that isn't fair, because at such times probably no bait would be of much use. I intend to give potato a really fair trial in future, especially at Temple Pool.

You will be amused to hear that the morning after we left that eel at Arlesey, the capture of an eel of 'about 3 lb.' was reported. Unfortunately, the exact weight could not be ascertained, as the captor left it on the bank while he went into the village for a meal, and when he returned the eel had been partially eaten by rats!

Best of luck,

DICK

From Harry Sheckell

Grimsby

Dear Mr. Walker,

Your letter to me I read with great interest, but I cannot claim to know more about carp fishing than the other fellow. It is true I spent thirty years fishing for carp before I 'packed up' at the beginning of the war, and I have not wetted a line since. My biggest fish were two of between 16 and 17 lb., caught in 1938 and 1939, and I cannot be dogmatic in any way in an expression of my views upon the subject. I have fished for carp with all types of bait, in a number of waters, and many factors must be taken into account if one wishes to be successful in catching big ones. It is little use fishing in what is usually known as maggot or worm waters with paste and potatoes, and vice versa. Again, the difficulties attendant upon carp fishing when such fish as eels, bream and roach are in abundance requires a great deal of patience and a tremendous amount of good fortune, as these nuisances will not let baits alone. There is not much doubt that round here the best baits are paste and potatoes, but I have read of very big carp indeed being taken with a bunch of maggots as bait. It all depends upon the waters and the food that the fish are accustomed to feed upon. Carp are bottom feeders and 'suck' the bait into mouths that can be distended to take extremely large baits. Paste bait so far as I am concerned means 'large lumps'—as the song has it—as big as a walnut, and potatoes, par-boiled, of approximately the same size. I groundbait with similar pieces round and near—though not so large—with very occasionally ground bread or biscuit as attraction, as I think carp, like other fish, are attracted by 'cloud' ground-baiting. Unless the hook bait is nibbled by small fish I seldom—and I mean seldom—take it out of the water. As to methods of fishing, I am a disbeliever in 'far out'! My experience leads me to believe that carp, when on the move, keep near to the edge of the weeds and reeds round the confines of the water, and so I place my baits carefully near the reeds. I always fish ledger in the following fashion. Hook, size around 6 or 8 on fine wire, no gut trace. Wire trace say 2 feet long, tied direct on to line. Ledger is a round bullet with large hole through it. This I place about two feet from hook, with a split shot underneath it. I then place float about 6 feet above the depth of the water and keep the line above it fairly taut. All this preparation has for its object the luring of the fish into thinking that the bait has nothing attached to it. If good fortune comes your way and the bait is taken a big fish moves very slowly indeed at first and you can perceive his actions by the movement of the float lying flat on the surface of the water. The fish does not give his 'rush' until he feels there is something not to his liking, and the fisherman has time to be prepared for the strike or 'hold' if only he keeps the float in view all the time. This might seem to you to be nonsense, but it is the method *I* have found to be practical and successful and I am very particular as to the way I draw the line in when laying the bait and I try to arrange matters so that the line between float and lead is taut and at an angle of about thirty degrees to the bottom.

You write you are being fortunate sometime in August in the fishing of a water from which giant carp have been landed this season. The little advice I would give is that you find out if at all possible *the baits used* and *the methods adopted by the fishermen*. It is little used theorizing about carp fishing. It is a case of doing it. For goodness' sake—if you allow me to say so—do not go in for what I call 'patent baits'. I have tried them all out, paste flavoured with aniseed and a dozen and one other things; honey paste that nearly always flops off the hook, cherries and various other lures mentioned in books, mainly by writers who have never caught carp and possibly would not know them if they saw them.

The best way is to use your own common sense. No one in this world or the next can tell you all there is to be known about carp and their capture. I have been dead lucky, I always say, and I wish you and your friends in the south the same good fortune as I have enjoyed. I am in retirement after fifty years of school teaching and sports and games mixed up with politics and everything else to keep an active man happy, and I am definitely content now to be a 'looker-on' and well-wisher to others.

I have let my pen run on, but must conclude with the well worn tag 'Tight lines'.

Sincerely yours,
H. W. SHECKELL

From Harry Sheckell

Grimsby

Dear Mr. Walker,

Your letter has both interested and amused me. I have been through all the ideas and thoughts that apparently have bemused you, having lain awake at nights for hours and puzzling myself as to what new methods I could devise to catch a monster carp. Often enough the next outing has been a complete blank. It is all so like making a century at cricket one day and a 'duck' the next. From the information you give it certainly seems that you are better off for carp than we are here. The only ponds or pits that contain carp in this district were stocked years ago by a Mr. Ford who had fish hatcheries at a village twelve miles from here. He was possibly the best known breeder of fish in the whole country and it was a thousand pities that his place just outside Caistor was not kept up after his death. He stocked the ponds at the Dukeries and other mansions. Possibly the fish you are catching came from his place.

I have read of carp hundreds of years old, but to me it seems nonsense. One thing I am certain about is that King Carp cannot fight like the ordinary carp. Weight for weight they are simply not in it, their conformation being all against them.

My biggest fish was caught on ordinary flour (not bread) paste. The fish sucked it up, went slowly away and when I held tight, partially hooked itself, and then the fight began. I believe in landing fish in the shortest possible time and it was not long before the fish was landed in the very big and deep net kept for the purpose. One required help with the landing net, which was a veritable monster, made on the Docks here, the like of which could not be carried by the ordinary angler unless he used a pantechnicon. Rod used always—a Milward 'Cormorant', two piece, 11 foot, a great weapon in my view.

The 'bubbles' query cannot be answered by me. It has puzzled me and I have given it up. By the way, I noticed one day that the carp's two eyes are not set. When we had a seven-pounder on the bank a friend of mine, one of the best roach-bream match anglers in the kingdom, drew my attention to the fact that one eye was pointed up and the other down. I thought for a moment that he was 'crackers' but this fish he held was certainly as described.

As to crusts of bread, this game I tried at Tubbs' Pit, but never hooked a fish. The beggars seemed to know the crust that held the hook and kept off, whilst the other crusts disappeared as they floated across the pond.

I am quite puzzled with what you say about Croxby. I was a pre-war angler there and fish came to the net very seldom. Since my time some fool or other has put roach in, or they have got in from somewhere or other.

Like all carp fishermen who really get bitten with the bug I used to want big ones or nothing at all. So far as the effects of weather or season go, all my experience goes to show that they can be caught at any time. You as well as I must have caught them when you least expected to do so. *They are utterly unpredictable in their likes and dislikes so far as I am any judge.*

A word on gut traces. I tried gut all manner of ways and means. I am certain that at times I was 'broken' by the fish rolling over and cutting the trace with the dorsal fin and so I said—no more traces. Hence my wire, hooks, and tie-on to line. I do not like to think of fish swimming about with a yard or two of gut and hook in their mouths, and also I reckon that as big ones are hooked but seldom it was bad policy risking a break.

My last word is that I never fished 'straight out' from my pitch. I always laid the bait near the weeds *in the face of the wind or flow of water* so that the line lay parallel to the bank and fairly taut. I did not like a long, drifting line, as I thought a wily fish like the carp might be disturbed by it.

You have certainly caught your share of carp and I should have thought you would do better in your quest in home waters, rather than trying in other waters. However, I believe I know how you feel and I hope you will get your twenty-pounder. I felt sure I should have done so had the war not spoiled things. The first world war spoiled my cricket. The second one my fishing. But I am still a good looker-on and remain content.

Once more—'tight lines'.

Sincerely yours,

H. W. SHECKELL

Dear Dick,

Thanks for sending Harry Sheckell's letters—they are most interesting. I must pay him a visit some time. I would like a chat with him. After thirty years of carp fishing he must have learned quite a lot and I am always willing to take the short cut and learn by other people's experiences. There are a number of points in his letters against which I have put a mental question mark, and which I intend to discuss with him when we meet. He says that it is little use fishing in maggot or worm waters with paste and potato and vice versa, but my experience at Croxby last Monday morning proves that one cannot be dogmatic even on that point. Croxby is undoubtedly a 'paste and potato water' and yet my brother and I fished from 4 a.m. to 10 a.m. without a single run from a carp—fishing with paste and potato. Then we changed to lobs and for an hour the sport was fast and furious. On my first cast with a lob—at random, not at a bubbler—the bait was taken while it was sinking and I got a fish of 6¼ lb. I played another for some time before the hook tore out. A third either broke the eye of the hook or opened it sufficiently for the nylon to pull through. A fourth run I missed. My brother missed two runs—undoubtedly carp. Six runs in one hour on worms after six hours' unsuccessful fishing with the accepted baits!

I do not like the idea of wire, although I have never fished with it. I believe that banjo wire has greater cutting properties than nylon or gut, but in a water in which the main snag is water lilies, even wire would not be much use if a fish once got into them—and of course it is pointless to use wire of a greater breaking strain than the reel line. I think your suggestion is probably the best—where the cutting properties of wire would be of no avail—to tie the hook direct on to the reel line. It strikes me that it is *most* important to have *all* the tackle on the bottom within a very considerable distance of the bait, and for that reason I don't like the idea of a float. Apart from being something to watch—and what is wrong with watching the rod tip, or the reel, or the coiled line?—I cannot see that it offers any advantage unless perhaps—as you have suggested—when fishing far out, and even then I am doubtful. And without a float the bullet becomes unnecessary. There *might* be something to be said for a float when fishing a long line, in that it would indicate when a fish runs towards the rod, but on our usual tackle this would be shown by a sudden slackening of the line. Anyway, Sheckell does not believe in fishing far out and in some circumstances I agree; but the 15 lb. carp from Woldale, whose photograph I sent, was taken '*nearly in the middle of the pond*' according to the Keeper—at *4 p.m.* on potato, *with several other people fishing* at the same time. (The underlining is my idea of the special circumstances which justified fishing a long line in that particular case.) Rough weather might be another, assuming that the water in the middle was deeper than elsewhere.

Far be it from me to suggest that H.S. is wrong in his methods. As I say, after thirty years of carp fishing he must have learned a great deal and I would be the last to deny the truth of his general observations concerning carp. The question of tackle is largely, I think, a matter of personal preference—if a man is satisfied with his tackle and has confidence in it he usually fishes well—and it is on this point that our opinions differ.

I was particularly pleased to read what he has to say about the carp at Tubbs' Pit taking floating crust. If, as he says, the carp in that water are so well educated that they can detect a hook in a piece of floating crust (in daytime, presumably) what is wrong with margin-fishing with crust at night? I imagine that water is fairly deep and that night fishing with crust would be effective. I hope to try it shortly.

Last week I had a long talk with the Head Keeper at Woldale and he has agreed to groundbait a pitch up for me and to keep it baited up for the rest of the season. I have promised him a bonus for every carp that I catch from the baited pitch, so that should be some incentive for him to do the job thoroughly and to keep quiet about it! I only hope he doesn't over-do the ground-baiting.

John and I are making another assault on Woldale at the weekend, weather permitting. We'll see if the groundbaiting has made any difference.

Sincerely,

MAURICE

Dear Maurice,

For a possible explanation as to why the carp at Croxby suddenly preferred lobs, see *Confessions of a Carp-Fisher*, page 58, lines 8, 9 and 10. Refer also Sheringham's account, where Woodruff—using lobs—'hoped that after the rain there might be a chance of a fish that evening'. There were *two* chances, both taken!

I don't like the idea of wire, either. I can visualize situations in which it might be desirable, but not many. Anyway, if I do use wire I'll use a high-tensile wire. Banjo strings are the best kind I have ever tried and silver nitrate kills the glint most effectively. I always carry a couple of traces of banjo 2nd made up, in case I have reason to use them. Where water-lilies are bad, they definitely *do* increase your chances, and what they cut with a 14 lb. fish at the other end is sometimes amazing! Common error is using stout *twisted* wire, which won't cut as well as nylon or gut.

The afternoon catch of a fourteen-pounder strikes me as fluky. I've had a similar experience myself (e.g. 'Pickle-Barrel')[1], but I would not like to draw any conclusion except perhaps that, as Sheckell says, carp are utterly unpredictable. I don't like to take that line, though, because I believe that the more we find out about carp, the more we *can* predict what they're likely to do, and hence catch more.

Pete and I have been talking about carp a good deal this afternoon and we are both emphatic that margin-fishing is at least among the most effective carp-fishing methods. It is the only one that completely solves the tackle problem, and that in itself is a tremendous advantage. Also, we know of no water where carp will not, at some time or other, eat bread. At Woldale the only carp I hooked both took the crust. If those common carp would take it I see no reason whatever why the bigger fish shouldn't. I think that method, generally speaking (and forgetting temporarily the problem of bubblers) might be the *best to use at Woldale*, except if other anglers were there. (Incidentally, my first small carp there showed his face while four anglers were present and was landed before dark.)

You will be amused to hear that the monster carp at Lackey's Leap are accused of *taking wildfowl off their nests*! Pete, however, while scoffing at the idea of carp eating *ducks*, says he wouldn't be surprised if big carp took *eggs*, if reasonably accessible, and reminds me of a Brickhill carp which we saw take a crust fully three inches from the water's edge, on the *land* side! 'B.B.', when fishing with me at Brickhill, had a carp take his crust which, to

1 See *Be Quiet and Go a-Angling*, by Michael Traherne (Lutterworth).

avoid the rudd, he had drawn up three or four inches above the surface. I saw this myself. We were rather surprised!

I agree with you about floats and bullets and would never advocate the latter. I think it is absolutely asking for failure to use lumps of lead. I can, however, see reason in a float under certain circumstances. There is far less resistance to a running fish and a much cleaner strike if the line is floating instead of sunk. And you can tell much more what's happening down below if you have a float. If I wanted to strike quickly—as I might if I were trying mud-balls—I think I'd use a float. I wonder how many bites we get without ever knowing it! The first big fish I failed to hook at Woldale would have failed to register a bite had I not seen the bait actually taken, but he'd have been hooked if I'd struck at the right time. I don't use a float often, as you know, but I think there might be advantage in doing so at times.

You will observe that Sheckell used a Milward 'Cormorant' rod, which is a light roach rod, and one which couldn't put more than about a 3 to 4 ounce pressure on a fish. I can't see the point of using such a fragile rod in conjunction with a wire trace. The rod would have very little stopping power. It is far less powerful than my 'Avon' rod, though it's excellent for the work for which it was intended.

I think you are right in your diagnosis of Tubbs' pit. It is extraordinary how hidebound anglers are. I well remember, at Brickhill Pond years ago, how the carp would take loose floating crust, and that in full view of a dozen or more fishermen. Then wallop would go half-a-dozen float-tackles among the bits of crust. When eventually it was demonstrated that floating crust would catch fish if fished without the conventional float and lead, we found that only one or two people fished that way, and even they had a pike-bung attached to give weight for casting. Hardly anyone ever margin fished at Brickhill except Pete and I, because we stopped fishing if anyone else arrived—not because we wanted secrets but because it was useless unless done under quiet conditions. The only others who ever tried it were T——, who lost rod, reel and all at the first trial and never tried again (in 1946) and 'B.B.', who had five fish in as many days in 1947, besides being broken once and missing several offers, owing partly to taut line, which caused the bread to be sucked off the hook.

You ought to catch some carp with systematic groundbaiting, especially as the 'indifferent-bubbling' season is on its way out. Bubblers become more susceptible at the end of August and through September. At Temple Pool we find the fish feed around and below the island in September and early October, where the water is deeper, which is what one might logically expect.

During the war I had a course of sniper training and was shown how visible is the human face. At Woldale I think a carp, which might have taken my bait, didn't, and bunked, because it saw me. I certainly wasn't moving and I imagine it was my face the fish objected to (hardly to be wondered at!). I can imagine the carp dashing off to tell the others who he'd seen. (They probably all read the *Fishing Gazette* and I expect my articles on carp-fishing gave them a nasty jolt.) I'm wondering whether it would be advantageous to disguise oneself as a keeper or as someone whom they know can't fish. Or perhaps one might wear a bee-keeper's veil with a few green and brown strands of wool run through it, so they can't see it's a human at all? It isn't the first time it's been suggested. I think I'll try this at Temple Pool sometime.

Tench record broken—now 8 lb. 8 ozs., a substantial increase. You must get after those Woldale tench next June; groundbaiting by keeper, plus bonus on fish, ought to work wonders. Get John to try mudballing for his indifferent bubbler-tench. If it worked it might help our carp-knowledge. The two fish have very similar habits indeed, except that the tench is less cunning.

I wonder whether a hearty raking might not attract carp as well as tench? I don't for a moment suppose that a carp would bite within a few minutes of raking, as tench often do, but a thorough raking in the evening might produce a carp or two the following morning, or in the night. I like fishing a well-dragged pitch; at least one is reasonably certain that the bait is visible and not hidden among weed or silt; though carp are quite capable of smelling-out a bait, even if it *is* hidden.

Did I tell you that 1,500 assorted mirror and 'golden' carp

have been put in Arlesey Lake? By 'golden' I expect they mean common. I went to Arlesey yesterday evening, but saw no sign of anything except roach, of which I caught many, all about 8–9 inches. I used the 15-ft. rod, which works very well when one gets used to it.

When you asked about snails I forgot to tell you I had caught carp on black slugs at Brickhill, pre-war. I fished them right at the edge of the water, where the grass hung over. They are a good-sized bait and conceal a No. 4 hook well enough. You might try slinging one at a Woldale bubbler some time.

I am intrigued by this bubbler problem and I think researches would pay. After all, one knows one is fishing where the carp are, and that the carp are feeding. It ought only to need the right bait to catch them. They might take water snails. I'm sure they can be caught if only the magic bait can be found.

Best of luck,

DICK

Dear Dick,

The groundbaiting at Woldale has paid dividends already. John and I went over as usual on Saturday evening about 7 p.m. and as there were several people fishing we decided to have a walk round and look at the Decoy Pond. When we came back we saw that one fellow was fast into a good fish. His landing net was quite inadequate and I lent him mine; in trying to get the fish himself he broke his rod—a lightish 3-piece—at the top ferrule. It was a nice fish, a mirror carp of 14 lb. 2 ozs., in beautiful condition, but not quite so aldermanic as my big one. It was very heavily scaled, too—almost completely covered, except on the belly—very much on the lines of what I imagine your Temple Pool mirror-common hybrids are like. That fish was caught in my ground-baited pitch—on potato with a very large coffin-lead and 11 lb. nylon monofil line—and I understand from the keeper that a common carp of about 6½ lb. was taken from the same spot earlier in the afternoon.

John and I started fishing about 9 p.m. when the tumult and the shouting had died, and the captains and the kings departed.

I fished with potato on one rod and paste on the other, and about 10 p.m. had a run on the potato which I missed because, I think, the potato was too hard. After that experience I made a nick in the potato with my pen-knife along the line through which the hook would pull on striking—thuswise:

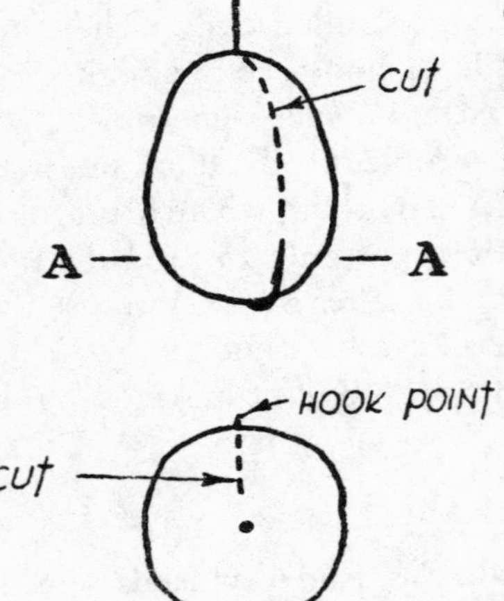

SECTION A-A

No more runs were forthcoming before we retired to the car for a sleep about midnight. We overslept and didn't recommence fishing until about 5 a.m. when it was broad daylight. At 5.30 a.m. I had a run on potato on my carp rod, which produced a very nice fish of 15 lb. 14 ozs. I didn't think there was much chance of another run that morning, but I threaded on another potato and cast out again in the same spot and in about half an hour had a fish of exactly 14 lb. There were no more runs before we packed up at 8 a.m. to catch John's train, but when we left the carp were still very obviously feeding in my pitch. On the whole a very satisfactory outing—for me! John, fishing with paste, had one run which took several yards of line off his reel but it was so fast that he had no time to strike before the fish dropped his bait.

It is interesting to note that both my fish took potato, the one on Saturday evening took potato, and the long thin fish whose photograph I sent you took potato. My rod baited with paste remained undisturbed, and John, using paste, had only one run. It is too early yet to draw any conclusions, but I think it does indicate that the Woldale carp will take potato as least as well as paste. The groundbaiting may be responsible in some measure, but as the groundbait consists of equal parts of potato and soaked bread I assume that it would condition fish equally to paste and potato.

The groundbaiting had another very marked effect. Both my runs—and the one I missed—were very slow and deliberate and I am quite certain that the fish suspected nothing amiss. They had, presumably, grown accustomed to picking up potato in that spot—after five nights of groundbaiting—and to them my bait was just another potato. John's run, in an unbaited pitch—*his* choice, by the way—was in marked contrast. The fish obviously suspected something wrong, set off at lightning speed and dropped the bait after travelling a few yards. The groundbaiting continues, but I have given strict instructions as to the amount to be dumped in nightly. I don't want it to be overdone and have potatoes rotting on the bottom.

I was delighted with the way my carp rod stopped the fish. It is the first time that I have had a good fish on it, and they were both landed in under ten minutes. They were, apparently, none the worse for their experience and after being photographed and having a scale removed they swam away most cheerfully. The smaller fish was very lightly scaled and was not in such good condition as the larger one—at least it was not so well proportioned. The heavier fish was, in fact, the shorter of the two, and it had some huge scales. The scale which I took is $3\frac{1}{8}$ inches long and $1\frac{1}{2}$ inches broad—considerably bigger than the largest scale from my seventeen-pounder.

I talked for a few minutes to the chap who caught the carp on Saturday evening. He asked me if I knew Harry Sheckell. I told him that I knew *of* him and he proceeded to tell me how he had met Harry a few days before and had read with great interest three letters which Harry had received from 'some fellow down south who' (you will be interested to learn) 'knows what he is talking about when it comes to carp fishing'!

The pond near home should prove quite entertaining. I had a couple of hours there last Friday night and I think floating crust, margin-fished, should be very effective. There were several people fishing when I arrived and I didn't start fishing until they departed about 10 p.m. I packed up about midnight without having any takers, but the 'clooping' was beginning in real earnest when I came away.

I have yet to catch a fish on floating crust and so I am not qualified to express an opinion as to its effectiveness, but it certainly appears to overcome the tackle problem. If only we can find the answer to the bubbler problem it may prove to be even more effective, because then one can present one's bait to the fish instead of waiting for the fish to come to the bait.

What Pete says about the possibility of carp taking eggs is very interesting. Didn't you say that a keeper had once told you that the yolk of a hard-boiled egg was a good bait?

That record tench must have been a magnificent fish. According to the Sunday paper in which I read of it, it was caught on a No. 16 hook on 6x gut—quite a good effort!

I hope this week-end to have a crack at a private lake near Lincoln, which my brother had got permission to fish. According to reports it contains some very large carp—also some big perch, pike and trout. A strange mixture! It is also reputed to have very extensive beds of lilies. It sounds worth investigation.

Sincerely,

MAURICE

Dear Maurice,

Excellent show! This will shake 'B.B.', whose letters complain about poor chances owing to what he calls lateness of the season. We are now reaching the end of the 'indifferent bubbler' period and this, as well as the groundbaiting, may have something to do with the fish feeding more readily. All the same, I am forced to revise my views on potato and I would say you have sufficient evidence to rate it *above* paste at Woldale. After all, four on potato to one on paste is pretty convincing, without counting my small ones or the unfruitful runs. I don't think there is much need to experiment with margin-fishing if you can get three runs at one outing! I agree that further experiments on bubblers are indicated, though. Of course it's too late this season; if you see bubblers from now on you have a good chance with ordinary baits.

When you say that the carp were still feeding when you left at 8 a.m. do you mean they were bubbling in your pitch, or was it swirls?

I'm glad the carp rod stood up well. I haven't seen anything to beat it and the 'Felton' for carp-fishing yet.[1] There have been times when I've wished it longer or shorter, but I don't think it could be bettered *for all-round purposes* without considerable thought and experiment. Yours is the stouter version, and later you must make a lighter one—ten minutes on a sixteen-pounder is a bit *too* quick! I bet that when you got stuck into the first one John thought he'd miss his train!

I assume you've decided that 20 lb. is stuffing size?

What was the name of that anti-insect cream you had? I got eaten alive by the Oughton Pond last week. No carp-fishing for me this week-end—I am fishing for our club in a three-cornered team match—tiddler-snatching.

Whereabouts did you have groundbaited? If other anglers find out about it, it won't be so good, especially if several carp get running about with yards of nylon attached, which is what happened at Brickhill when Pete (I think it was) did some extensive groundbaiting and his pitch was discovered.

Angling in Still Waters is half-done; I've done carp, tench, perch, bream and rudd.

I'm greatly flattered by the opinion on my letters to Sheckell, which in fact consisted largely of questions!

'B.B.' will be here next week; we start for Lackey's Leap on the 27th. He looks on it as a reconnaissance—says it's too late in the season to hope for a big fish! The keeper has been tipped

[1] I now use a "Mitchell" reel.

to bait a pitch and has been doing so for a week already. I don't know what with! Probably roast duck. I am preparing tackle both mighty and delicate. Season too late! Pooh! The best part of the season is only just commencing. You'll find out if you keep after those Woldale fish that they feed better and better until the first frost, and you won't need to start quite so early either. Don't forget to try lobs towards the end if potato fails.

I have made a doughty gaff in case nets prove too small. We have to remove all fish caught in the interests of the wildfowl(!) so I shan't hesitate to use the gaff if the net proves inadequate. I've ordered 4 lb. of burnt alum and saltpetre. That scalpel you gave me was fine on my goldfish, which looks even better than the perch (you remember I told you of a queer carp? It was an uncoloured goldfish). I've got the eye on it, and on the bream, much better. I painted the *back* of the perspex black, put the eye in and painted the coloured iris on *outside*, then several coats of cellulose. Both fish had easily-detachable scales, so it was a good exercise. I didn't use paper on the skin à la Joyce, but cellulosed the show side before skinning, two coats, as soon as the fish were surface dry. The bream stank like a polecat and nearly made me sick. It really was *rank*, and not because it had been dead long; it hadn't.

It would seem that your Woldale carp are all one brood—14 lb., 14 lb. 14 ozs., 14 lb., 14 lb. 12 oz., 15 lb. 14 ozs., 17 lb.—all very close together and as far as I can judge even closer for length. After seeing the picture of the thin fish I'm inclined to revise my estimate of those I stupidly failed to hook. They may not have been the 20 lb. plus which I at first thought, though the first one was the dickens of a width. I wish you'd seen 'Pickle-Barrel' closer at Temple Pool, as you would have been able to add your opinion to mine and 'B.B.'s'. He isn't *all* that long—30 to 36 inches—but he is the only carp I ever saw that *looked* deep-bodied when swimming normally; his width is amazing!

I intend to try potato at Temple Pool!

We failed to win the match yesterday, but I am glad to say I had highest individual weight, a magnificent total of 3 lb. 12 oz. 14 drm., consisting of roach, dace, perch, chub, bleak, bream and bream-roach hybrids, best fish $3\frac{1}{2}$ oz.! All on yellow maggots. They wouldn't touch white or pink ones.

You ought to fish in one or two matches, just for the experience. There's nothing like versatility.

I'll be away from 27th to 31st.

Good luck,

DICK

Dear Dick,

If the weather is favourable at the week-end I propose to go to Woldale again—alone this time. John is going after some tench—and we may have some more evidence to shake 'B.B.' I hope! I want to establish three things if I can: (1) that carp *do* feed more readily towards the end of the season, as is the case with the majority of creatures which go into semi-hibernation during the winter (2) that potato is the most effective bait—for bottom fishing at Woldale (3) that systematic groundbaiting is really effective. (The two fish on my last visit may have been a fluke!)

I was talking to Joker the other day and he had some interesting information on carp. I suspect that he bred carp in Denmark, although I was only with him for a few minutes and most of our talk was about trout—of which more later—so I was unable to follow up the carp topic. One scrap of information that he let fall interested me particularly—that when carp are grown and fattened for the table they are not fed in small regular doses as are trout, but that a *large* quantity of food (cereal or potato) is dumped into the water occasionally—as much as a ton at a time. The fact that the food decomposes in the water before it is all eaten does not deter the carp—they eat it just the same. Doesn't this indicate an easier and possibly more effective method of groundbaiting for carp, particularly in large lakes, than the method usually adopted—of regular small doses. In a water the size of say Arlesey Lake, a large quantity of groundbait dumped in one spot, say, every week, would stand a better chance of attracting carp than a small amount dumped in nightly. It would not be gobbled up by roach, bream, etc., before the carp had a chance of getting a good taste. The objection may be raised that by this method one would be *feeding* the fish and not merely *attracting* them to the pitch, but I don't think the carp would be attracted for long if there was nothing for them to feed on. You hold similar views on the subject, I think. A heavily baited pitch would establish a regular, and, so long as the baiting was maintained, a permanent feeding ground. I've no doubt there are objections to such a method of groundbaiting—possibly the stale food in the water may have a harmful effect on other fish—but if it could be done it would appear to have distinct advantages, particularly in large waters or waters that are too inaccessible for regular groundbaiting. I shall be interested to hear what you think about it.

Our visit to Norton Place on Sunday was a dismal failure. The lake is quite big, with a wide fringe of lilies all round and no bank fishing is possible. It looks an ideal place for carp and is reputed to hold some big ones, but so far as I can gather none have been caught and I neither saw nor heard any evidence of carp.

John and I went over to Woldale last night and thoroughly dragged a pitch which we fished early this morning. But our efforts were not rewarded by any tench. Lobs were instantly seized by small perch and paste by roach, so that we got fed up and came home earlier than we had intended.

If the published information is correct, that new record tench was taken on a No. 16 hook with the *tail* of a *small* worm as bait. That might appear to lend some substance to our theory that the indifferent bubblers are after some small creature in the mud—probably blood-worms as you suggest—and that they can be caught by a *small* bait which possibly resembles the natural food. Unfortunately we can't use a small bait for carp, but I feel sure that your idea of mud-balling with blood-worms or very small red worms would be effective. We must try it next year.

Another interesting fact about my two carp which I don't think I mentioned in my last letter—both were hooked well inside the mouth—the first right at the back of the roof of the mouth and the other in the roof of the mouth only a little further forward which, I think, proves that they were quite unsuspecting.

It must be, then, the *bait* that arouses a carp's suspicions and *not* the *tackle*—at least not such tackle as I was using which was, incidentally, a .016″ camouflaged nylon cast and No. 4 hook which you gave me at Temple Pool. Overcome the carp's suspicions of unnatural baits and the battle of wits is more than half won!

Of course ten minutes is a bit quick for a sixteen-pounder; but I played those fish really *hard*. I wanted to see just what the tackle was capable of and I was most agreeably surprised with what I discovered. In future I don't propose to use quite such a heavy hand, but I do agree that a slightly lighter version of the carp rod would be more suitable at Woldale—at least when fishing in my baited pitch. Perhaps you would be good enough to give me the tapers when you give me the details of your spinning and brook rods. There's no hurry—I shall have no time for rod-making until the late Autumn.

I think it is coincidence that all the carp from Woldale (mirrors) of which we have knowledge have been of approximately the same size. I am certain there are much bigger fish than that. When we left a week last Sunday morning the sun was on the water and there were at least a dozen carp basking in the 'bay', and there was a wide variety of sizes. Also, what about the fish that I saw in May which was, I'm sure, at least three feet long and of tremendous width; and what about the one that took your worm and rejected it? You had a good look at that fish at close quarters and I can't imagine your making such a bad guess as to its size. I heard to-day of a 27-pounder which was caught at Woldale recently and returned to the water, but I doubt the truth of that story—not because I don't think there may be 27-pounders in Woldale, but because I cannot imagine any local angler catching a record fish and returning it with so little publicity. No! I think that was a version of my 17-pounder which had grown in the re-telling!—but I must ask the keeper when I see him at the week-end.

My baited pitch is a close secret. Other people do fish it, of course, but not for carp.

I'm sending a tin of 'Dimp' anti-insect cream in case you can't get any locally. You'll probably need it next week. I have found it most effective.

All the very best of luck for your trip to Lackey's Leap. I shall look forward to hearing from you.

Sincerely,

MAURICE

Dear Maurice,

Thank you for the boots, which arrived quite safely. We start to-morrow morning and I've just finished rounding-up the provisions.

What Joker says about feeding carp is most interesting. It may be that the feed of potatoes and cereal is put in *uncooked*, in which case it would not go sour for a long time. You might check on this point. Of course one would have to have some idea of the rate at which the stuff is consumed, otherwise one's potato would very likely lie among a couple of hundred others and stand a correspondingly small chance of being taken. My technique in matches is to give plenty of feed but in such a form that the hook-bait represents a 'plum', i.e. it offers an easier meal than that of the groundbait. If one groundbaited with *lots* of potato, it would be better chopped up into fairly small bits, so that the hook-spud was the biggest piece.

The keeper at Lackey's Leap has been groundbaiting since the first week in August, so if groundbaiting *is* a good thing, we ought to do well.

What I can't understand about the effects of groundbaiting and your experience at Woldale is this: you say that the bites and the way in which the carp were hooked showed that the fish were not suspicious—right, I agree. Now the cast and hook were identical with those we used at Woldale before with paste. It would be reasonable to infer that the carp then *were* suspicious? Why, then, is this so? The groundbait included bread, etc., and I threw in paste *as such*. Can it be that free offerings of bread, etc., are soon consumed by the roach and bream, but the potatoes stay long enough for the carp to eat plenty and thus allay their suspicions? In which case, the advantage of potato lies entirely in its immunity to the attacks of roach, etc., does it not? Isn't that what I said about potato some considerable time ago? What I mean is that in an unbaited water, *or* one in which only carp existed (e.g. Beechmere) paste would be as good as potato, and maybe better.

I went tench-fishing at Southill on Tuesday, but only small perch bit, until I spun with a little Vibro and caught a jack of about 4 lb. which bit me blinkin' finger—blood all over the place!

Of course you shall have the taper of the light carp rod: Yours is like (*b*); the light one (*a*).

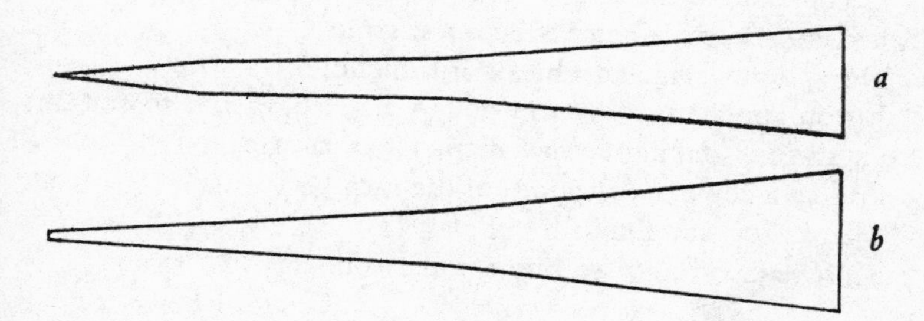

It gives better casting with light baits, and you can use tackle as light as 6 lb. b.s. without fear on it. The heavier design, like yours, was intended for much worse conditions than Woldale and designed for 12 lb. line to 18 lb. if necessary.

I am glad to hear you are going to have a shot at rod-building and I hope that will include designing. It all hinges on the moment of inertia of the cross-section, which is, of course, a function of its dimensions.

The deflection of a cantilever beam

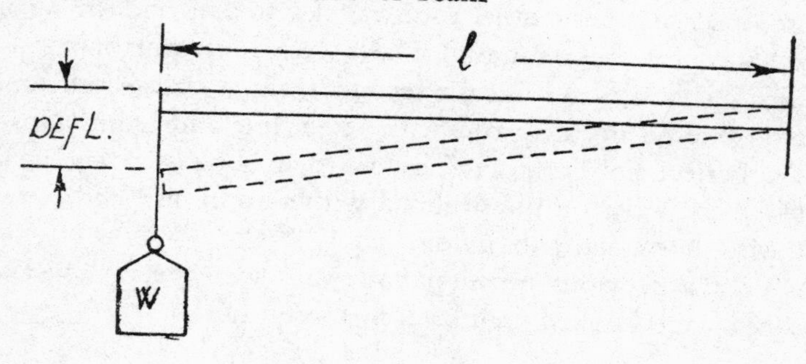

$$= \frac{wl^3}{3EI}, \text{ where}$$

w = load
l = length
I = moment of inertia which is proportional to *diameter* to the fourth power
E = modulus of elasticity, which can be assumed constant as it is a function of the stress/strain characteristics of the material.

If you double the length of a rod, you will get 8 times the deflection if the diameter is kept the same.

Now, don't panic at a bit of arithmetic!

If you apply this, you can design any length rod to suit any strength line—taking *average* diameter of course.

I'd like a copy of the photo of the carp very much.

Thanks for the 'Dimp'!

Must dash off now to buy a toilet roll.

Good luck,

DICK

Dear Dick,

Either 'B.B.' is on the wrong track or I am extremely lucky, because I caught another brace of carp last Sunday morning. It was a lone vigil this time.

I started fishing at 4 a.m., in bright moonlight, and hooked my first fish at 4.30 a.m. It took about 15–20 minutes to get it into the net, which was quite a tricky business in the half-light. My second run, on the other rod, was at 5.30 a.m. and this again took about twenty minutes. They were both mirror carp—the first 14 lb. 13 ozs. and the second 15 lb. 4 ozs.—both took potato—one on my carp rod with 11 lb. line and 'your' No. 4 Model Perfect hook on .016″ nylon (that hook is doing well, isn't it?), the other on the steel rod with a 10 lb. line and No. 4 eyed M.P. hook on $6\frac{3}{4}$ lb. nylon.

As on the previous occasion both runs were very slow and both fish were hooked well back in the mouth.

I fished on until 8 a.m. but had no more runs, and returned the fish after taking several photographs of them from different angles, and after taking some scales which I am enclosing.

On Sunday we set off for a picnic, but there was such a cold wind that we eventually decided to go to Woldale and eat our lunch in the car. There were several carp in evidence and I spent about half an hour watching two real whoppers. I had plenty of time to have a really good look at them from all angles, both with and without binoculars and I am quite sure they were much bigger than the ones I have caught. One of the fish was actually feeding—at least I can think of no other reason for his movements. He was in the shallow water of the 'bay'—he would cruise slowly along with his dorsal fin occasionally breaking the surface, then he would put his nose down, his tail would wave just below the surface, causing a great swirl, and up would come a lot of bubbles. Then he would level off, move on slowly a few feet and down he would go again. The fish undoubtedly congregate in that bay during the daytime and it may be that they could be caught there. It would mean a long cast out into the middle of the bay, but it could be done.

Another interesting point. We have never done much good at Woldale in the evening and at night. The only fish that we have hooked at night was one which John had last year, which broke him on the strike—at 11.30 p.m. The five fish which I have caught there this year have all been taken in the early morning—4.45 a.m., 5.30 a.m., 6 a.m., 4.30 a.m. and 5.30 a.m.—and in each case I have had a run within half-an-hour or so of starting fishing—even last Sunday, in moonlight.

When I see Joker again, which I hope to do before long, I will see what further information I can gather about carp, and I will certainly find out if they are fed with raw or cooked potatoes, etc.

The point you raise about groundbaiting is most interesting, and I think you have hit the nail on the head. I had, as I think I mentioned, come to the conclusion that it must be the bait and not the tackle which excites the carp's suspicions, but I had missed the significance of your point. I think it must be a fact that where bream, roach, etc., exist, they devour bread groundbait before the carp have a chance of eating sufficient to allay their suspicions—but that where potatoes are mixed with the bread they are left almost exclusively for the carp. Last year I went over to Woldale every night for a week and ground-baited up a pitch—the same that I am fishing this year—with bread and bran and small balls of paste. Fishing with paste at the end of that week—Saturday night, Sunday morning—I didn't have one run.

I'm surprised at you letting a pike bite your finger! I have two scratches about an inch long on the back of my right hand as I write—caused by the primary dorsal fin-ray of one of my carp on Sunday. It started to flap about while I was photographing it and in pacifying it the saw-edge of its fin was dragged across my hand.

Thanks for the formula for deflection of a cantilever beam. I am with you so far, but I'm afraid I am awfully thick in matters mathematical. How does one apply the formula to rod design? Does one first of all decide upon the desired curve of the rod at a given load and then, working from the butt at intervals, calculate the reduction in diameter necessary to give the desired deflection? If so, how? I'm sorry to be so dumb, but I have always been a duffer at maths. You must hurry and get your book into print!

I think you said you would be returning from Lackey's Leap to-day. I am looking forward very much to hearing your report and I hope you have some good news for me.

Best of luck,

MAURICE

XII

September Letters

Dear Maurice,

You seem to have got the measure of the Woldale carp. I am interested in the sizes, as I have a theory about this. I've noticed on all carp waters where I've fished that there is a sort of 'average run' of fish which one catches; occasionally one gets a fish much larger. At Temple Pool, for example, the 'average run' this year has been 4 to 7 lb. (It has increased each year I've fished there.) I think the carp only breed occasionally and only when their numbers are *low*. Hence, a generation much of a size, plus a few bigger ones which are the parents. At Woldale I fancy a generation was bred soon after the fish were put in (many years ago) and these 15-pounders you're getting are Woldale bred; the *monsters* you've seen are probably the original stock. I imagine you will get a twenty-pounder sooner or later.

Next, the weed disappeared at Woldale. I think it was eaten by the carp. I think that they reached their maximum condition by the beginning of July, then the weed was all eaten and condition fell off. The keeper at Lackey's Leap says the weed grows before the carp become active. They commence eating it after spawning, i.e. in late May, and have cleared up the lot by July at latest. They thus get it when it is young and fresh and full of protein.

Third point. I discussed mud-balling with Pete and while I was away he had a day breaming at Offord. Bream were bubbling and he couldn't get a bite; he had several smallish roach on gentles, but no bream. So he enclosed his gentles in a *walnut-sized ball of mud* and caught more bream from 2 lb. to 4 lb. than he could remember to count. He says he had a vigorous bite at every cast and never missed one. I think this is a terrific event, and most encouraging. It now wants trying on bubbling carp and tench.

Those Woldale fish obviously prefer the bay, and it might be well next year to bait up nearer that end. You could work the old trail dodge—throw some of the bait in a line so the fish work along it to the main feast, which is where you fish.

Now about the Lackey's Leap trip. I rather suspect that the 27½-pounder was caught in the close season! The keeper hadn't a clue about close seasons. The fish was caught, he says, the *second week in June*. Although no angler, the keeper strikes me as a genuine chap. He looks exactly like John Bull; he needs only a billycock and Union Jack waistcoat.

The lake is about five acres. The water is the colour and 'texture' (?) of Woldale, but deeper. There are places up to 20 ft. but plenty of shallows too. No visible weed. Rough plan attached.

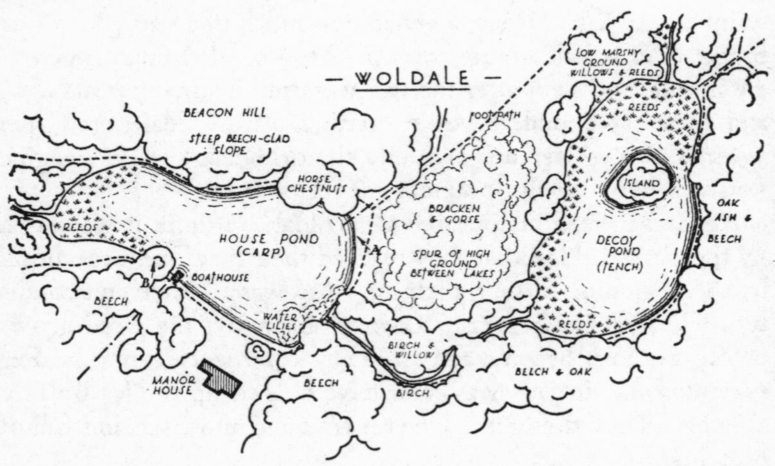

The fish are all common carp and even more stealthy than those at Woldale. Except for an odd fish leaping far out, I saw none at all except what we caught. I had five on paste and was broken by another. Weights 9½, 9½, 10½, 11½, and ¾ lb. I also had a terrific run which I didn't know had taken place until I reeled up and found 70 yards of line out. This, and the break, took place in the dark. All fish on 6 lb. line and .012″ nylon, size 6 hooks. 'B.B.' had one, 8½ lb., on potato, 12 lb. tackle and size 2 hook.

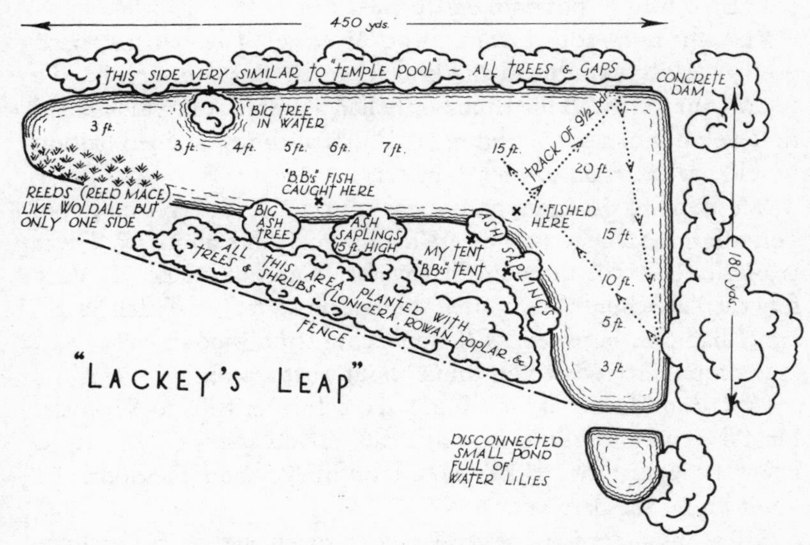

The fish were all very long and thin and fought like tigers, except the first (10½ lb.) which was sluggish. The 11½ lb. fish was 27½″ long and the 10½ lb. one was 27″. They should have weighed fifteen or sixteen pounds in good condition. (See remarks on weed-eating.) I say they were thin, but don't imagine they were *sick*! They were lovely clean-looking bright fish, and I've never met faster ones, not even at Croxby. The 9½-pounder had a neat knot round the big front dorsal spine: and we really thought 'twenty-pounder at last!'. If I had had much less than 150 yards on the reel I'd have been in trouble, I think. He took 115 yards (measured) in the first rush. See his track on the plan. I've never had a tougher battle with a fish in my life; had no control of him whatever; he went just where he liked. On his second tack I had a good cross strain on, rod fairly doubled and line 'twangy' (you know how it feels) and he just

didn't deviate at all. I thought I'd got a real monster! The hook was in his mouth all right, but there was a yard of slack between it and the knot round the fin. He tried to get into a sunken tree, but 'B.B.' threw potatoes and turned him.

I caught numerous bream, as at Woldale. I baited my pitch pretty heavily with bread and boiled potato, but although I had a potato out nearly all the time I only had a nibble at it which failed to develop into a proper bite. No doubt a more sustained baiting would get them on to potato better.

We hope to go again early next season. 'B.B.' says he hopes you might be able to join us. What do you think about it? There is ample room for three on that water. Can you make it? Very few carp are caught, only nine this season so far, of which 'B.B.' and I had five between us (I don't count the ¾-pounder!).

Let me know what you think about next season.

I still don't know what's doing about further trips to Woldale, but I'll let you know as soon as I can. The Lackey's Leap trip is being broadcast by 'B.B.' next month, Midland Regional. I don't know the date yet.

After an interval of several weeks tench are again feeding. Tell John he can start tenching again, as the indifferent bubbling season is now over!

I'll send you the Lackey's Leap pictures as soon as I get prints. Terrific bubblings at Lackey's Leap—never seen so much anywhere. They were *mostly* indifferent, but not all!

Rod-design. I don't think it would be a good thing to *try* to design a rod entirely mathematically. What I think is important is to know the formulae so that one can see how a *change* will affect the result. For example, since the deflection varies as the *cube* of the length $\left(\frac{wl^3}{3EI}\right)$ you can deduce how much influence a small alteration in length will have. Double the length gives eight times the deflection; see? Also, the moment of inertia (I) for a hexagon is $0.06d^4$, where d is diameter (flat to flat), so that doubling the diameter of a given rod would reduce the deflection to one-sixteenth. All this for a given taper. The taper itself gives the *action* you want. The steeper it is, the more bend in the tip and the less in the butt, and vice-versa. This is all you need to know as a basis for design.

Good luck,

DICK

Dear Dick,

I am very pleased to learn that your visit to Lackey's Leap was a success, even if you didn't break any records. It's not surprising that your 9½-pounder put up a terrific fight, with your line attached to the middle of his back—you *would* be disappointed when you saw his size. You said in an earlier letter that all the fish that you caught there had to be killed—is that, in fact, true? It seems a dreadful pity if it is—there are not so many carp in the country that we can afford to wipe them out like that. If it can be managed I would love to join you and 'B.B.' in your visit to Lackey's Leap next season.

Our Woldale visit last week-end was a complete blank—not a single run. I was not really surprised, though—it was a very cold night. There were more carp jumping than I have seen on any night this year—to keep warm, no doubt!—but there was no sign of feeding carp. Not a single bubble. Another angler was fishing when we arrived on Saturday night and stayed until dusk—also without success. He had four rods out at intervals of about 50 yards. All tight lines with centre-pin reels on check. He relies on the sound of the check to tell him when he has a run—and then he has to run himself! He was using heavy tackle, too; nothing less than 16-pound line. He tells me that there have been five specimen carp caught from Tubbs' Pit this season, in the 15–16 pound category—one by Harry Sheckell! I am waiting for a really warm spell before I try my luck there. My present permit limits me to three visits only and I don't want to waste them.

Your theory that the carp grub up all the weed is most interesting. Certainly, of the five carp that I have caught at Woldale, the best conditioned one was the first—the 17-pounder—which was caught, you remember, on the 2nd July, soon after the disappearance of the weed. Does your experience in other waters confirm this theory? I seem to remember a good deal of weed at Temple Pool, but perhaps it was not an edible variety. There was quite a lot of weed at Croxby in May and early June, which seems to have disappeared completely now.

Pete's experience at mud-balling is very encouraging. I might try it out on some tench at the week-end. Unless, and until, we get a warmer spell I don't think it will be much good fishing at Woldale—the water is so shallow that I think the carp are particularly susceptible to changes of temperature, and it has been really cold at nights for the past week. John and I propose to have a shot at a pond at Thorpe St. Peter—about eight miles east of Spilsby. It is an old brickpit which is reputed to contain some big tench and also some carp. The owner claims that it was stocked with tench several years ago and that a considerable number of large fish were introduced at that time, including a number over 6 lb. One fish of 5 pounds-odd has been caught this year, but very few others. John has fished there a few times and he says the bubbling is terrific, so mud-balling might prove effective. So far as I can gather, only two carp are known to have been taken from the pond—one about 8½ lb. on rod and line and one about 10 lb. in an eel-trap! Both common carp. Anyway, it will be interesting and being fairly deep it may provide us with better sport than Woldale at the present time.

Tench are strange creatures. John is completely baffled by them. He has fished for them a lot this season in waters that we know hold a lot of tench, with every possible variation of tackle and all the *usual* baits, and his total bag has been three fish—all under two pounds. There have been *very* few tench caught this year in these parts. Have you any explanation for the bad tench years which seem to occur fairly frequently? Is it that some years the climatic conditions are such as to promote the growth in the water of certain forms of life upon which tench feed to the exclusion of everything else, while at other times this natural food is not so prolific, due to adverse climatic conditions, and the fish are more easily tempted with artificial baits? Also, why is it that even in a bad season one can sometimes catch two or three fish very quickly—within a few minutes of each other—

and then catch no more fish in that water for the rest of the season? I know several people who have had that experience. Another point, from John's experience in past seasons—and it has also been my experience in a lesser degree—one can start fishing for tench at dawn on a perfect summer's morning, tench are bubbling all over the pond—there are no other bottom-feeding fish in the water—one fishes for probably three hours without a nibble; then three or four bites in very quick succession and no more, even though the bubbling continues. John is convinced that tench are more difficult to catch than carp. He must try mud-balling next season—that may be the answer.

Will you let me know when 'B.B.' is broadcasting? The printers may still be on strike but even if we have a *Radio Times* it is most unlikely that I should notice the broadcast, and I would like to hear it.

I do hope you can manage a trip to Woldale with Pete before the season ends. We are sure to have a warm spell before the season finishes and if we do I have a feeling that the fishing should be good.

Thanks for the elaboration on the mechanics of rod building and design. I can follow you up to a point, but I'm afraid I still don't see how one sets about designing a rod from scratch. I'm very stupid about such things, as I said before.

I shall look forward to seeing the Lackey's Leap photographs.

Sincerely,

MAURICE

Dear Maurice,

The broadcast is September 19th, Tuesday, 10 p.m. Midland Regional.

We killed the two best fish, and I've stuffed them. The keeper says, quite rightly, that although it would be impossible to remove all the carp, he thinks the water is overstocked at present and no harm would be done if some were removed. He does not really think that the carp are a serious menace to his ducks! He suggested that a reasonable compromise would be to set a 10 lb. size limit (but he was in no way insistent) and so we killed the 10½ and 11½ lb. fish. I find these bigger fish fairly easy to stuff. That scalpel you gave me has proved invaluable.

Lackey's Leap strikes me as very much like the shape of things to come at Croxby, i.e. too many and too thin, except that at Lackey's Leap the situation has arisen later in the life of the fish and you get big thin fish instead of little thin fish!

Thanks for the photograph. The fish look nice fat ones—much fatter than Lackey's Leap torpedoes. I'll send you some prints of my lot when I can get them done.

I take a very poor view indeed of the angler with four rods and if I found any such methods on waters within my bailiffing jurisdiction, they'd soon be stopped. It is quite wrong for one angler to take up four pitches on a water—and then to go pounding round if he gets a run. What's more, it's illegal in the Ouse and Cam area.

Temple Pool weed is, I think, inedible in bulk. The fish may eat shoots, they probably do, but not the whole plant. The weed at Woldale and Croxby is a much softer weed—I don't know its name, but it's the same as at Lackey's Leap. I think the carp clear up nearly all of this kind where they exist in numbers.

I went to Temple Pool yesterday. It turned warm at the week-end and the fish fed well. We had a spell of rank bad luck. Bob was with me. We both had six or seven good runs and missed them all; then I caught a little fat mirror of 2½ lb. Then Bob got into a big fish, about 12 lb. I should think, and after playing it for about five minutes it dived under the bank and went three times round a submerged branch, which was eventually landed minus the fish. After all the shemozzle—up at the shallow end—we went down above the island. The water was gin-clear there—it was muddy at the other end—and the bottom could be seen clearly. There were several fish swimming about, including three big ones from 12 lb. to 18 lb. or so. I put out a worm and the biggest one of the lot followed it down, took it and swam off quite unconcernedly. When I struck he shot into the thickest weeds and there shed the hook. Half an hour later another big one—about 14 or 15 lb.—did the same thing. Then Bob hooked a smaller fish which ran straight towards him and got rid of the hook. We went home at about 12.30, one $2\frac{1}{2}$-pounder being the bag. It's now in the Oughton Pond. Our hooks were all dead sharp and everything appeared to be in order. Bait was lobs. I just can't understand it! Just one of those days, I suppose. I don't think I've ever had so many bites in a morning.

It's funny about the tench in your part of the world, because hereabouts it's been one of the best tench seasons ever. 'B.B.' says it's been bad in his district. I haven't been out after tench much, but I've had some sport every time I've been and my smallest has been 3 lb. 6 ozs. They've been getting plenty on the Ouse, too, all sizes up to about 3 lb. or so. I don't profess to be able to give any reason. 'B.B.' says that in lakes where the level alters, big tench can only be caught when the water is low. This *is* the case on lakes where he fishes, near his home. At Southill Park the level this year is the highest it has been for at least ten years, and the fishing has been better than ever known. At least as regards tench. So what? I have never found tench as capricious as other people do and I usually get one or two when I go after them; of course when the weather is cold you don't expect to do much with *any* still-water fish. Indifferent bubbling is common to nearly all, if not quite all, bottom-feeding fish and I *think* we know the reason and *perhaps* the answer. I had intended to try mud-balling at Temple Pool yesterday, but the fish weren't indifferent!

Rod-design. I have never *tried* designing a rod from scratch. I've always worked on the lines of modification of an existing design on reasonably scientific lines. But you *could* do it from scratch. You know the total deflection

$= \frac{wl^3}{3EI.}$ Now, for a hexagon, $I = 0.06\,d^4$, so deflection $= \frac{wl^3}{0.18Ed^4}$

You could find E $\frac{\text{stress}}{\text{strain}}$ either by a stress/strain experiment or better still, by finding the deflection of a bit of split cane of known length and diameter with a known load and substituting in the formula. If deflection $\delta_n = \frac{wl^3}{0.18Ed^4}$, then $E = \frac{wl^3}{0.18d^4\delta_n}$, doesn't it?

But I take the view that if you remember that the deflection varies directly as the cube of the length and inversely as the fourth power of the diameter, you can fiddle a known design anyhow you like.

Example: a carp rod is ten feet long and has a butt diameter of $\frac{9}{16}''$ and a tip diameter of $\frac{5}{32}''$. It is found satisfactory for use with a 12 lb. line. It is desired to build one for use with a 6 lb. line; i.e. we want double the deflection for a given load. We are going to double the deflection and keep the length constant.

δ_n varies as $\frac{1}{d^4}$, so the new diameter will have to be $\sqrt[4]{\frac{1}{2}} \times$ original diameter $\left(d^4 \times \frac{1}{\delta_n}, d \times \sqrt[4]{\frac{1}{\delta_n}}\right)$, i.e. multiply all diameters by $\sqrt[4]{\frac{1}{2}}$, i.e. by 0.84 approx. This gives butt diameter 0.473″ and tip diameter 0.131″.

Of course, rod-tapers are not usually straight, so in practice you must measure the diameter of your original rod at close intervals throughout its length, say every six inches or closer, and multiply each diameter by the factor given by the formula, in this case 0.84. It helps to plot a graph of the taper the diameter co-ordinate being about 100 times that of the length. By greatly exaggerating the variation in taper, this shows you the intention of the designer.

I don't know what will happen about a further visit to Woldale, as I am overwhelmed with work at present. I should like very much to come again!

I'm enclosing some of the Lackey's Leap photographs. When you've had a look at them could you send them on to 'B.B.', as he wants illustrations for an article in *Country Sportsman?*

I went to Temple Pool yesterday (Sunday) roach-fishing, as my wife ran out of fish for the cats. I used about 7 lb. of groundbait, well out, and fished with paste and groundbait mixed, on a 14 hook on .006″ French nylon. Result, 13 lb. of roach up to 1½ lb., and one carp 3½ lb. I *hooked* four carp in all! There were several rooting in the groundbait all morning (I was there 7.30–12.30). The water was pretty clear, as it usually is at this time of year, and I could see the groundbait lying on the bottom, and the carp eating it. I used a small two-shot float which the carp didn't seem to mind. The carp I *did* land was the only one that didn't bolt straight into the weeds; he ran down the lake and then turned inwards. It was quite a battle on such fine tackle.

I shall be glad to see your latest photographs.

Yours,

DICK

Dear Dick,

Our trip to Thorpe last Sunday produced one very small bream! I have no doubt there are some good tench in the pond—there were lots of very tenchy bubbles—but they were not interested in any of the baits that we offered them, including little red worms in mud-balls. Weather permitting, I hope to have another go at Woldale this week-end.

You had a very eventful morning at Temple Pool last Sunday. Isn't it infuriating to miss one run after another for no apparent reason. Too bad about the big ones that were hooked but got away.

Many thanks for the elaboration on rod-design. I can follow you, which speaks well for your lucid explanation. Thanks also for the data for the light carp and spinning rods. I must get cracking shortly. Can you please, some time, give me similar information with regard to the little brook rod of yours?

I've had another evening worming for trout on the little stream we fished and got five around the ½-pound mark—and several smaller ones.

I'm afraid this will have to be a shorter letter than usual as I have to attend a meeting in a few minutes.

Sincerely,

MAURICE

Dear Maurice,

Thank you for the photographs, which are very good.

It doesn't look as if I shall see Woldale again this year, though I certainly mean to next season.

I might manage to get a free week-end in October, probably

From extreme Butt—inches.	Light Carp rod for 6–10 lb. line.	8 ft. Salmon spinning (Ogden Smith)	8 ft. Salmon spinning (Foster)
0	¾-inch dowel	.220″	.250″
6		.216″	.237″
12		.212″	.225″
18	.250″	.207″	.215″
24	.233″	.202″	.207″
30	.220″	.195″	.200″
36	.207″	.186″	.195″
42	.197″	.175″	.192″
48	.186″	.163″	.175″
54	.175″	.148″	.162″
60	.165″	.135″	.152″
66	.154″	.127″	.142″
72	.145″	.117″	.132″
78	.136″	.107″	.122″
84	.127″	.092″	.112″
90	.121″	.072″	.092″
96	.115″	.070″	.082″
102	.104″		
108	.092″		
114	.075″		
120	.060″		
	Two-piece	Two-piece	Two-piece

Dimensions of light carp rod and two spinning rods.

All measurements taken thus:

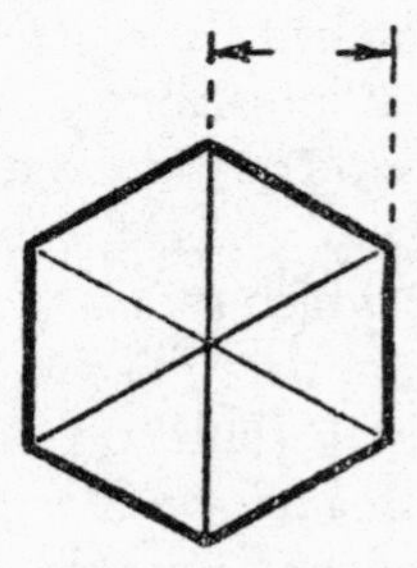

To obtain width across flats, i.e.:

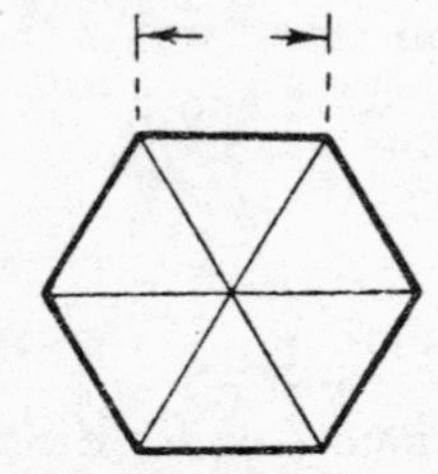

multiply figures by 1.155.

late, but I expect the carp will be down by then. I had thought of having a look at the Royalty fishery. It ought to be dealt with some time, and I want a big chub to stuff, while a barbel of 12 lb. or so wouldn't come amiss! I suppose you couldn't manage to get away for a long week-end?

I've been thinking about that little trout brook that you fish. You ought to read a book called *Loved River* by Jukes—if you haven't already done so. It has tons of valuable information about dams, groynes, etc. You could make a marvellous little fishery there with five pounds' worth of wire-netting and lots of sweat. I wish I lived near it, and could help you.

It will soon be time to think about pike and chub. Apart from our visit to Thimbleby Mill I haven't been chub-fishing this season, and I usually try to get at least one four-pounder each year.

The fish in the Oughton Pond seem to be thriving, to judge from the bubbling and mud-stirring that goes on there. I intend to feed them up next spring with large quantities of lobworms, bread, potatoes, etc. It will be interesting to see if they will breed there; I expect the tench will, but I don't know about the carp. There are seven good-sized fish of each species there now. I am still striving to get a lease on a disused gravel-pit, but the owners all seem to suspect some ulterior motive—I think they imagine I must have found a vein of gold in their pits, or something like that!

I'm going to make a new carp landing net on similar lines to yours, but not *quite* so large. I think I shall make it twenty inches in diameter, and with a jointed 6 foot handle. Perhaps a certain amount of cork or balsa to make it lighter *in the water* might help; I mean to experiment with this idea.

When are you going to produce some more articles for *Fishing Gazette*?

Yours,

DICK

Dear Dick,

Will you please let me have 'B.B.'s' address so that I can send the photographs on to him? They are very good indeed. Could I have prints of the one of you holding the two fish, the rear view of 'B.B.', and the one with the horses, to add to my collection?

My week-end was not uneventful in spite of the storm. I arrived at Woldale Lake on Saturday evening about 7 p.m. and fished until dark without a run. Then I baited up the pitch with soaked bread and broken potato. As the weather was so rough and it was quite cold I decided it might be as well to try a new pitch, in the corner by the chestnut tree—where you caught your second common carp—where I think the water is deeper. I started fishing again about 5 a.m. while it was still dark. While I was baiting up my second rod I had a run on the first, which had not been cast out five minutes. The fish ran out the yard or so of line that I had pulled off the reel and also pulled several yards off the reel against the check, but before I could reach the rod and strike the fish dropped the bait and departed. Miss number one! About half-an-hour later I had another run and this time I connected. I played the fish, which was a mirror in the 14–15 pounds category, for about ten minutes and was drawing it over the net when the hook came away and fish No. 2 departed. When I examined the hook I found that the point had been turned over—thus:

presumably by contact with some hard part of the fish's anatomy, and the hook had not penetrated properly.

About half-an-hour later I had another run and again I connected. I skipped very quickly round to the end of the pond and played out the fish from a position by the dam. It was a common carp of 11½ lb. and he put up a grand fight—much faster than any of the mirrors I have caught there. He made several determined rushes towards the overhanging chestnut tree, but I managed to turn him each time and netted him after about fifteen minutes. He was a most beautiful fish, very fat and chubby, in proportion exactly like my seventeen-pounder, and in beautiful condition; perfectly clean without a mark or a blemish and the most beautiful golden-bronze colour. I seriously considered bringing it home and having a shot at stuffing it, but thought better of it. It was not a big fish by Woldale standards and it seemed a pity to practise on such a lovely fish, so back he went to grow bigger.

About 7.30 a.m. I had another run—I struck while the line was running out steadily, but for some unaccountable reason I failed to connect. Miss No. 3!

Four runs in two and a half hours on a very stormy morning was far more than I had expected. In fact it was more than I have ever had in one morning's fishing at Woldale. Does it not confirm your theory that carp feed until the weather becomes so cold as to put them down for the winter? It seems to me only logical that it should be so.

I fished on until about 8.30 a.m. without any more runs and then packed up and came home for breakfast.

It is interesting to note that, except for my first (and biggest) fish, all the carp that I have caught at Woldale have been taken in the early morning after groundbaiting fairly heavily the night before. Admittedly four were caught in a pitch that had been systematically groundbaited for some time previously, but after my experience last week-end in a pitch that had not been pre-baited, I am wondering how much of my success has been due to pre-baiting. I certainly think that systematic groundbaiting increases one's chances of success, but I am wondering now to what extent this is so. Another small point, which might be of some importance—when making up my groundbait I always soak the bread in the water in which I have boiled my potatoes. No doubt this increases its 'flavouring' properties, and therefore adds to its attractiveness.

I would like to read 'B.B.'s' article in *Country Sportsman*. Will you let me know when it is published and I will try to get a copy?

You had a very active day at Temple Pool last Sunday. The cats will be waxing fat!

Congratulations on your 3½ lb. carp on .006″ monofil! It was no mean feat.

Too bad you can't make Woldale again this year. We must

make plans well in advance for next year's visit, so that I can get the keeper briefed and everything 'laid on'. I'd love to come with you to Christchurch, but I'm afraid I can't manage it. Perhaps another year. I hope you get your specimen chub and barbel.

I shall look forward to seeing your new landing net, when made. If I hadn't a car my net would be a terrible encumbrance, but as it is I could not wish for anything better. It may be a bit on the big side, but that is a great advantage when I have to net my own fish.

When the dark winter nights prevent me from working in the garden and I am not quite so busy I shall have a crack at doing some articles for the *Fishing Gazette*, if I can think of something to write about!

Sincerely,

MAURICE

Dear Maurice,

I am having some more prints of the Lackey's Leap trip done and will let you have yours as soon as they are ready. I don't think they are very good; the negatives are badly scratched. I think the camera needs interior cleaning.

You appear to have the Woldale carp thoroughly taped, and no doubt you will easily appreciate how I could run up such a score with Brickhill Pond just round the corner from my house. Goodness knows what you could do at Woldale if you could be there every morning before going to work!

I have always held that the tail-end of the season is a good time for catching carp. It has been so on every water I've fished, right up until the first real frost. After there has been a frost there isn't much more to hope for. You will know when the carp are down, because the water will become clear. There is a chance of an odd fish for some time after that, but it's a long chance.

I should think the point of your hook was turned over against the throat teeth of the fish. I have a set of these teeth which came from the carp I stuffed; they are proper ivory molars, and they do not work against a gristly plate as the books say, but against a hard bony plate. You've been finding that the fish take the potato well down, and I should think in this case the fish had started chewing. I had a hook completely crushed by a carp once, probably in a similar way.

I am not at all sure that very long-term groundbaiting is necessary. If the fish get potatoes often enough, so that they can eat a few with impunity now and again, I think a baiting the evening before fishing is enough. What I'm trying to say is that they don't need feeding every day; once a week ought to be enough to keep them happy about eating potatoes or whatever the bait is to be. I think we must recognize that groundbaiting serves two purposes; attraction and education. For the former, the groundbait only needs putting in just before fishing commences; the greater the density of carp-population the more true this is. For education, the fish need feeding only just often enough to keep them eating that kind of food without suspicion.

I think your early morning success is due to more than the morning's being the best time (which it undoubtedly is). You've been packing up at 8.30 a.m. on most occasions and you might have had more if you'd stayed on, unless other people arrived; the fish usually feed until much later than 8.30 a.m. if undisturbed, especially towards the end of the season. Late evening and night-fishing has not been so productive, as it might have been in your case, because this is early and mid-season work, mostly with margin-bread which you didn't try much, and also, you didn't find how effective potato was at Woldale until the time for night fishing had about finished. Although there appears to be little doubt that potato is the best all-round bait at Woldale, I still think things could be done with marginal bread, and if we get some hot weather and sweaty nights next season I should advise you to give it another trial, especially when you can have two rods in action.

I showed one of your letters to a friend the other day and he says why don't we collect up all the letters that have passed between us and publish them as a book? This sounds a distinct possibility to me; what are your reactions?

Good luck,

DICK

PS. I think I've discovered how to get a reasonably good metallic appearance on a goldy or silvery fish. After the fish is dry and one or two coats of varnish have been put on, a state is arrived at where the margin of each scale is varnished but the middle is (although covered with varnish) still rough, or perhaps *matt* would be a better way to describe the condition. Anyway, several more coats are needed to get a wet shiny look. But if at the matt stage you apply bronze powder, *the finest grade obtainable*, with a *finger*, it sticks to the roughish part of each scale but *not to the smooth part*. (For a silvery fish, of course, aluminium powder would be used.) Then continue successive coats of varnish. I've done this on my 11½ lb. carp and it looks very good—not 'gilded' as you might suppose. I want a chub of about 4 to 5 pounds to try next.

Harry Sheckell says he did *not* catch any carp and has not been fishing since 1939, but perhaps his brother may have been to Tubbs' Pit. When are you going? Don't leave it *too* late! The carp you netted out for his pal was *eaten*! I hope the captor got a bellyache.

D.

XIII

October Letters

Dear Dick,

I've no more carp to report. I repeated the performance of the previous week-end—groundbaited and tackled up on Saturday afternoon, home to bed and returned early on Sunday morning. It simply poured with rain all day on Sunday, but as I had to go to Woldale to collect my gear, I thought I might as well fish for an hour or so. I started fishing about 5 a.m. and had a run about 5.30, but in the dark I fumbled and knocked the rod before I could pick it up to strike, with the result, of course, that the fish dropped the bait. There were no more runs before I packed up about 8 a.m.

For the past week the weather has been very definitely autumnal—cold nights, wind, heavy rain and glimmers of sunshine—and I suspect that the Woldale carp will have gone down for the winter. If the weather is reasonable this week-end I intend to have one more try, and if I don't have a run I shall pack up carping until next year. Then I propose to have a crack at the chub in the Bain and the pike and perch at Revesby. I think Revesby would interest you—could you manage a long week-end, or perhaps a few days around Christmas?

The Lackey's Leap photographs have gone off to 'B.B.'. He should have received them by now. I told him that I understood that I might be able to accompany you both on your visit to Lackey's Leap next year, which I would like to do *if it can be arranged*.

I entirely agree with what you say about morning fishing. I am quite sure the carp feed after 8.30 a.m.—on many occasions I have seen abundant evidence of feeding carp when I have been leaving.

The idea of publishing our letters in book form sounds quite attractive. I have all yours, and they really do make very interesting reading—I was reading some of the 'back numbers' only a few days ago. My letters, I am sure, are not so instructive, but they would preserve continuity. It would be a novel way of presenting information, and some of our experiences and anecdotes might, I think, make interesting reading and leaven the heavier technical stuff! I shall look forward to hearing more of what you think about this.

Your idea for obtaining a metallic shine on stuffed fish sounds very good. If I can get a reasonable chub, I must try my hand at it.

Best wishes,

MAURICE

Dear Maurice,

Don't consider the Woldale carp asleep yet! I have known big fish active right up until November in seasons where a warm spell set in in October, as if often does. The first really sharp frost is the finisher as a rule.

Wind and rain are not good, but the September gales are frequently following by a warm spell, and often really big fish are taken then.

I think we *could* do something with these letters. I have all yours, I think, but they'll need some sorting! I'll start searching them out to-night and try to get them in some sort of order.

From my own point of view our correspondence has proved a case of rather laborious discovery by me that you, who wrote initially in a novice-like way—or should I say a *modest* way—proved to be a very efficient and observant angler, who eventually succeeded in wiping my eye to the tune of one carp bigger than I've *ever* caught, and five to beat any I've had since 1946! I think this develops itself without any alteration to the existing letters, and would undoubtedly cause readers a good deal of glee!

Good luck,

DICK

PS. I am enclosing two letters I had from Mr. D. F. Leney, of The Surrey Trout Farm, after my articles on carp appeared in the *Fishing Gazette*. Note what he says about carp-breeding.

The Surrey Trout Farm,
Haslemere

Dear Mr. Water Rail,

I have seldom read a more helpful and better fishing article than your recent one on How to Catch Carp, in the *Fishing Gazette*. Without piling i on, I wish there could be more such.

But there seems to be a fly in all ointment, for your last paragraph really does throw mud at those fish breeders who honestly try to do the best for their clients!

Ever since 1925 I have been distributing King Carp (Mirror

and Leather varieties), Common (all-scaled) Carp and the Jap HiGoi or true Golden Carp (all with barbules) and the numbers must have run into many thousands. On very very few occasions have we had any Prussian or Crucian carp or bronze, unturned goldfish, and NEVER, NEVER have we tried to palm them off to anyone for angling. We appreciate only too well how marvellous the results may be from the true fast and heavy growing King Carp, and we have numerous clients who still clamour for them—Alas, supplies fall far short. English summers fall lamentably short of the warmth required for easy and successful breeding and present sterling restrictions preclude getting any in from the Continent.

I am well aware that frequently 'Carp' are advertised which only prove to be bronze (uncoloured) goldfish or Prussians, and are utterly worthless. Personally, I have very seldom found the true deep, narrow bodied Crucian offered; it is quite a different type to the Prussian Carp.

I think perhaps the enclosed print from a pre *Great* War list will interest you, a fish of 12 lb. netted from a large lake near here. At the beginning of the last war I left a few yearling King Carp of 4–5″ in some trout ponds in Derbyshire. They remained amongst the trout all the war, cleaning up the bottom and scraps of uneaten meat and fish left by the trout. When I returned in 1945, I took the two giants remaining to the London Zoo's aquarium; they weighed 15 lb. and 7 lb. The largest King Carp that I have ever handled alive was 20 lb. which I personally brought from the Continent for the early opening days of the Zoo's aquarium. Nowadays on the Continent they are crossing King Carp with the Jap Golden Carp to get a very hardy, coppery-bronze fish, all scales, which they say bites better than the King Carp; this I doubt, but it is a very beautiful fish, but I fancy less hardy over here.

Pre-war we used to find that good 2-year King Carp of between 8 and 11 inches used to make 3–4 lb. fish in their 5th year when put into canals and lakes in the Midlands, and even better growth say in the southern counties.

You do well in your article to stress the greater fun to be got from carp stocking, against numbers of tiny roach, perch, etc. You could well include the Common or Green Tench, about which perhaps you will also write later! They are far slower growers than any carp, but when one gets hold of a 3–4 lb. one, what beautiful fish they are. I have a small stock of the true golden variety, like bananas, but they, too, are very shy breeders, though they throw true to colour.

Please pardon my intrusion, but your article seemed to call for an appreciation and a slight remonstrance!

Yours truly,
D. F. LENEY
Managing Director

The Surrey Trout Farm,
Haslemere

Dear Mr. Walker,

Very many thanks for your long letter. I *do* know only too well that some distributors of fish (I refuse to call them breeders) have supplied Prussian and bronze uncoloured goldfish to clubs. I hold no brief for competitors, but I consider the clubs should have known better than to accept such junk or should have applied to a reputable firm!

The Mirror and Leather types are one and the same, under the heading of King Carp. There is no difference in rate of growth, weight of fish, of hardiness of either type; there is no pure strain of either though I have no doubt that if several generations were selected of one or the other, you could establish a large proportion of the particular type. I believe those with the fewest scales are the most prized by the Jewish housewife, for the table. I do know that those with greatest 'leather area' travel and handle better, especially with fish of over say ¾ lb. for the fish are apt to snap off the big scales when they twitch or thresh about when netted and handled. I have seen King Carp covered entirely with large scales, of far larger size than the scales of the typical English Common Carp. King Common and the Jap HiGoi (or Golden) Carp cross easily. King Carp grow faster and larger than the common carp and this probably helps in their freer biting habits. You say this is not generally known, but perhaps it has been forgotten that the King Carp has been evolved primarily for edible purposes—to produce a tender fleshed, fat and heavy fish for its length and fast growing (from the economic production standard)—by Continental breeders.

It is a great pity that insufficient distinction has been made between the 'Carp' listed in *Where to Fish*, or by the captors in the first case. I had been of the impression that the Mapperley Carp were all King Carp and I think a number of the big fish listed in the last edition of the 1949–50 *Where to Fish* might prove to be such.

To breed well, Carp must have sunwarmed shallows, with a thick growth of water plants or marginal rushes, from 2 feet shallowing to say 6 inches—in a sunwarmed corner of the pond, where the water will warm up to the maximum about May. Added to which one must have a sufficiently long and settled spell of warm weather to warm the water and induce the fish to spawn, AND no great change in temperatures after that which may chill either eggs or fry. It is helpful too, if there are good beds of water plants in the deeper water below the spawning places, which will help shelter the fry as they grow and scatter afield. Consequently I am afraid that frequently a season's spawning will come to nothing, owing to our quick-changing weather. Special small ponds are made on the Continent in which the breeders are placed to spawn as soon as suitable weather comes along; the breeders are removed after spawning, so that they do not mop up the eggs, and the tiny fry are dipped out into large suitable growing ponds, holding no other fish *whatsoever* (sticklebacks included!) for the rest of the summer. The presence of shoals of perch means death to many fry; and I consider that shoals of roach, bream, etc., will all militate against a large and successful crop of carp fry.

Really suitable ponds are few and far between for natural carp breeding. My opinion is that the best results are where there are carp alone in a pond. One comes across pools which teem with these small growing Prussian carp, bronze uncoloured goldfish, crosses between these kinds, and small ponds (comparatively) which teem with only tench. This last fish breeds best in similar conditions, rather later in the year. On the whole, the deeper waters of old gravel and clay pits are unsuitable for breeding, unless they possess sufficient sunwarmed shallows. The more experience one gets, the more I find it advisable not to try to lay down hard and fast rules as to how or when fish will breed or behave; so much differs with the peculiar character of each water, coupled with the weather conditions, and the particular growths of vegetation each year. Once one gets the Carp to, say, 4 inches average their first autumn, as most of the Continental stock attains, one has strong hardy fish, able to adapt themselves and carry through their first winter safely. Tench are slower growing and are usually only about 2 inches average their first winter.

Well, I must apologize for such a dissertation, and I can only plead that I think you are as interested in the natural history side of the fish as I am. By profession I am a trout farmer, but by inclination I have always had a very soft spot for Carp, Tench and their varieties, as well as the Golden varieties of Orfe and Rudd—but that is 'another story' and it's time I dried up! One day I look forward to meeting you and continuing the matter!

Every good wish for your future thirty pounder.

Yours sincerely,

D. F. LENEY

Dear 'B.B.', February, 1951

You remember I wrote to you some time ago about the possibilities of publishing some letters that have passed between Maurice Ingham and me? We've collected them and sorted them out. I think it would be a good idea if you had a look through them, and if you think they would be of interest to other anglers, we'll go ahead with the idea of publication.

Reading through these letters, I find several references to the big perch at Arlesey lake and the difficulty of catching them. You've seen the lake yourself and know how deep and clear the water is, and you will remember how baffled I've always been by the conditions there! You'll probably be amused to hear that this January I became so angry at my continual failure to find the answer to this problem, that I spent a whole icy-cold day plumbing the depth at various distances from the bank, in order to gain some idea of the contours of the bottom. I did it by casting out a plummet and timing how long it took it to sink to the bottom!

All the books say that perch are hungrier and easier to catch in the early months of the year, and I thought if I could locate the fish I might tempt one. Thought I, these perch will be in the warmest part of the lake. Chilled surface water sinks, and flows down the slopes of the sides and bed of the lake. Therefore, the fish will not be near the banks, nor will they be in the uttermost depths. *But,* they will be near bottom *somewhere.* The plumbing revealed that there were six under-water ridges, sloping down to the bottom; ramps used when the pit was being worked, I imagine. It seemed to me likely that these ridges would divide the flow of chilled water to the depths, and that at some point along each ridge there would be a warm spot. Accordingly, on January 14th I went armed with ledger tackle and lobworms, determined to see if the theory was sound.

Well, the theory *is* sound! I had eight good bites, and having missed seven by striking too soon, I let the eighth fish run well away before tightening. The result was a fine perch of 4 lb. 2 oz., the biggest I've ever caught.

A week later I tried the same spot again, had two bites and landed both fish, 3 lb. 1 oz. each. On the 24th I tried a third time and had the best catch of perch I've ever seen—six fish, 2 lb. 14 ozs.; 3 lb. 2 ozs. (two); 3 lb. 4 ozs.; 3 lb. 5 ozs.; and 3 lb. 10 ozs., besides losing three others which got me round what I suspect is a steel hawser on the bottom. One of these felt much heavier than anything I've landed from that spot. If it wasn't a pike—which is a possibility—it must have been a really monstrous perch. I tried everything to clear it, including leaving the line slack for an hour, but all in vain.

The following week-ends were impossible—half-an-inch of ice all over the lake, then a hurricane; but yesterday I tried again, in spite of ice-margins 30 yards wide, and got two more, 3 lb. 1 oz., and 2 lb. 14 ozs. I just pulled them up to the edge of the thin ice and they smashed their own way through; fortunately it was quite thin.

Until this season I had never caught a perch over 2 lb. 13 ozs.; since October last I've had twelve bigger, including ten over 3 lb.! (I had one of 3 lb. 1 oz. at Southill, in late October, on a floating plug.) I've 'set-up' the Southill fish, and the 3 lb. 10 oz. and 4 lb. 2 oz. fish from Arlesey. The latter won the *News of the World* reel, by the way.

All these Arlesey fish were caught ledgering with a big lob-worm, on .010″ diameter perlon monofil, ¾ oz. lead and size 6 Model Perfect hooks, except the 4-pounder, which was on a size 6 crystal. It's necessary to make a pretty long cast, at least fifty yards, and it has to be accurate, too. I check by landmarks on the opposite bank, as I did when we caught the carp at Lackey's Leap.

Probably a live gudgeon or a small roach would be even more attractive than a lobworm, but you know I am not very happy about live-baiting. There might be trouble from pike, too. I've tried working a small spoon down deep, where the perch are, without any result. The depth is considerable where I caught the fish—forty feet or more—and when landed the fish are distressed by the change of pressure and tend to float belly-up; it is important to release them at once or they are liable to die.

Both the fish I stuffed were females and to judge from their appearance all the others were, too. I've been examining the scales from some of the fish, and they are most interesting. I imagine the annual rings are spawning marks, since in all cases the first seems to have been made when the fish was about 5 to 6 oz. in weight. If one assumes (as seems probable) that the fish first spawned at three years old, the 4 lb. 2 oz. fish would have been eight years old next May; the 3 lb. 10 oz. fish was a year younger. The spacing of the annual rings is very even and indicates that the fish had by no means finished growing. I haven't the least doubt that there are much bigger perch in Arlesey Lake than any I've succeeded in catching.

Maurice has been down for a try at them, but we were both

defeated by appalling weather. It poured icy rain all day and both of us lost fish through our hands being so numb from cold and wet that the reel-handle slipped from our fingers. We had several runs, but in most cases the bait was dropped before the fish had gone far. I imagine that the general wetness of everything caused the lines to cling to the rods and check the fish enough to arouse their suspicions. Anyhow, we caught nothing.

I've been using a 'Mitchell' fixed spool reel for this perch-fishing, and like it very much indeed, and I think it will do well for carp. One could use .012″ perlon, which lifts 9 lb., or .014″ (11 lb.) for heavy fish. The Mitchell takes 200 yards of the 11 lb. stuff.

Maurice and I are looking forward to joining you in the assault on Lackey's Leap next summer. We'll have that thirty-pounder yet!

Best wishes,

DICK

Conclusion

SINCE these letters were written, many fishing seasons have come and gone, and in them so many things have happened that it would be wrong to allow this book to go to press without mentioning some of them.

In June, 1951, four anglers sat on the famous embankment at Mapperley, where the then record carp of 26 lb. was caught by the late Albert Buckley. Those four anglers were Denys Watkins-Pitchford, John Norman, Maurice Ingham, and me, and we formed the Carpcatchers' Club. Jack Smith and Harry Grief were invited to join soon afterwards, and later, Bob Richards, Peter Thomas and Bernard Venables were made members.

The pooling of knowledge that began with the correspondence you have just read has had results beyond our dreams.

In October, 1951, Bob Richards smashed Albert Buckley's

record with a carp of 31 lb. 4 oz. which was sent to me to be stuffed. In June, 1952, Peter Thomas—'Pete' of earlier pages—surpassed the old record with another great fish of 28 lb. 10 oz. In July of the same year, Maurice achieved his ambition to catch a twenty-pounder, with one of 24 lb. 12 oz., and I mine, with one of two pounds less, a day later and on another water. And in September, 1952, I caught, with essential help from Pete, an almost unbelievable monster, a common carp of 44 lb., which now holds the record for the species. I wonder for how long? We have seen carp bigger, and they will one day be caught.

Nowadays, carp weighing upwards of 20 lb. or more are caught so often that the modern angler may think that fish of the size Maurice and I were catching in 1950 are small fry. Remember that in those days, fewer than a dozen carp over 10 lb. in weight were caught in an average season in the whole of Britain. The deliberate pursuit of big fish, now regarded as a commonplace branch of angling, was then almost unheard of; Maurice and I were groping our way out of the dark.

I make no apology for the space in this book which is devoted to carp-fishing. Although, as has been explained, our letters were not written with any intention of publication, it would have been possible to delete some of the matter dealing with carp. We did not do so because we both believe that if a man can catch big carp, he can catch anything, and if our letters help other anglers towards a better understanding of carp, they cannot but help in other branches of angling as well.

If in referring to some aspects of modern angling, we have been a little too harsh and outspoken, we must ask to be forgiven. If we growl at incompetent and lazy people now and then, it is not because we wish them ill, nor is it because we consider ourselves superior beings. I have sometimes wondered if we do not take our fishing too seriously—if others who care little whether they are successful or not may not derive more pleasure from their fishing than we do. We are fanatical anglers, and that is hard to change.

Perhaps the greatest attraction of angling is that it demands so much thought, and perseverance, and skill, without imposing penalties for failure. Surgeons and statesmen and sailors often become anglers, and it may be that in angling they can exercise the qualities that bring success in their trades, without the accompanying tremendous responsibilities. The choice of a lure, in fishing, may involve the angler in emotion and indecision every whit as great for the moment as if he were Foreign Secretary, or navigator of a battleship, but the consequences of a mistake are insignificant except, it may be, in their effect on the mind; for no layman can believe or understand the state of mind of a man when he grasps a rod with a limp, hookless line and gazes speechless—yes, speechless—at the water in which a great fish swims free after its successful fight.

Certainly, no man can ever feel himself more successful than the angler who, happily, does all well and is rewarded by the sight of the fish of his lifetime safely brought to bank. It is pure elation, and I can wish nothing better to those who read this book.

RICHARD WALKER

July, 1964